The ACTFL Foreign Language Education Series

Foreign Language Standards:
Linking Research, Theories, and Practices

June K. Phillips
Editor

Robert M. Terry
Associate Editor

Joanne Burnett
Alvino Fantini
Joan Kelly Hall
Dale L. Lange
Mary Ann Lyman-Hager
Myriam Met
June K. Phillips

Published by National Textbook Company
in conjunction with the American Council on the Teaching of Foreign Languages

Acknowledgments begin on page 265, which is to be
considered an extension of this copyright.

ISBN: 0-8442-9375-X

Published by National Textbook Company,
a division of NTC/Contemporary Publishing Group, Inc.
4255 West Touhy Avenue,
Lincolnwood (Chicago), Illinois 60646-1975 U.S.A.
890 VP 0987654321

Contents

Standards for Foreign Language Learning

Communication

Communicate in Languages Other than English

Standard 1.1: Students engage in conversations, provide and obtain information, express feelings and emotions, and exchange opinions.

Standard 1.2: Students understand and interpret written and spoken language on a variety of topics.

Standard 1.3: Students present information, concepts, and ideas to an audience of listeners or readers on a variety of topics.

Cultures

Gain Knowledge and Understanding of Other Cultures

Standard 2.1: Students demonstrate an understanding of the relationship between the practices and perspectives of the culture studied.

Standard 2.2: Students demonstrate an understanding of the relationship between the products and perspectives of the culture studied.

Connections

Connect with Other Disciplines and Acquire Information

Standard 3.1: Students reinforce and further their knowledge of other disciplines through the foreign language.

Standard 3.2: Students acquire information and recognize the distinctive viewpoints that are only available through the foreign language and its cultures.

Comparisons

Develop Insight into the Nature of Language and Culture

Standard 4.1: Students demonstrate understanding of the nature of language through comparisons of the language studied and their own.

Standard 4.2: Students demonstrate understanding of the concept of culture through comparisons of the cultures studied and their own.

Communities

Participate in Multilingual Communities at Home and Around the World

Standard 5.1: Students use the language both within and beyond the school setting.

Standard 5.2: Students show evidence of becoming lifelong learners by using the language for personal enjoyment and enrichment.

Standards for Foreign Language Learning 1996: 9.

Introduction

Standards for World Languages— On a Firm Foundation*

June K. Phillips
Weber State University

From whence do standards come? In industry, when standards are used to assess product quality, precision may be established on features of measurement and accuracy, such as railroad gauges, chemical compounds, or wattage. The assessment of conformity to the standard rests on criteria upon which independent judges will universally agree. When standards are used to assess performance quality, competency may reflect variables that include artistry, functionality, audience or user response, and individuality. Judgment relies on agreed-upon interpretations and applications of criteria. In an endeavor such as playing the piano, progress toward a high performance standard counts for something, whereas a prescription drug that is a close approximation of the formula has no value at all. Quality assurance takes on a different dimension in car manufacturing than in education.

Content standards, upon which performance standards are assessed, lie at the heart of education reforms undertaken during these transitional years to the next century. The design of content standards for our discipline required that the profession articulate its best judgment of *what students should know*

---

*See pages iv and v for a listing of the five goal areas and the eleven standards found in the *Standards for Foreign Language Learning: Preparing for the 21st Century* (1996).

June K. Phillips (Ph.D., The Ohio State University) is dean of Arts and Humanities at Weber State University in Utah. She served as director for the national standards project and is editing the language-specific document for the National Standards in Foreign Language Education Collaborative Project. She chairs the Foreign Language Academic Advisory Committee for the College Board. She is a former chair of the Northeast Conference on the Teaching of Foreign Languages and has served on the executive council of ACTFL.

and be able to do as a result of their study of world languages. Content standards, while not curriculum per se, do exert influence on the experiences students should have in the classroom and the pedagogical approaches their teachers employ. Content standards must become the basis for the new assessments that will judge student competencies in terms of quality and progress toward high and challenging performance standards.

The history of *Goals 2000: Educate America Act* and the national standards development process in world languages has been adequately documented elsewhere (see Phillips 1994; Phillips and Draper 1994; Phillips and Lafayette 1996). The professional consensus achieved with the publication of *Standards for Foreign Language Learning: Preparing for the 21st Century* (1996) has been transformed into an energetic collaboration among eleven organizations, which are developing language-specific standards and which, as a collaborative project, are participating in teacher education standards development. The project has been accepted for membership in the National Council for Accreditation of Teacher Education (NCATE) and will provide the financial support for sustaining that membership. Since the 1996 publication of the national standards, numerous states have begun the parallel process of designing state standards and the concomitant curricular frameworks. Virtually every state's standards strongly align with the national ones; most do so word for word, and others have slightly modified wording or organization.

During the standards development process, much effort had been aimed at achieving a strong national consensus. That challenge was successfully met as individuals from education, government, and business embraced the standards and over fifty professional and state organizations endorsed them officially. Certainly a primary reason for this consensus lies with the extensive dissemination activities that occurred as the standards were being drafted and with the subsequent familiarization workshops that have been conducted nationwide. Equally important, although not as uniformly established throughout the profession, another basis for consensus lies in the fact that the standards are grounded in a combination of solid research, strong and sequential curriculum, and effective instructional practices.

The student standards are challenging—as are the implied standards for teaching. At present, however, standards are too frequently being greeted with expressions of verification such as, "I do that" or "That is what I do with my students." Less often, one hears "That is what my students are doing or learning" or "My students perform those tasks at a high level of competency." More comments on the order of "I hadn't thought of learning that way" or "I see how I need to change what we do in class" would signify that teachers have recognized and begun to struggle with the real challenges of the standards. The major shift inherent in the standards requires teachers to focus more on what students are learning than on what they are teaching— making output what counts rather than input. The reality is that these standards are based on a number of research and theoretical models that must provoke new thinking on the part of world languages teachers. To effectively make the myriad instructional decisions that standards-focused programs demand, teachers have to understand the premises and processes upon which the acquisition of linguistic, cultural, interdisciplinary, and comparative competencies lie. It is imperative that as teachers, we move from using the standards to verify present practice to using them to improve student performance. This volume is intended to facilitate that process by examining in depth the theories, models, and research that underlie the very different and challenging vision for learning the world languages embodied in the standards of Communication, Cultures, Connections, Comparisons, and Communities.

Professionalization through Standards

Standards broadened the content range of language learning by venturing well beyond the traditional four skills of listening, speaking, reading, and writing and the occasional study of culture. The new frameworks for communication and culture in *Standards for Foreign Language Learning: Preparing for the 21st Century* (1996) dramatically change the paradigms under which teachers have been operating even within traditional content areas (Communication and Cultures). The addition of goals and standards that encourage students to use new languages to explore interdisciplinary content (Connections), to develop insights into the very nature of language and culture as systems or patterns (Comparisons), and to search actively to test their new competencies in venues beyond the school (Communities) legitimize the occasional forays that foreign language classes took into these areas. The representation of all five goals as interlocking circles signifies that all should be systematically incorporated into language instruction at all levels.

To understand more fully the rationale for the Five Cs and how they play out in instruction, teachers must be willing to dedicate themselves to intensive work with the theoretical principles that form the basis for standards-driven learning. They must abandon the temptation to look only at the surface of activities and classroom scenarios. Given their busy schedules and the preponderance of short-term professional development workshops, it is not surprising that teachers gravitate toward the hands-on, practical kinds of inservice programs. However, that level of professional development inadequately addresses the complexity of language and cultures learning that accompanies the longer sequences and the diverse students in today's—and tomorrow's—classrooms. At conferences, in workshops, in the articles in this volume, it may seem appealing to skip the expository information on models drawn from research in order to access the classroom examples more quickly. But I urge readers to take the time to delve into those theoretical principles, for that is the basis for the important instructional decisions that you will need to make for yourself and for your students.

At a recent education conference, Willis Hawley (1998) chided the profession for not having adequately built a research foundation for teaching and for relying less on systematic research than other professions do. He urged the use of standards, given their focus on student learning, to develop a new consensus promoting research that places the learner at the center and focuses on "solving authentic problems identified through systematic analysis of student learning." Hawley further expressed the challenge of professional development as one that is "not a question of what teachers *want* to know but of what they *need* to know" if they are to be effective leaders in today's classrooms.

This volume in The ACTFL Foreign Language Education Series seeks to enrich the knowledge base in support of the standards by examining what we know about student learning in the interlocking domains of communication, cultures, connections, and comparisons in particular so that students can use those competencies and contents effectively in communities. Before anticipating the topics authors will develop, this introduction will posit some of the other new areas that future standards-focused initiatives will have to address.

Longer Sequences for Learners

The great majority of articles in the professional literature for foreign language learning concentrates on first- and second-year programs, whether in schools or in higher education. Because most students in the United States have had limited opportunities for doing advanced work and because most teaching time has been spent on early stages of learning, neither theoretical nor classroom-action research has widely investigated advanced learning or learning over time, for example, from the elementary school through high school. Even those students who began foreign language learning at a younger age often found their study interrupted at some grade-level cluster—e.g., middle school—or they were recycled, with several "new beginnings" due to failures of articulation.

Earlier Starts for Language Instruction

A body of research on younger learners—i.e., elementary-age children—especially in immersion or partial immersion programs is beginning to accumulate. We are still a long way from knowing what levels of competency are being developed in elementary school programs with much less contact time; as new assessments appropriate to that age group provide evidence of performance, that knowledge gap may be at least partially filled (see Thompson 1995). The Younger Learner Project, sponsored by the American Council on the Teaching of Foreign Languages (ACTFL), will soon release a draft version of proficiency guidelines that should be helpful as programs expand at this level of instruction. Some of the key research that must follow the implementation of programs in elementary schools revolves around articulation so that gains made in early learning programs are adequately assessed and more importantly, drawn upon at the subsequent levels of instruction to grow competencies sequentially.

The advocacy for an "early start" in the study of world languages that was embodied in the standards publication has resulted in numerous state actions to promote that undertaking. Within the past year, commissioners for education or state boards in Connecticut and New Jersey issued calls or mandates for instruction in elementary schools. Utah's state education commissioner wants to lengthen the school day to accommodate language study. The success of these initiatives rests on several factors: (1) a pool of competent teachers with elementary preparation, (2) wise choices of program models, (3) use of standards and assessments that communicate learning, and (4) willingness of teachers at the next level to articulate with programs. In the past, we have unfortunately seen resistance to articulation, which perpetuates the new beginner syndrome. As a unified profession interested in language learning, it behooves us to familiarize ourselves with learning at all levels so that we can properly embrace students who come to us from programs at younger levels. Adjustments will have to made for learners who are continuing with a single language and for those who begin a new language, i.e., who add a layer to their studies. Both are very different learners than are monolinguals with their first encounter with a new system.

Advanced-Level Programs

Just as research has been sparse with younger learners so has it been with advanced learners in classroom settings. The implied promise in a commitment to longer sequences of study would be learners who communicate more proficiently in a range of tasks and who interact more adeptly in the culture. The old paradigm of learning language to learn literature after having learned language (defined as a certain number of lower-division courses) with relatively little overlap reflects an insufficient view of either domain. In Byrnes's (1998) work restructuring the undergraduate curriculum at Georgetown with her colleagues, the byword is "literature from the beginning, language through the end." This conceptualization meets quite fully the spirit of the standards, which emphasizes children's and adolescent literature in early grades and achievements in a wide range of content areas for advanced students. Many have decried the curricular rift that faces advancing learners in colleges and universities—and that is sometimes replicated in high schools when the only option for advanced study may be Advanced Placement Literature—when faculty have not collaborated for compatible missions. Bernhardt (1997) predicts that

> Programs that hold to the illusion of a two-year language program that brings about linguistic accuracy and then leads to some sort of "real language use" will go the way of the other dinosaurs. Language and literature departments must begin to accept the reality of length of learning time; that reality entails a knowledge of second language acquisition, which tells us to expect a developmental progression in accuracy and knowledge in students. Further, language departments must begin to communicate to the rest of the university what the students can and cannot do after each level of the curriculum. Students can do a lot of things with the language that we have given them over a year or two. But they cannot do everything linguistically or conceptually that upper-level study demands. They must continue to refine their language skills, if they didn't have to do so, there would be no need for the so-called upper-level curriculum (16).

While the national standards were developed under a federal program for K–12, all but two of the language-specific collaborating organizations[1] have subsequently adopted them as guidelines for K–16. Dissemination efforts into college and university departments of languages and literatures must be increased so that the seamless curriculum called for in the standards becomes a reality for learners. To further improve advanced level instruction, research into how learners do indeed refine skills, expand vocabulary, develop more discourse styles, and deal with nuance and abstract ideas must be undertaken. Many of the instructional approaches that are effective for beginning learners are not suitable for advanced learners, and a documented teaching repertoire at those higher levels is meager.

New Paradigms for Familiar Goals

In anticipation of the chapters in this volume by Hall and by Lange, it might be useful to set the stage for the standards frameworks that these authors explicate in terms of research, conceptual models, and classroom practices. From the outset, the National Standards Task Force,[2] knew that there would be standards that encompassed communication and culture as a minimum. In the course of the drafting, it became obvious that the traditional way of thinking about four separate and separated skills of listening, speaking, reading, and writing did not reflect how learners learn or how people communicate. Even with the methodological changes of past decades, this basic skill paradigm had held. Most recently, as functional or communicative language and proficiency guidelines emerged as curricular influences and moved the profession to value more highly real-world language and authentic tasks, we still clung to a skill-based paradigm.

If one looks at all the discipline-based standards publications, certain cross-disciplinary concepts become apparent. Many documents contain a standard or standards that address "communication"—for example, mathematics as communication. The foreign language group also examined the discipline of communication, and that study convinced it to consider more fully the context and cognitive demands of communication rather than designation by skill. The resulting "Framework of Communicative Modes" (see *SFLL* 1996:33) forms the foundation for three standards that describe learning performances as Interpersonal, Interpretive, and Presentational. Hall prefers to label these as "domains" in her chapter. The key concept that requires teachers to restructure their curriculum, their pedagogy, and their assessment practices lies in the fact that listening is not done in a vacuum. Listening is either part of an interpersonal mode where negotiated meaning with an individual is occurring, or it is an interpretive task performed from live or recorded audio, or audiovisual materials, where the cognitive strategies to make meaning without the ability to get clarification from the presenter determines the learning task. The other skills likewise each exist in two modes, and the marked difference resides in the opportunity to negotiate meaning through two-way interpersonal exchanges or through one-way negotiation with text (interpretive) or one-way expression of content and perspective (presentational). This slight but consequential shift pushes the researchers and the practitioners to think differently—to think modes or domains, not skills. Words like "reading" or "speaking" can no longer stand alone; they must be accompanied by the idea of reading to interpret fixed text or reading as an interpersonal enterprise, where the writer can be contacted as to meaning.

Framework for the Study of Culture

The National Standards Task Force felt that, as with communication, the time was right to take a fresh look at how culture had been treated in foreign language classrooms. In spite of much lip service over the years, culture remained at the periphery of instruction, most frequently referred to as a fifth skill, a capsule, a cultural note at the bottom of a textbook page, or a Friday "fun" activity. To categorize the field in some way, the terms "big C" and "little c" had been devised to signify the great works of civilization in contrast to daily patterns of life. Teachers taught the culture as they knew it; students learned items randomly, not as connected threads or themes. In most courses no systemic process was visible that enabled students to observe cultural manifestations; to analyze the patterns of behavior; to hypothesize about origins, usage, or context; and to understand the perspectives of the people in the target cultures. In sum, most cultural content learned was fact or act in isolation from how it related to the values and attitudes of a person or a people.

The new framework for culture adopts a stance more reflective of the anthropologist. By envisioning the study of cultures as one that examines *products* and *practices* in order to gain insights into *perspectives,* the task force hopes to focus attention on important and defining issues. A society may produce items and behave in ways that are incidental to its real values; too often this kind of material was the focus of cultural content. The result was that students learned trivialized aspects of cultures, which tend to accentuate the differences, not the similarities. But societies do hold dear essential perspectives that are manifested in their tangible and intangible products and in the practices of individuals and groups. Fantini's chapter on cross-cultural comparisons provides us with a more positive approach to leading students to think about the target cultures and their own. Teachers are encouraged to work with the full triangular model so that students examine the linkages among the three categories. Another advantage of this framework is that it does not make teachers responsible for knowing everything there is to know about a given culture. Instead, teachers can promote the process of observing and withholding judgments until perspectives can be confirmed; in turn, that will lead students toward more divergent and critical thinking as well as more tolerant and accepting attitudes toward other cultures. Because the foreign language profession had not fully integrated culture into its teaching, it relied more on lists of features for instruction than on models for learning generated by the research.

The Curricular Weave: Whys and Wherefores

For the most meaningful reading of this volume, educators should be familiar with *Standards for Foreign Language Learning: Preparing for the 21st Century* (1996). This publication illustrates the relationship among the goals expressed by the Five Cs, the eleven standards themselves, and the curricular experiences that enable students to achieve at a high level of performance. The authors of this ACTFL volume were not asked to address explicitly the elements of the weave, yet as they synthesized research and provided classroom examples, these elements can easily be discerned. The curricular weave (*SFLL:* 29) identifies both content and processes that undergird the standards and goals, as well as the role of technology.

- Content areas include the language system, cultural knowledge, and content from other school disciplines.
- Processes include communication strategies, learning strategies, and critical thinking skills.
- Technology includes a system for direct communication with language users, a source of materials, and an instructional delivery system.

As learners work with standards, they will be drawing on many of these areas simultaneously. Their experiences in these areas should always have a clear standards focus, for the performance assessments measure progress toward the standard. The teacher may also choose to evaluate the curricular underpinnings as part of diagnosing student progress.

Following is an example of the curricular weave linked with standards-based assessment.

> **Standards: Interpersonal, Interpretive, Presentational, Cultural Practices, Making Connections, Acquiring New Information**
>
> Intermediate-level students have been asked to search the Internet (technology) for information on the Maurice Papon trial (cultural, current events, and historical content), which took place in 1997–1998 in France. First, they shared in class information they knew about war crimes from World War II and some of the issues involved. Students scanned documents to find those they self-assessed as being in their range of comprehensibility (learning strategy, language system). Actual documents they used were historical time lines, short journalistic reports of the AFP-type (*Agence France Presse*). In small groups, students selected documents to read; they summarized their understandings in a journal and noted places where they had only part of the message so that the teacher could direct their inquiry. From the summaries, they prepared a synopsis—oral, visual, written—for the class;

groups worked with topics that covered the history, the individual, the justice system in France, and the witnesses. The final activity was a minitrial (language system, cultural content, communication strategies, critical thinking) and judgment. In their journals, individuals reflected on the issue of punishing war criminals (critical thinking, language system).

In this example, there are multiple opportunities for assessment based on the standards: the quality of the *interpretation* of the documents from the Web; the *presentation* of information to classmates; the *cultural practices* in terms of the conduct of justice; the *connections* to history and current events *knowledge* gained; and the effectiveness of the *interpersonal* communication in the mock trial.

As readers think about the research, theories, and practices provided by the authors in this volume, they will also want to draw upon elements in the curricular weave as they implement standards in classrooms. These elements, it must be remembered, are means to standards, not ends in themselves.

On the Horizon: New Assessments

It comes as no surprise that a variety of new assessments will be required to transform content standards to performance standards that answer the question, "How good is good enough?" These new assessments will have to be designed, piloted, reviewed, and revised many times, given the changing psychometrics that must be adapted. Assessments will not be primarily of the forced-choice design that lends itself so readily to statistical analysis and traditional measures of reliability and validity. Wiggins (1993, 1998) and Wiggins and Kline (1998) have set out the challenge for the profession, and multiple efforts are under way. ACTFL has a task force investigating assessments appropriate to standards operating under the title, *Beyond the OPI*.[3] While the national standards project was charged solely with developing content standards, many of the state standards-setting efforts are also responsible for performance standards and recommendations for testing. Communication among these projects could ease the burden of unnecessary replication of effort in the expectation that useful and usable assessments would arise that would measure the standards that are common to all.

In their chapters, where appropriate, the authors have shared their thinking on directions that assessments might take in the goal areas about which they write. Assessment will be a continuing topic as the profession moves forward with student standards as well as with standards for entry-level and for experienced teachers.

World Languages for *ALL* Students? What Does That Mean?

The Statement of Philosophy that opens the standards document clearly confirms that "ALL students will develop and maintain proficiency in English and at least one other language, modern or classical." The philosophy statement elaborates the conditions that would render language learning achievable by all students by proposing that:

All students can be successful language and culture learners, and they

- must have access to language and culture study that is integrated into the entire school experience,
- benefit from the development and maintenance of proficiency in more than one language,
- learn in a variety of ways and settings, and
- acquire proficiency at varied rates. (*SFLL:* 7)

Many teachers will find it much easier to embrace this philosophy in thought than in deed. Most teachers were trained to teach students who fit the mold of the ideal, although the last decades have already provided a more diverse student body, especially with programs in elementary and middle schools. Lindquist and Rosen (1997:5) remind us of the exclusiveness of our discipline and theirs that went on for many years: "It has almost become a cliché that mathematics is for all students, but, as with foreign languages, this has not always been true. Instead, for centuries, mathematics was the province of the intellectual elite." Likewise, foreign languages was once the domain of the college preparatory curriculum or open to students with "good grades" in English. If our profession truly believes that all students should experience the study of another language throughout their school years, then we must accept the challenge of teaching them for success, not dooming them to failure.

As we work with students who have physical and learning challenges, who come from a variety of ethnic, social, and economic backgrounds, who possess different learning styles, talents, and interests, we will need to create more research to help us help them be successful language learners. No one chapter, no one book can capture the essence of all this diversity; this body of information will have to accumulate bit by bit over time. In this volume, Lyman-Hager and Burnett examine one small piece of the giant puzzle, readers using computer-generated texts so that teachers can gain insights into how they learn to interpret. Language learning has always been complex—as it expands in school programs, layers of complexity will be added.

Linking Research, Theories, and Practices

Professional development around standards can take a giant leap forward for teachers who choose to immerse themselves in the chapters that follow. One's understanding of the standards will be richer for having probed and reflected upon the supporting research that serves as a foundation for student learning. The authors have also provided models that bridge the theory-practice gap and give examples of how standards-focused instruction might look in classrooms.

Joan Kelly Hall urges us to look at communication not just as an external event that students do but as an ongoing negotiation in the very conduct of our classes. Competency in the communicative standards, especially the interpersonal, can be built through teacher-student interactions, but this requires sometimes painful analysis of our typical classroom dialogue. Hall explores various theories of communicative competence, shares some classroom ethnographies, and makes solid recommendations for classroom research and practice.

Dale L. Lange synthesizes research on cultures learning, examines critically some of the culture guidelines available to date, and shares several models for cultural awareness with relevance for teaching and curriculum. Those models are exemplary in that they are vehicles for teaching toward the perspectives anticipated in the standards and are related to the large themes that can be spiraled throughout a long learning sequence.

Myriam Met helps us understand the importance of students' having meaningful content as they learn a new language. Constructivist theory supports the Connections standards, and the opportunities for integrating world languages into school curriculum abound. The strongest program examples currently lie in elementary and middle school programs, with at least one higher education model in Foreign Languages Across the Curriculum programs.

Alvino Fantini tackles the Comparisons goal and looks at both language and cultures from the intercultural perspective. His visual representations of the intersection of first- and second- language and cultures study is a powerful tool for enabling teachers to advance this goal in their classrooms. Fantini brings us information from related disciplines of English as a Second Language and cross-cultural communication.

Mary Ann Lyman-Hager and Joanne Burnett demonstrate an important use of technology as we build a research field that will help us teach a variety of learners. In their focused case study, they gain insights into how readers read by using technology as an analytical tool that lets us get into the processes of the learner. This example of intensive research on a specific task shows that dealing with diversity will require very specific experiments. There is no chapter in this volume that addresses the Communities goal, not because that goal is of lesser importance—indeed, it may well be the culminating reason for language study for most students. At this beginning stage of work with standards, the Communities goal is an application for which we have yet to generate much research; as more opportunities for work in the field are generated, there will be many research questions to pursue.

To repeat the beginning—the standards were not designed without foundation. At first reading, the sentences that comprise the standards may seem simple, but one must penetrate the surface to interpret and implement the instructional changes envisioned. Linda Darling-Hammond (1998) credits standards with the potential for "a powerful pedagogy that connects to learners." She calls for a two-way pedagogy, and by that she means that we must educate teachers not just "to know how to do, but to know what learners are thinking." The foreign language standards have the capacity to form that powerful pedagogy—but that power cannot be activated until we accept the challenge to link research, theory, and practice to promote student learning.

NOTES

1. The National Standards in Foreign Language Education Collaborative Project brings together for standards-related projects the American Association of Teachers of French, the American Association of Teachers of German, the American Association of Teachers of Italian, the American Association of Teachers of Spanish and Portuguese, the American Classical League, the American Council of Teachers of Russian, the American Council on the Teaching of Foreign Languages, the Chinese Language Association of Secondary-Elementary Schools & Chinese Language Teachers Association, the National Council of Secondary Teachers of Japanese & Association of Teachers of Japanese. The Project's activities are coordinated through the AATG, 112 Haddontowne Court # 104, Cherry Hill, NJ 08034.

2. Members of the National Standards Task Force were June K. Phillips, Project Director; Christine Brown, Chair; Marty Abbott, Keith Cothrun, Beverly Harris-Schenz, Denise Mesa, Genelle Morain, Marjorie Tussing, A. Ronald Walton, John Webb, Thomas Welch, and Guadalupe Valdés.

3. The Oral Proficiency Interview is a global assessment to measure speaking proficiency. The interview and rating system is linked to the ACTFL Proficiency Guidelines for speaking and uses inter-rater reliability as a source of reliability. It serves as a leading example of how task-based performance might be assessed in other domains.

REFERENCES

Bernhardt, Elizabeth B. 1997. "Victim Narratives or Victimizing Narratives? Discussion of the Reinvention of Language Departments and Language Programs." *ADFL Bulletin* 29,1:13–19.
Byrnes, Heidi. 1998. Personal communication.

Darling-Hammond, Linda. 1998. *The Vision of Teacher Education Linked to Student Learning.* Presentation at the National Academy on the Alignment of Standards and Teacher Development for Student Learning. Washington, DC.

Hawley, Willis. 1998. *A Dialogue: The Policy of Systemic Education Reform.* Presentation at the National Academy on the Alignment of Standards and Teacher Development for Student Learning. Washington, DC.

Lindquist, Mary Montgomery, and Linda P. Rosen. 1997. "Professional Collaboration: A Perspective from the Mathematics Standards," pp. 1–20 in June K. Phillips, ed., *Collaborations: Meeting New Goals, New Realities. Northeast Conference Reports.* Lincolnwood, IL: National Textbook Company.

National Standards in Foreign Language Education Project. 1996. *Standards for Foreign Language Learning: Preparing for the 21st Century.* Yonkers, NY: Author.

Phillips, June K. 1994. "The Challenge of Setting National Standards for the Study of Foreign Languages," pp. 1–5 in Robert M. Terry, ed., *Dimension: Language '94. Changing Images in Foreign Languages.* Valdosta, GA: Southern Conference on Language Teaching.

——— and Jamie B. Draper. 1994. "National Standards and Assessments: What Does It Mean for the Study of Second Languages in the Schools?" pp. 1–8 in Gale K. Crouse, ed., *Meeting New Challenges in the Foreign Language Classroom.* Report of the Central States Conference on the Teaching of Foreign Languages. Lincolnwood, IL: National Textbook Company.

——— and Robert C. Lafayette. 1996. "Reactions to the Catalyst: Implications for Our Professional Structure," pp. 197–209 in Robert C. Lafayette, ed., *National Standards: A Catalyst for Reform.* ACTFL Foreign Language Education Series. Lincolnwood, IL: National Textbook Company.

Thompson, Lynn, compiler. 1995. *K–8 Foreign Language Assessment: A Bibliography.* Washington, DC: Center for Applied Linguistics.

Wiggins, Grant P. 1993. *Assessing Student Performance: Exploring the Purpose and Limits of Testing.* San Francisco: Jossey-Bass.

———. 1998. *Educative Assessment: Designing Assessments to Inform and Improve Student Performance.* San Francisco: Jossey-Bass.

——— and Everett Kline. 1998. *Understanding by Design.* Presentation at the National Standards Foreign Language Education Collaborative Project Seminar. Yonkers, NY.

2

The Communication Standards

Joan Kelly Hall
University of Georgia

Introduction

Success in meeting the social, political, and economic challenges in our linguistically and culturally diverse communities depends in large part on the ability of teachers to prepare students studying other languages to meet the communicative demands of these challenges. Such preparation requires minimally that communication become one of the central principles around which foreign language study is organized.

This chapter presents an overview of the theories and empirical research that support the Communication goal and its three standards and lays out a pedagogy of foreign language learning that leads learners toward meeting these standards. To achieve this, the chapter is divided into three parts. In Part One the theoretical premises and empirical findings related to the concepts of communication, communicative competence, and communicative development, on which the Communication Standards are based, are presented. Part Two presents a review of the research on classroom discourse and other features found to support communicative development in classrooms. A review of some recent research on teacher and student use of the target language in foreign language classrooms is also included. Part Three provides a frame for a pedagogy of foreign language learning organized around the Communication goal and its standards. In the first and second sections of Part Three, some implications for reconfiguring classroom-based

Joan Kelly Hall (Ph.D. SUNY Albany, 1990), associate professor in the Department of Language Education and faculty member of the Linguistics Program at the University of Georgia, teaches courses in first- and second-language development, theories, and practices for teaching second and foreign languages, and multicultural communication. Her recent research interests include classroom-based second- and foreign-language learning, and intercultural communication. She has articles appearing in such journals as *Applied Linguistics, Foreign Language Annals, Issues in Applied Linguistics, Modern Language Journal, Journal of Linguistic Anthropology,* and *Research on Language and Social Interaction.*

foreign language learning drawn from the reviews of research are provided. I then discuss the three domains[1] of the Communication Standards in more detail, suggesting some general instructional considerations for each. After a short discussion on assessment needs, the chapter concludes with the raising of some issues and concerns related to research and professional development that are in need of further attention in our move to transform foreign language learning.

Part One: Communication, Communicative Competence, and Communicative Development

Communication

Communication is at the heart of all social life. It is in our communication with others that we develop, articulate, and manage our individual identities, our interpersonal relationships, and our memberships in our communities (Blum-Kulka 1997; Carbaugh 1996; Gumperz 1981, 1992; Halliday 1994; Hymes 1972; Vygotsky 1978). As we communicate, we set goals, negotiate the means to reach them, and reconceptualize those we have set. Research on communication (e.g., Carey 1989; Gumperz 1992; Hall 1959, 1983; Heath 1983; Hymes 1972; Purves 1990; Scollon & Scollon 1996) makes it clear that much of what we do when we communicate with others is conventionalized. In other words, in going about our everyday business, we participate in recurring intellectual and practical activities in which the goals of the activities, our roles, and the language we use as we play these roles and attempt to accomplish the goals, are familiar to us.

We approach all of our communicative activities, even seemingly mundane ones such as those we associate with banking, like withdrawing money or opening an account, with a set of communicative plans, i.e., "socially constructed models for solutions of communicative problems" (Luckmann 1995:181). We share the content of these plans with other members of our sociocultural groups and communities. These plans lay out for us what the expected or typical goals of any activity are likely to be. The goals, in turn, frame the role relationships of those involved in the activity and thereby provide some common ground for knowing what each participant can appropriately, or conventionally, say and do. When we participate in communicative activities, we use the plans as navigational tools to help us synchronize our actions and interpretations with others and thus reach a mutually recognizable idea of what is going on in the activity (Edwards 1995; Luckmann 1995). When we walk into a classroom as experienced teachers, for example, we have a set of expected goals and know what we as teachers can legitimately say and do. Moreover, we anticipate what students' responses and other actions are likely to be. If someone utters "raise your hands," a typical teacher-student role relationship is called to mind, along with expectations about the activity taking place and the kinds of linguistic actions that are likely to follow. Likewise, the utterance, "Did you hear what happened to Fred?" invokes certain expectations in the listeners about the kind of activity that is likely to follow (e.g., a recounting of an unexpected occurrence to someone who is known to the participants), the kinds of social roles and relationships that exist among the interactants (close friends or associates), and the kinds of language that would be considered both appropriate and inappropriate to use.

These plans then function as maps of our sociocultural worlds and contain significant sociocultural knowledge about our communicative activities. As we participate in our activities, we learn to attend to and use that knowledge so that we may become adept at communicating in our activities in ways that are considered appropriate and thus understandable to our social groups. There are few communicative moments in our daily lives about which we do not have some kind of communicative plan to help us decide "what is going on" and work through the activity, figuring out, for example, what counts as an appropriate utterance, what to do to resolve uncertainties, and so on.

Communicative plans and activities are nested within and shaped by our memberships in various social institutions. Family, school, church, community, and the workplace are significant social institutions that give shape and in turn are shaped by the social identities through which we participate in our communicative activities. In activities that are typically associated with schooling—such as faculty meetings, club advising, classroom teaching, and parent-teacher conferencing, we take on such roles as students, teachers, administrators, and staff members. In communicative activities typically associated with families, we are parents, children, cousins, or in-laws, and we communicate with each other in our activities through these identities.

Although we may not always be able to articulate clearly our worldview, beliefs, and values, they nonetheless help shape the expectations we use to judge our social institutions, our communicative activities, and our individual participation within them as appropriate and relevant. Figure 1 depicts this sociocultural perspective of communication. As shown here, the linguistic resources we use to communicate are shaped by, and help to shape, the goal-based plans of our communicative activities. These activities in turn are shaped by and help to shape the role relationships we develop as part of our membership in important social institutions, and more generally, the beliefs and values that we, as members of sociocultural communities, hold.

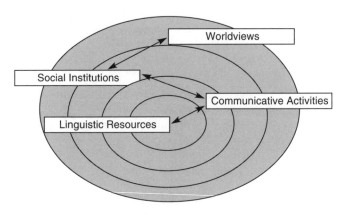

Figure 1
Sociocultural Perspective of Communication

To recap, communication is the means by which we create and live through our sociocultural world. It is a fundamentally interpersonal phenomenon in that much of the language we use on a day-to-day basis is situated within and framed by the myriad of intellectual and practical activities that constitute, and are constituted by, our social institutions. Thus, much of our individual language use is conventionalized, tied to the goals of our activities and our socially constructed roles as members of our various institutions. The conventionality allows us to participate in social life and connect with others in mutually intelligible ways, and thereby helps us to both sustain and transform the goals, values, and customs of our sociocultural groups and communities (Wertsch 1991).

As stated earlier, our communicative activities are fundamentally pragmatic and are organized around particular socioculturally defined goals. While there can be a variety of ways to group these goals, the Communication goal contains three macro domains that frame the purposes for learning to communicate in another language and define the standards: the interpersonal, the interpretive, and the presentational domains. The *interpersonal domain* frames those communicative activities accomplished through direct interaction with others for the purposes of creating and maintaining interpersonal relationships and/or accomplishing a particular task. The *interpretive domain* encompasses activities involving understanding spoken and written texts for the purposes of developing new meanings, new ideas, new feelings, and new experiences and using them to transform those we have. The *presentational domain* frames those communicative activities in which the primary purpose is to present or express ideas, information, feelings, and experiences through both the spoken and written word.

Effective participation in any of the activities constituting these three communicative domains requires the development of *communicative competence*. A brief overview of the history of this term as it has developed in the field of foreign language education and a description of its components is provided in the next section.

Communicative Competence

The concept of communicative competence was first made popular by Dell Hymes more than three decades ago (1964; 1972). Hymes argued that one's competence to use language effectively and appropriately is intimately linked to one's knowledge of such social conditions as the setting, the participants, and the goals or purposes for which the language is being used. He labeled this knowledge *communicative competence*. This concept is a significant reconceptualization of the concept of linguistic competence as first proposed by Chomsky (1965). According to Chomsky, linguistic competence consists of innate, mental, structural systems that exist apart from any contexts of use. Hymes, however, considered the nature of competence to be fundamentally pragmatic, and argued instead that competence could only be explained in terms of the social knowledge shared by members of a speech community. It is this social knowledge that shapes and gives meaning to linguistic forms. He stated, "It is not enough for the child to be able to produce any grammatical utterance. It would have to remain speechless if it could not connect utterances to their contexts of use" (1964:110). Hymes's early assertions about the nature of communicative competence have been backed up and in many ways extended by a great deal of empirical research in a variety of cultural settings (e.g., Goodwin 1990; Heath 1983; Philips 1983; Ochs 1988; Schiefflin 1990). The findings from these studies show the varied and complex ways in which our communicative competence is "inherently linked to the cultural, institutional, and historical settings" of our social worlds (Wertsch 1994: 203).

In the fields of second- and foreign-language learning, Canale and Swain (1980) made one of the earliest attempts to develop a theoretical framework of communicative competence for the purposes of curriculum design and evaluation. Integrating various perspectives, they proposed a model of communicative competence that contains four components: grammatical competence, sociolinguistic competence, discourse competence, and strategic competence. More recently, Bachman (1990) proposed a model that, while similar to Canale and Swain's, contains just two primary components, language competence and strategic competence. The first component is further divided into two areas, organizational knowledge and pragmatic knowledge, while strategic competence is broken into three: assessment, planning, and execution. Building upon these two previous models, Celce-Murcia, Zoltan, and Thurrell (1995) have proposed a third model of communicative competence. Because it takes into consideration some of the most recent research on communicative competence, their model is by far the most comprehensive. In it, communicative competence is arranged into five interrelated areas of knowledge: discourse competence, linguistic competence, sociocultural competence, actional competence, and strategic competence.

Discourse competence, considered the core of communicative competence, deals with "the selection, sequencing, and arrangement of words, structures, sentences and utterances to achieve a unified spoken or written text" (Celce-Murcia et al., 1995:13). As seen in the model depicted in Figure 2, it is placed at the center, surrounded by the other competences, since it is here where the microlevel lexico-grammatical building blocks intersect with

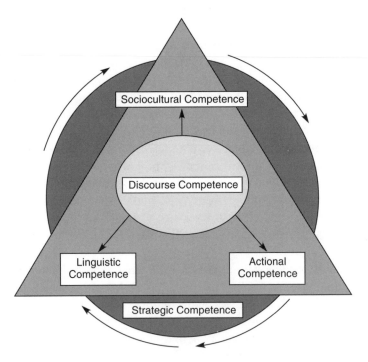

Figure 2
Communicative Competence (Celce-Murcia et al., 1995)

the more macrolevel dimensions of sociocultural context and communicative intent in the expression and interpretation of meaning.

Giving shape to and being shaped by discourse competence are three additional components: *sociocultural competence, linguistic competence, and actional competence.* Sociocultural competence includes knowledge about such extralinguistic factors as the context, stylistic appropriateness, and the nonverbal and other background cultural knowledge that communicators rely on to understand and contribute to any particular communicative activity. Linguistic competence consists of knowledge of such linguistic systems as the syntactic, the morphological, the lexical, the phonological, and the orthographic. Actional competence is defined as the ability to match "actional intent with linguistic form" (Celce-Murcia et al. 1995:17) and includes the knowledge of how a variety of communicative purposes—such as expressing opinions, displaying attention, showing satisfaction, etc.—are linguistically encoded. Weaving through these four competences is the last component, *strategic competence.* Celce-Murcia et al. (1995) define this as a set of skills for negotiating and resolving communicative problems as well as for compensating for communicative deficiencies in any of the other four components.

In sum, our ability to communicate depends on our development of communicative competence. This competence encompasses a variety of skills and knowledge that include far more than just linguistic knowledge. The significance of this concept to the field of foreign language learning has grown over the years, shaping its instructional goals and approaches. There have been several attempts at constructing an adequate model for these purposes, the most recent and most comprehensive being the five-component model designed by Celce-Murcia et al. Still to be considered is the process by which we develop such competence. I take this up in the next section.

Communicative Development

There is substantial research (Berman & Slobin 1994; Levy & Nelson 1994; Ninio & Snow 1996; Pine 1994; Shatz & McCloskey 1984; Sokolov & Snow 1994; Tomasello et al. 1993; Vygotsky 1978) that locates the source of children's communicative development in their engagement in communicative activities with their caregivers or more expert communicators. Among other findings, it has been shown that the communicative skills and knowledge that children learn are dependent on their experiences in regularly occurring, goal-directed communicative activities, with assisted guidance from more-competent participants. These expert communicators not only provide the children with a substantial amount of input in which they make salient the more important cues to the children, but they also provide verbal instructions that direct the children to perceive these cues and make connections between them and their contexts.

Initially, as children and adults interact, the adults assume responsibility for doing most of the communicative work. Over time and with the guided help of the adults, the children learn to recognize the activity taking place and the relevant linguistic cues and their meanings. Their initial linguistic actions begin to approximate the conventional forms used by the more expert participants. As the children take more responsibility for the realization of an activity, they build up habits of language use and expectations about their communicative values. These habits and expectations are shaped into prototypical linguistic action patterns that are ultimately internalized by the children. In this way they become the cognitive tools with which the children make sense of and participate in their communicative worlds. The ability to recognize what is going on and to contribute independently to a communicative activity constitutes a major accomplishment in children's communicative development and facilitates the development of more-complex and creative communicative behaviors.

Because different communicative activities are comprised of different arrangements of linguistic resources, different conditions for communicative development are created (Wertsch 1991). In turn, these different conditions, the varied means of assistance in recognizing and using the linguistic cues, and the children's individual responses to them give rise to distinct developmental outcomes. A study by Pine (1994) nicely illustrates this process. In a microanalysis of mother-child interaction Pine shows how the different placements of syntactic elements in the talk of different mothers provided different learning conditions for their children. As a result of being provided with different models of language use, the children's understanding and ability to use these elements in communicative situations also differed. In another study that looked at caregiver-child talk (Tomasello et al. 1990), it was shown how children develop different understandings of communication from their participation in different communicative contexts. In looking at the differences between mother-child and father-child interaction, the authors found that when conversational breakdowns occurred, children elaborated upon their utterances if their mothers did not initially acknowledge them, while they repeated their utterances or abandoned talk if their fathers did not acknowledge them. The authors concluded that through extended interactions with each parent the children learned to assume different intentions in their parents' nonacknowledgments. Because mothers usually followed up on their children's utterances when a breakdown in communication occurred, the children learned to interpret their mother's lack of initial acknowledgment as a need for more information and so learned to elaborate. On the other hand, because fathers usually did not return to the conversation after a breakdown, the children learned to interpret their fathers' nonacknowledgments as a lack of interest and so learned to give up. Findings from these studies make clear the developmental consequences that arise from differences in communicative activities.

To recap, the fundamental base of all language development is communicative action. Children develop the knowledge and skills needed for competent communication through participation in communicative activities with more expert communicators. Over time and with help children learn to approximate the conventional forms used by the more expert participants to express similar communicative intents. Eventually, as these forms become internalized, they are used by the children to help them in understanding what is going on at any communicative moment and in the creation of their individual communicative actions. Since communicative development is fundamentally tied to children's communicative activities, both the form and direction that individual growth takes depend on the communicative environments in which they are involved, the kinds of assistance that more-capable communicators provide them in using and interpreting the uses of the linguistic and other resources, and their individual responses to their involvement.

Because schools are important social institutions, the activities formed in their classrooms play an especially significant role in development. Moreover, because many classroom activities are created through teacher-student discourse, the school's role is especially consequential to the creation of communicative learning environments and ultimately to the shaping of individual learners' development. In Part Two, I discuss the role that classroom discourse plays in communicative development and the implications for foreign language learning.

Part Two: Classroom Discourse and Its Role in Learning

Classroom Discourse

Classroom discourse is the oral interaction that occurs between teachers and students and among students in classrooms. To be successful at learning, students must develop the communicative competence that is specific to the discourse of their classroom activities. They need to know, for example, how to listen or appear to listen at appropriate times, how to bid for a turn at speaking, and when and with whom it is appropriate to speak. They also need to know how to locate the cues that are used by the teacher in her talk to find the "right" answers and how to display their knowledge in ways that are deemed appropriate by the teacher (Edwards & Westgate 1994).

Research on classroom discourse (Baker 1992; Bowers & Flinders 1990; Cazden 1988; Gutierrez 1994; Gutierrez, Rymes, & Larson 1995; Lemke 1988; Mehan 1979; Nystrand 1997; Patthey-Chavez et al. 1995; Smagorinsky 1993; Wells 1996) provides compelling evidence linking students' involvement in their classroom interaction to their communicative development. Taken together, the findings from these studies show how teachers and students develop consequential patterns of interaction in their classroom discourse. These patterns are consequential in that they establish the norms and expectations for the participation of the teachers and students, and more generally, the communicative activities through which knowledge is organized and learning accomplished. Differences in teacher-student discourse across classrooms, and within the same classroom and same activities, in the kinds of learning opportunities teachers make available to their students in their interactions with them lead to distinct individual developmental outcomes.

A study by Smagorinsky (1993) highlights this intrinsic link between learning and classroom discourse. He compared the discourse of two communicative activities whose purpose was to discuss literature in two high school English classrooms. He found that in each classroom the students' beliefs about the nature of the activity of "literature discussion" and their own discussions of literature in small groups reflected to a large extent the ways in which each teacher shaped the discussions on literature in his large group discussions. He concludes that the different ways in which literature discussions were accomplished in the two classrooms created different communities of learners with different understandings of what it meant to "discuss literature" and thus with different communicative skills for doing so.

Since oral communication is both the medium of learning and an object of pedagogical attention in foreign language classrooms, the discourse of these classrooms plays an especially significant role in the development of learners' communicative competence, shaping both their understanding of, and ability to interact in, the target language. Since language teachers are considered to be the expert users of the target language, and because they are usually the primary if not the only source of the target language for foreign language learners, at least in the beginning years, their management of the discourse is crucial. Through the various kinds of interaction patterns and norms for participating in classroom interactions that foreign language teachers establish in their classrooms they help to establish the fundamental sources of their learners' communicative development.

My own investigations of communicative development in a high school Spanish language classroom (Hall in press) provide evidence of the connection between foreign language teacher talk and foreign language learning. In an examination of teacher interaction with different students in one particular communicative activity, I found that the students' communicative development in Spanish depended to a great extent on the different ways the teacher interacted with each of them and on the different opportunities for involvement that he made available to them. The participation of one student, to whom the teacher gave ample opportunity to add to and direct the classroom interaction over the course of a semester, increased and the student reported that his interest in speaking Spanish did as well. On the other hand, the participation of two other students, who attempted to participate in the classroom interaction as often as the first student, was limited by the teacher to short responses or ignored altogether. Over time these two students became inattentive and occasionally disruptive, and they reported at the end of the semester that they found speaking Spanish difficult and thus were less enthusiastic about learning it. I concluded that these differences in student abilities and interests were largely tied to the opportunities for participating in the classroom interaction that the teacher made available to them.

Much research on classroom discourse has shown that although discourse activities may differ from classroom to classroom and school to school, one particular pattern, commonly referred to as the I-R-E, or recitation script, typifies the discourse of Western schooling, from kindergarten to the university. In the next section, I provide an overview of this pattern.

Typical Pattern of Classroom Discourse

The teacher-led three-part sequence of I-R-E, or teacher initiation > student response > teacher evaluation, is the most common pattern of discourse found in all kinds of classrooms. The set of moves involves the teacher asking a question to which she usually already knows the answer. The typical purpose of such questioning is to direct a student to display some bit of knowledge so that the teacher can ascertain whether the student knows the material. The student is expected to provide a brief but "correct" response to the question, which is then evaluated by the teacher with such typical remarks as "Good," "That's right," or "No, that's not right." The teacher then asks either a follow-up question of the same student or the same or a related question of another student. This pattern is exemplified in Excerpt 1.

Excerpt 1

1. Teacher: Mary, what is the answer to number 1?
2.   Mary: Banana.
3. Teacher: Yes, that's right, it is. Regina, what do you have for number 2?
4. Regina: I put apples.
5. Teacher: Apples? Tom what did you put?

In this excerpt, the teacher begins by asking a student to respond to a question, which the student does. The teacher's "Yes, that's right" in line 3 is a positive evaluation of Mary's response. The teacher follows this with a related question to another student. Like Mary, Regina gives a short response. In line 5 the teacher repeats the student's response using a rising intonation. Repeating a student's response in this way is a typical cue used by teachers in the I-R-E to indicate that the student response is incorrect and thus needs to be repaired (McHoul 1990). The teacher then puts the same question to a different student.

Excerpt 2 illustrates an I-R-E pattern typically found in a foreign language classroom.

Excerpt 2[2]

1.   Teacher: *¿Te gusta cantar?*
       (Do you like to sing?)

2. Mercedes: *Sí.*
       (Yes.)

3.   Teacher: *Oh sí, a ti te gusta cantar. ¿Te gusta cantar?*
       (Oh yes, you like to sing. Do you like to sing?)

4.   Andrea: *Sí me gusta cantar.*
       (Yes, I like to sing.)

5.   Teacher: *Muy bien, muy bien, sí. Y Jamaal, ¿Te gusta cantar?*
       (Very well, very well, yes. And Jamaal, do you like to sing?)

In this excerpt the teacher begins by directing a question to a student, to which the student gives a short response. In line 3 the teacher repeats the student's response and then reformulates it into a more syntactically complete one, thus providing feedback to the students on what the teacher considers an appropriate response to his question. He then asks the same question to a second student, who succeeds in providing him with the expected response.

With his *muy bien* in line 5 the teacher positively evaluates Andrea's response and moves on to pose the same question to another student.

Extensive research has examined the consequences of participation in this particular pattern of classroom discourse. Using data from her own and others' classrooms, Cazden (1988), for example, shows how the use of the I-R-E pattern of interaction in reading lessons more often facilitated teacher control of the interaction rather than student learning of the content of the lesson. Similarly, based on examinations of classroom discourse from several classrooms, Barnes (1992) found that the frequent use of the I-R-E pattern of discourse reflected a constricted, transmission model of learning. In this model the teacher is assumed to be the sole authority and learning is unidirectional, with bits of knowledge moving in a narrow path from the teacher to the student. The extended use of this pattern, Barnes argues, does not allow for complex ways of communicating between the teacher and students.

More recently, in a study of "journal sharing" in three different classrooms Gutierrez (1994) found that in those classes in which the activity was based on a strict use of the I-R-E pattern, the teacher did most of the talking. Thus, Gutierrez argues, the children in this group had few opportunities to participate in the activity and thereby expand their learning about the topics on which the journal sharings were based. In classes using different discourse scripts for the activity, students were encouraged to ask questions and to respond to and elaborate upon each other's contributions. In addition, the teacher more often expanded upon rather than evaluated the student responses. Thus, students were more actively involved in the activity, more topically related discourse was produced, and greater opportunities for joint problem solving were created.

My own investigations of a high school foreign language classroom (Hall 1995) revealed similar findings on the I-R-E. In an instructional activity whose goal was to provide opportunities for students to practice speaking Spanish, I found that the teacher used an I-R-E pattern of interaction almost exclusively. He was most often the initiator of the sequence, and his responses to the students, the third part of the three-part sequence, were almost always an evaluation of the grammatical correctness of their responses to his initial question or comment. The sample of classroom interaction found in Excerpt 2, above, typifies the kind of interaction that took place in this activity over the course of an academic semester. His strict adherence to this pattern of discourse led to mechanical, topically disjointed talk and limited student involvement. I concluded that extended engagement in this activity was unlikely to lead to the learners' development of the communicative competence needed to speak Spanish in any context outside this particular classroom activity.

Perhaps the most comprehensive examination of the consequences of the I-R-E to date is the study of 112 eighth- and ninth-grade language arts and English classes by Nystrand (1997). He found that the overwhelming majority of teachers used the recitation script almost exclusively in their classrooms and that its use was negatively correlated with learning. Students whose learning was accomplished almost exclusively through the recitation script were less able to recall and understand the topical content than were the students who were involved in more topically related open discussions. Moreover, he found that the use of the I-R-E was more prevalent in lower-track classes, leading, he argues, to significant inequalities in student opportunities to achieve.

In a comparison of the I-R-E pattern and other, more open patterns that stimulated learning Wells (1993, 1996) found that what differed most often was how the third part of the I-R-E sequence was realized. When the third part was only an evaluative comment, like "That's right" or "Very good," it stifled rather than maximized student participation. However, when the third part followed up on a student's response, such as a comment that added to or offered an example or explanation of the student response, or invited the student to make such a move, e.g., "That's an interesting point. Why do you think it happened that way?" or "Who agrees with what Jim said?" it stimulated active student talk and thereby helped to move the topical discussion along. Examinations of teacher-student discourse in such content areas as English (Lee 1993, 1995; Miller 1996), math (Forman 1996), science (Warren & Roseberry 1996), and foreign language (Toth 1997) support and extend these findings. In looking at teacher involvement in classroom discourse these studies found that teacher-led, topically connected questions and comments that expanded upon student responses and challenged their thinking were positively correlated with learning.

Given these findings, we can conclude, as does Wells (1993), that creating conditions for student learning in classroom discourse does not depend on whether the teacher controls the discourse but on the direction the interaction takes. In cases where teacher-produced questions and comments are limited to evaluating student displays of knowledge, and student contributions are limited to short responses to teacher queries, the classroom discourse is not likely to lead to active student involvement and complex communicative development. However, in cases in which teacher questions and comments are probing and open-ended, and in which students are allowed to ask questions and expand on the talk in addition to responding to the teacher, the classroom discourse facilitates learning. Wells argues that the choices teachers make about the kinds of interactional patterns they use in their classrooms are linked to their pedagogical beliefs. Teachers who view themselves as leaders of communities of inquiry, who view students as active agents in the learning process and thus take their involvement seriously, are more likely to engage their students in intellectually challenging interactions. Teachers who perceive themselves as authorities of knowledge and students as passive recipients of their knowledge are more likely to use the standard I-R-E.

Using the findings from the research on classroom discourse, Tharp and Gallimore (1988; 1991) and their colleagues (Goldenberg 1991; Rueda, Goldenberg & Gallimore 1992; Patthey-Chavez, Clare & Gallimore 1995) have developed a protocol for establishing a particular pattern of teacher-student interaction, labeled "instructional conversations," whose purpose is to foster learning. A discussion of these conversations and their relevance to learning to communicate in another language is taken up in the next section.

Instructional Conversations

"Instructional conversations" (ICs) are a developmentally rich pattern of teacher-student interaction whose purpose is to assist students' understandings of and ability to communicate about concepts and ideas that are central to their learning. ICs stand in marked contrast to the more traditional recitation pattern discussed above. The concept of ICs is based on Vygotsky's (1978) notion of the ZPD, or zone of proximal development, which is the level at which one can do something only with the assistance of a more capable other. Individual movement from dependence to independence in one's ability to perform in a given activity depends on assisted performance, or what we more commonly call teaching. ICs are one form of assisted performance.

ICs are based on the idea that classroom discourse that engages students in productive interaction helps them to develop complex knowledge and behaviors at the same time that it helps them assume responsibility for their own learning. Extended negotiation of the concepts and ideas with those more knowledgeable, such as their teachers, helps students to internalize the meanings of these concepts. It also helps them to connect their own experiences to the concepts, and thus develop deeper conceptual understandings as well as the communicative behaviors needed to display and use this knowledge in academic and other activities. ICs have been found to be especially useful for the analysis of literary or other kinds of texts, including films, for learning and understanding complex concepts, and for discussing issues from multiple perspectives (Goldenberg 1991).

ICs are marked by several features. First, the focus is always a particular topic or theme that is both interesting to the students and intellectually challenging. Second, the discussion is managed in such a way that all class members are highly involved. This does not mean that the teacher does most of the talking or maintains tight control of the students' turns at speaking, as happens with the use of I-R-E. Conversely, it does not mean that the teacher relinquishes her role, leaving participation in the discussion to be decided by the more talkative and assertive class members. Rather, the teacher acts as discussion leader and facilitator, allowing students to initiate turns while making sure that all student voices are included in the discussion and, when necessary, drawing out and helping students to draw out their ideas. Finally, the teacher helps the students link their background experiences and prior knowledge to the current discussion by making sure that the contributions are highly responsive and interconnected and that they build upon each other through challenging or extending previous turns.

Several communicative actions by which teachers can help to facilitate students' conceptual and communicative development in the ICs have been identified. These are summarized here.

a. *Modeling:* This provides the students with exemplary communicative and cognitive behaviors associated with the doing of a particular activity that students observe, note, and imitate. Research on modeling (Bandura 1977) has shown it to be an effective means of establishing abstract or rule-governed behavior. By watching what others do or having a model to work from, we learn, among other things, judgmental orientations, linguistic styles, conceptual schemes, information-processing strategies, cognitive operations, and standards of conduct.

In modeling, a teacher may talk aloud her thinking on a particular issue or task, letting students listen to how she connects given information to new information, how she constructs an argument to defend a position, or how she thinks through the solving of a problem or exercise. As she does, she provide students not only with the cognitive strategies they need to engage in the activity but, just as importantly, with the words, phrases, and other linguistic cues the students are likely to need to accomplish the task on their own. Reciprocal Teaching (Palincsar, Brown, & Campione 1993) is an example of one instructional activity in which modeling plays a central role. Here, the teacher first models the use of those strategies that have been shown to be necessary to successful reading comprehension, by "asking a question about a text," "summarizing," "clarifying a point," and "predicting what is to happen." She then guides the students in these same tasks, gradually decreasing her help as their abilities develop.

b. *Feeding back:* This communicative behavior provides students with clear information on the standards against which their performances are to be compared and how well their actions at a given point in time compare to them. Students have the opportunity to compare their own performances and self-correct. Research (e.g., White & Kistner 1992) suggests that teachers need to be judicious in their use of feedback to individual students, since their feedback influences the formation of students' perceptions of themselves and others as learners. The more positively framed the feedback is, the more positive the students' perceptions are likely to be. This means, then, that providing an explicit model of an expected performance and telling a student what she can do to improve her performance will yield more positive results than giving a vague indication, or no indication, and/or making negative comments about the student's attempts at performing to the standard.

c. *Contingency managing:* This means of assisting performance is closely related to feeding back and involves arranging rewards and punishments to follow learners' behaviors. The primary focus is on rewarding positive behaviors rather than punishing undesired ones.

d. *Directing:* This focuses the learners' attention on what is to be learned in a task or activity and directly teaches a skill or concept. As Rueda, Goldenberg, and Gallimore point out (1992), this does not mean teaching skills or concepts apart from any context, but within and as part of a larger activity. Rather than having students try to figure out how to do something on their own, it is sometimes helpful to provide the students at the beginning with the information and/or the particular linguistic tools they need to complete a task successfully. This can be done through lectures, demonstrations, and coaching. Evidence from research on direct teaching in first-language content classes (e.g., Light & Butterworth 1993; Stone & Forman 1988) and in second-language learning (e.g., Schmidt 1994) shows that direct teaching helps focus the learners' attention on those features of the activity they are expected to learn and doing so facilitates both cognitive and linguistic growth.

e. *Questioning:* Assisting students' performance through questioning is the most characteristic means of assistance in formal learning. Teacher questions have two functions, both of which are essential to supporting learners' development. The first is to help students work through the task or activity (assisting function) by, for example, eliciting extended student discussion on a particular topic or helping students activate relevant background knowledge. The second function of teacher questions is to allow the teacher to see where the learner is in terms of her understanding and ability to perform without assistance (assessing function).

f. *Explaining:* This involves explaining and justifying the underlying conceptual or schematic structures of what is being learned. Doing so helps the learners organize and make sense of new information, knowledge, or skills and subsequently integrate it with what they already know. As research on learning (Detterman & Sternberg 1993) demonstrates, explicitly showing students how information applies in new contexts and providing them with frameworks for organizing the new information greatly facilitates their learning.

g. *Task structuring:* This last means of assistance consists of teasing apart the various components of a task and arranging them so that they are cognitively, communicatively, and in other ways accessible to the learners and at the same time challenging. Tasks that are too easy can lead to frustration, lack of motivation, and disinterest in much the same way that tasks that are too large or too difficult can. The goal of task structuring is to provide students with tasks that they can do only with help from others and, through the other means of assisted performance, to move them to a state of independence.

In sum, the use of ICs in classroom interaction helps to promote student learning in ways that the more traditional recitation script of I-R-E does not. Through the ways in which they weave instruction into their conversations with students, teachers help them make connections and build upon what they already know. Teachers also make their own thinking explicit, modeling for the students the strategies they use to work through an issue, solve a problem, or accomplish a task. Students then are able to develop a shared base of knowledge and skills upon which more-complex knowledge can be built. For their part, the students' involvement in extended talk in and through their classroom activities allows them to be active participants in their own development. As a final note, as beneficial to learning as they have been shown to be, ICs are not meant to replace all other methods of instruction. Rather, as Goldenberg (1991) suggests, they are particularly suited for such educational goals as "helping students comprehend texts, learn complex concepts, and consider various perspectives on issues" (17).

In addition to creating and sustaining complex webs of learning through the use of classroom discourse, other instructional practices have been shown to promote learning in classrooms. In the next section I provide a brief overview of these practices.

Features of Supportive Learning Environments

In recent studies of classroom learning (Cabello & Terrell 1994; Carlsen 1992; The New London Group 1996; Chang-Wells & Wells 1993), several features were found to promote the establishment of a classroom environment in which a high level of learning was supported and academic success was common. Perhaps most importantly, teachers in these classrooms were concerned with creating a community of learners characterized by the nurturing of learner engagement in meaningful activities that foster an atmosphere of trust, mutual respect, risk-taking, and exploration. Thus they made affective concerns as important as intellectual and academic ones. Some of the means for doing so included the use of personal anecdotes to make instruction more meaningful, the use of first-person plurals such as "we" and "let's" to refer to the entire group. They also used examples and materials that positively acknowledged the students' cultures, ages, and social communities, and incorporated routines in the classroom in which all students were given roles. Moreover, in these classrooms, teachers provided students with opportunities to be experts in something, thus helping them develop confidence in their abilities as learners. Finally, these teachers were able to articulate clearly the purposes of their instruction; their activities were goal-directed, and what students were to learn in these activities was clearly marked. In classrooms that were less supportive of learning, it was found that teachers provided few opportunities for students to be actively involved. Instead, these teachers tended to hold the floor for long periods of time, spending much of it trying to control the students' behavior rather than engaging them in learning. Moreover, their goals for student learning were often vaguely stated, if at all, and they relied heavily on the textbook as the primary source of learning.

To sum up, the interaction that occurs between teachers and students as they engage in their classroom activities shapes both what students learn and the process of learning itself. The most typical pattern of interaction, the I-R-E, is negatively associated with learning, since the different contributions often lack coherence and provide little cognitive or linguistic challenge to the students. On the other hand, teacher-led discourse that includes questions and comments that push students to think and connect their utterances to others in meaningful ways has been shown to facilitate student learning. One particularly productive pattern is the Instructional Conversation. Other behaviors that help to create supportive conditions for learning include finding ways to nurture both intellectual and affective development and being clear about the instructional goals and the standards for performance.

A last area to examine is the recent research that is specific to target language use in the discourse of foreign language classrooms.

Target Language Use

Recent literature on teacher talk (e.g., Krashen 1980, 1989) has urged the exclusive use of the target language in teacher-student interaction to provide "comprehensible input" and "linguistically rich environments." This environment is typically defined as including such features as semantically and syntactically simple constructions, repetitions, and rephrasings (Crookes & Gass 1993; Pica 1991, 1994). These claims about the foreign language classroom environment have led to the belief that as long as whatever the teacher says is in the target language and "comprehensible" as defined above, it is pedagogically useful. However, recent examinations of teacher talk (Hall 1995; Toth 1997) have raised questions about the nature of "comprehensible input" and its potential for learning. In the same study of a high school Spanish classroom reported upon earlier, I examined the linguistic construction of the teacher's utterances in his talk to his students. Although the teacher talk was replete with simple syntax and multiple repetitions and rephrasings, there was no attention to topic development. Instead, the conversation was limited to what I called "lexical chaining," the linking of utterances through the use of the same or similar words that had no connection to any larger topically related goal. While the teacher's talk was almost always exclusively in the target language, and contained those features thought to create "comprehensible input," it provided no basis upon which students could add to and extend the talk in any meaningful way. Thus, its potential as a meaningful and rich source of development was, at best, limited.

In a similar vein, Toth (1997) examined the discourse in a university-level Spanish classroom. He found that teacher utterances containing features conventionally associated with "comprehensible input" but not connected by some larger topical or goal-directed agenda violated learners' conversational expectations, negatively affecting their ability to participate in the conversation activity. These findings make it clear that to facilitate learners' communicative development through classroom discourse, teacher talk must not only be in the target language, but it must also be discursively comprehensible, organized around the mutual alignment to some larger, activity-based, communicatively meaningful goal.

Connected to the concern with teacher use of the target language is the concern with student use. As has been the case for teachers, the typical pedagogical stance has been to encourage exclusive use of the target language by the students from the beginning levels of instruction. A recent study of language use by students in a university Spanish class (Brooks & Donato 1994), however, raises some questions about this belief. In an examination of the ways in which students used English and Spanish in this classroom, they found that when confronted with an unfamiliar or difficult task, the students' use of English tended to increase. A closer look revealed that the students used English to talk about how to do the task (e.g., "Oh, ok, this is what we have to do"), and to mediate their own and each other's behavior in relation to what needed to be done (e.g., "I think we put a mark here"). As they gained experience and grew comfortable with what needed to be done, both their English use and their talk about the task decreased. The researchers concluded that the use of English by these students did not hinder their learning. Rather, it facilitated it by assisting them in organizing, planning, and coordinating their behavior and others' behavior in the accomplishment of the tasks. Given just this one study, it is difficult to make general claims about the use of English in foreign language classrooms. However, it does make apparent our need to look more closely at the uses to which both teachers and students put English and the target language as they engage in their classroom communicative activities.

Several significant implications for foreign language learning can be drawn from what we know about communicative development, classroom learning through teacher-student interaction, and the use of the target language. These are dealt with in Part Three. I also provide more detailed descriptions of each of the three communicative domains and include discussions on pedagogical considerations for creating classroom learning environments that encompass these domains and on assessment issues and concerns. I conclude by suggesting specific areas in both research and professional development in need of further attention.

Part Three: Organizing the Foreign Language Classroom for Communication

Implications for Designing a Pedagogy Based on the Communication Standards

What we know about the nature of communicative competence and communicative development both in and out of schools has several implications for understanding foreign language learning and designing a classroom environment organized around the standards of the Communication goal.

The first has to do with the purpose of foreign language learning. If the development of communicative competence is the underlying goal of foreign language learning, then, as the current research on communicative development shows, learning to communicate does not mean accumulating sets of context-free, structurally based linguistic units and vocabulary lists in the target language. Rather, it involves developing an understanding of and ability to use the symbolic tools and resources associated with meaningful and goal-directed communicative activities in the target language. These resources include the particular linguistic, actional or rhetorical, discursive, sociocultural, and strategic competences that are typical of the activities of interest and crucial to their realizations.

The activities themselves are crucial components of the developmental process. As pointed out in the discussions on communicative development and classroom discourse, both how and what our learners learn to do in the target language are tied to their classroom-based communicative activities, the linguistic resources of these activities, and the kinds and degree of participation made available to them. Thus, what we as foreign language teachers choose to do in the classroom is of great consequence to our learners' development of communicative competence. More to the point, in deciding which communicative activities to make available to our students and by defining appropriate and inappropriate displays of communicative behavior within them, we play a significant part in determining what the students subsequently develop in the target language.

It is apparent that a foreign language curriculum needs to be organized around meaningful, motivating, and cognitively challenging activities. This is a particularly noteworthy point for beginning levels of foreign language instruction, where such activities are not usually found. It is often assumed that if students do not have a certain level of communicative competence in the target language, they also do not have the cognitive capabilities or motivations to engage in extended talk or other complex activities. In classrooms where such assumptions are the norm we typically find such low-level activities as "Tell me what time it is," "What color is this?" or "What number am I holding now?" Teachers in these classrooms argue in their defense that because their students are at the beginning levels of instruction they are unable to sustain more-complex talk. However, as has been pointed out earlier, what students learn to do in their language classroom depends on what is made available to them in these environments. If there is little provided to be learned, there is little the students *can* learn. Thus limiting the options for student involvement to the activities of listing and labeling only limits their communicative development. To shape learners' communicative competence in the target language in ways that are considered to be appropriate to their social, academic, and other needs requires involving them in developmentally rich communicative activities that challenge their linguistic and cognitive capabilities.

Another implication has to do with learning itself. We know that it requires extended engagement in two interconnected processes. The first is constituted by long-term immersion in authentic versions of communicative activities that learners are expected to master with those who are considered experts (The New London Group 1996). As noted earlier, much of the knowledge and skills we need to be competent in a given activity depends on the opportunities we have had to experience participation in them. The more we do something with someone who is more expert, and the more the goals, plans, and tools for doing it are made clear to us, the more automatic our involvement becomes and the better we are at doing it ourselves (Vygotsky 1978). The experts serve as mentors to the learners, helping create risk-free environments where learners feel safe to explore and guiding them in their explorations. Such explorations provide students with opportunities to negotiate the rules of role-based language behavior and to try them out under different conditions in ways that are likely to have few negative social, academic, or other consequences for them. This in turn helps learners build up meaningful patterns of communicative behavior corresponding to various conditions that can subsequently be used to make sense of and participate in activities outside the classroom. Involving students in role-plays, sociodramas, and simulations are some of the many ways to create such learning opportunities in the classroom (Leontiev 1981).

Immersion in meaningful communicative activities is only part of the learning process. Learners also need systematic, analytic instruction that helps them to become conscious of and proficient in the use of the linguistic conventions considered essential to the realization of their communicative activities. Any activity involves a number of discrete acts. Writing a narrative, for example, involves not only knowing certain grammatical conventions. It also encompasses knowing the conventions of spelling, punctuation, vocabulary, how to organize the telling of events and ideas, and how to open and close the stories. Likewise, seeking information from someone involves more than appropriate use of certain grammatical and lexical items. To be successful, one needs to know the conventional ways to get the interlocutor's attention, to take turns, and to identify and resolve misdirected talk. Thus, instructional practices designed to provide learners with opportunities to practice these conventions are essential to their successful development of communicative competence.

Generally, such practices are structured around repeated rehearsal of the construction of the form or forms of a particular convention. A great deal of recent research in second- and foreign-language learning has focused on the instruction of one particular aspect of communicative competence, namely, grammar, although a few very recent studies have begun to look at methods for the overt teaching of specific speech acts as well (e.g., Bouton 1994; Lyster 1994; LoCastro 1997). The primary concern of these studies has been with finding the optimal practice conditions for student learning. Studies investigating "input enhancement" (e.g., VanPatten 1993; VanPatten & Cadierno 1993) and "consciousness-raising tasks" (e.g., Ellis 1992; Fotos 1994) have provided useful information on how to help students become conscious of and gain control of the syntactic aspects of the target language. Likewise, recent work on classroom tasks (Crookes & Gass 1993a, 1993b) has documented the conditions that foster the emergence of "negotiated interaction," which is assumed to lead to the successful acquisition of syntax and lexicon (see Pica 1994, for a review of this research). Finally, a body of research investigating the role that student "output" plays in raising students' awareness of linguistic forms (see, e.g., Donato 1994; Kowal & Swain 1994) demonstrates that such instructional practices can also lead to student learning.

In learning to become communicatively competent in a particular activity, then, the issue is not whether such conventions as grammar should be taught, but rather how we should teach them. The findings of the research mentioned above give us some ideas for designing instructional practices for doing so.

A final consideration in designing a pedagogy organized around the notions of communication and communicative development has to do with the three domains of the Communication goal. Although the interpersonal, the interpretive, and the presentational domains are oriented to different communicative purposes, they are not categorical. That is to say, they do not involve behaviors that are mutually exclusive. It is more realistic to think of the goals in terms of interconnected dimensions, each influencing and being influenced by the development of the other. Moreover, each domain encompasses social-, academic-, civic-, and business-related activities that are likely to involve not only conventional written and oral modalities but, given the influence of technology in our lives today, electronic ones as well. Finally, the domains and their constitutive activities do not exist in any kind of hierarchical relationship. Activities in the interpersonal domain are potentially as important as those related to the interpretive and presentational domains. Likewise, within each domain, social activities are potentially as important as those activities whose purposes are more business or academically oriented. All have the potential for the development of complex communicative behaviors.

Interpersonal Domain

This domain frames those communicative activities accomplished through direct interaction with others, and whose primary purpose is either "transactional" or "interactional" (Ramirez 1995). "Transactional" refers to those activities where one interlocutor seeks to obtain something from another, such as directions to an unfamiliar location, information on a new program, or help with one's homework. It also involves activities whose goal is to identify and resolve a problem or concern, such as the doctor-patient consultation during a health examination, or the negotiation of rules when playing a game.

Activities whose primary purpose is interactional are directed toward the establishment and maintenance of interpersonal relationships, and ultimately the development of an understanding of oneself and others, both in terms of each other's group memberships and as unique social beings. Included here are activities whose focus is on mutual acquaintanceship, such as encounters with new neighbors, classmates, or colleagues. Also included are those activities that are used to nurture family bonds, friendships, and other social relationships, such as mealtime talk, gossiping, chatting, "hanging out," and "dropping a line." All these activities, as mundane as they might seem, are crucial to the creation and sustenance of stable community life. While many of the activities framed by the interpersonal domain are accomplished through face-to-face interactions, such methods as personal letter writing, phone calling, electronic mail, audio, video and satellite exchanges, and other technology-related modalities are also used to conduct transactions and make connections with others.

There are two issues to be dealt with when making choices about the kinds of interpersonal activities to include in the curriculum. First, although the manner in which we conduct ourselves in our transactional and interactional activities may vary from group to group or within any group, the communicative means for their realization and the norms for participation in them are conventionalized. These conventions help us to decide the kinds of role relationships to expect, how to begin the activity, how to take a turn, which topics to include and which to avoid, where the interaction is likely to lead, and how to spot and resolve potential breakdowns in communication. This conventionality helps us to recognize what is happening at any particular communicative moment and thus how we might participate. As experienced members of our communities, for example, we can usually distinguish the activity of "recounting a past event" from that of "gossiping" and, based on that, we make our decisions about what to say and do, and what others might say and do.

As foreign language teachers we know that the communicative norms and linguistic conventions associated with these activities vary from group to group. The more different the groups are in terms of gender, race, socioeconomic status, age, ethnicity, and nationality, the more different their norms and conventions are likely to be. This being the case, the question becomes: What activities from which groups of native speakers of the target language are to be included as part of the curriculum?

Creating environments in our classrooms that promote the development of foreign language learning communities requires other kinds of activities in addition to those that are part of the target cultures. We also need activities that are particular to the social and academic culture of the foreign language classroom—activities that the teacher and students themselves create and maintain and through which they build relationships with each other. Spending the beginning of each class in an interpersonal activity in which teachers and students "chat" or "share something" with each other provides opportunities to use the target language in developing their individual identities as members of the class as well as to learn more about each other. As they develop a shared base of knowledge about each other, they can use it to build upon and extend the activity, using more complex communicative behaviors as they do.

Interpretive Domain

This domain frames communicative activities that are focused on developing an understanding of the intent of a variety of texts and through this, transforming one's understanding of the world. Although many of the texts with which we come into contact are written, at least in our academic communities, they can also be visual and/or audio. Television programs, films, radio broadcasts, and formal presentations are examples of texts that we encounter on a daily basis. The process of interpretation means more than decoding a set of written symbols or aural sounds. Rather, it is an interactive process between the written, visual, or audio texts and the individuals. In interpreting any kind of text, we draw upon our previous emotional and intellectual experiences and knowledge to give shape to and derive meaning from the textual signs and significant symbols. Our understandings in turn transform our past experiences and knowledge and help to create new frames for textual interpretations (Rosenblatt 1995/1938; Scholes 1989).

Rosenblatt (1995/1938) distinguishes two general purposes for reading, aesthetic and efferent. Although her frame is focused on the interpretation of written texts, it is a useful heuristic for understanding the purposes of other interpretive activities. Activities with an aesthetic purpose involve "reading" or "interpreting" for pleasure, where the focus is on the feelings, ideas, and attitudes that emerge during the readings. Viewing movies with friends, listening to music, and watching favorite television programs are examples of such activities. The purpose of efferent activities is to seek new information for the development of conceptual meaning. The focus here is on what can be carried away from the reading. Reading textbooks or newspapers, watching the evening news, surfing the Internet, or listening to a lecture are examples of interpretive activities with an efferent purpose. It should be noted that any text can be experienced for one or both purposes at the same time. I can listen to a speaker and become drawn into her presentation through her play with words and the cadence of her speech. At the same time that I am appreciating the aesthetic qualities of her presentation, I can learn something about the topic on which she is speaking. In any activity at any given moment, the purpose that takes precedence depends on the stance of the reader/interpreter and, at least in classrooms, the larger pedagogical purposes for which the activity is intended.

We know from research on the development of the ability to interpret texts in another language that background knowledge of the topic and familiarity with the genre of the text facilitate the process of interpretation (Bernhardt 1993; Carrell 1992). The knowledge about rhetorical structure and plot development that I develop through extended experience in reading mystery novels, for example, helps me make sense of and understand the action of a mystery novel I am reading for the first time. Moreover, it helps me anticipate what is likely to happen next and guess the meanings of unfamiliar words or phrases. Likewise, if I have some knowledge about the topic of, say, international politics, my ability to understand and glean information from a lecture on this topic is likely to be greater than it would be for someone who has little or no background knowledge. In general, then, the more experience and knowledge one has of a particular genre and topic, the easier it is to predict what is to come and to guess the meanings of unfamiliar words. Thus, the more familiar I am with the topic and rhetorical structure of any written, visual, or audio document, the easier it will be to understand it and connect it with what I already know.

As with activities in the interpersonal domain, the norms and conventions for organizing texts, both topically and rhetorically, and the ways we interpret them vary across groups. Thus, when making curricular decisions we need to consider three issues. First, whose texts from what target-language speaking groups are to be used? Second, whose norms and conventions for competent interpretation of the texts are the students expected to develop?

Third, what kinds of interpretive activities can teachers and students use to nurture the community of language learners they are developing in their classrooms?[3]

Presentational Domain

This domain frames communicative activities that involve the creation of texts through which we display what we know and explore what we do not. Our involvement in these activities helps us to make sense of our world, and of others and ourselves as participants within it.

The purposes for presentational activities can be grouped into five major types: descriptive, narrative, demonstrative, explanatory, and transformative (O'Hair, Friedrich, Wienmann, & Wienmann 1995). Descriptive activities are those in which our intent is to describe something—our experiences, our feelings, physical objects, places, people, or events. In narratives we tell a story, or recount an event. Through demonstrations we display our understanding of how something works or provide instructions on how to do something. In explanatory presentations our intent is to create an understanding or awareness of some phenomenon by providing empirical evidence or logical explanations that help to answer such questions as "why?" or "for what purpose?" The primary intent behind transformative presentations is to persuade an audience to rethink or recast an idea or understanding, or to consider an alternative.

The texts we create in our presentational activities can be oral, written, or multimodal. Examples include formal oral presentations on a scholarly topic, daily journals, notebooks or activity logs, performances of plays, poems, or songs, and the production of documentaries or other kinds of programs using a variety of media. In developing competence in these activities, learners need to be concerned with such conventions as the quality and development of ideas, the organization and presentation of content, the appropriateness of style and tone, grammar, spelling, and even the mechanics of production (e.g., handwriting).

As it is with the norms and conventions of activities associated with the other two domains, the linguistic conventions associated with activities in the presentational domain are culture-specific, varying from group to group. Thus, when making decisions about the types of presentational activities to include in the curriculum, the issues of whose norms and conventions are to be the expected standards of performance and what kinds of activities the teachers and students are able to create themselves must be considered.

In sum, a foreign language pedagogy that is based on the communication standard is activity-based, motivating, and challenging. Activities under all three communicative domains are included in classrooms from the beginning levels of instruction, and they move from activities that students know and are familiar with to those that involve them in the exploration of new worlds. Moreover, instructional goals are explicit, and students are provided with opportunities to be immersed in the activity as well as with opportunities to develop awareness of and expertise in the acts involved in the competent accomplishment of the activity. Being immersed in the activity gives learners a sense of the whole, and helps them develop fluency. Direct instruction and practice gives learners a sense of the particulars and helps them develop accuracy.

Because the activities we make available to our students in our foreign language classrooms fundamentally shape their development, the choices we make about the kinds of communicative activities to include in the curriculum are of great consequence. Thus, the process by which we make such decisions and the decisions themselves cannot be taken lightly. If our aim is to develop well-rounded language learners and users, then we need a wide variety of activities from all the basic institutions that encompass social life as lived by the myriad of target-language-speaking communities. At the same time, we need interpersonal, interpretive, and presentational activities that are created by teachers and students in the establishment of their classroom-based communities of foreign language learners.

A final issue to be considered is assessment. In the next section, I briefly discuss some concerns related to the assessment of communicative development that need to be considered when designing means to evaluate student learning in a foreign language curriculum in terms of the communication standards.

Assessment

The concept of assessment is perhaps best defined as "all of the information that may be obtained about students to promote effective instruction" (Fradd & McGee 1994:23). It is commonly used for the following purposes: (1) to determine the status of students' communicative development in order to place them at an appropriate level; (2) to monitor students' progress; (3) to determine the effectiveness of an instructional program or method; and (4) to determine whether students are meeting predetermined instructional goals. While in our classrooms and programs we may tend to use one assessment tool more than we use others, the consensus is that no single measure captures the full range of one's communicative development. Tools for assessing learner development are usually placed in two groups, those that provide a window onto an individual's process of development, and those that measure the outcomes. For a complete understanding of learning both are essential.

One useful tool for assessing communicative development is the portfolio, a systematic collection of work from multiple sources that represents an individual's development (Kieffer & Faust 1994). There are two kinds of portfolios. The first, formative portfolios, are collections of student work that show the student's development over time. Key elements of a formative portfolio include (1) samples of student work collected over a specified period of time, (2) a student self-assessment and reflections on his or her own development, (3) a teacher assessment, and (4) clearly stated criteria for the assessments. Self-assessments are especially useful as they provide students with the chance to become more aware of themselves as learners and their process of development. More specifically, they help students identify their strengths and weaknesses and develop personal goals, thus putting them in charge of their own learning (O'Malley & Pierce 1996). Peer assessments, while optional, are also useful as they provide opportunities for students to help and at the same time learn from each other. The second type of portfolio, the summative portfolio, is meant to showcase what the learner knows and can do. They typically contain a set of exemplars of student work from multiple sources along with a teacher assessment.

Portfolios generally focus on the assessment of individual learning. We know, however, that collaborative work is equally important to learners' development (Vygotsky 1978; Bodrova & Leong 1996). Working together creates a zone of proximal development in which the learners have opportunities to do something together that they are likely unable to do on their own. Thus it is useful to include as assessment measures group projects that showcase both the processes and products of group learning. In the construction of any tool used to measure students' communicative development, the principle of "authentic assessment" (O'Malley & Pierce 1996) must be kept in mind. To be authentic, assessment tools must reflect classroom activities in authentic ways. That is, the knowledge and skills that are being assessed must directly correspond to those the learners use to participate in their communicative activities, however they are constructed in their classrooms. Moreover, measures are needed to assess both fluency, the ability to participate competently in an activity, and accuracy, the knowledge of the particular conventions and norms needed for competent participation.

In addition to authentic assessment tools, standards of performance and criteria for judging student performance need to be developed. Having a clear idea of the standards against which student performance is to be judged and providing examples of work that are considered benchmarks of standard performance are the only ways that students will have a clear sense of where their learning is taking them and what they need to do to be successful (O'Malley & Pierce 1996). Criteria to judge student performance can take several forms, including checklists and rating scales.

The tradition in foreign language classrooms has been to assess learning with discrete-point grammar tests (Hadley 1993). Recently, the ACTFL Oral Proficiency Interview (OPI) or its variation, the SOPI (Simulated Oral Proficiency Interview), has become a popular means for evaluating learners' oral language development. The ACTFL Proficiency Guidelines were designed as a scale for rating language development in terms of the four skill areas of speaking, listening, reading, and writing. Unlike discrete-point tests these guidelines "are intended to be used for global assessment" (Hadley 1993:501) and thus do not attend explicitly to the particulars of an activity. Other, more informally produced, scales for evaluating student performance in a variety of activities, both oral and written (see examples in Hadley 1993; Lee & VanPatten 1995; Ramirez 1995; and Shrum & Glisan 1994), are also global in nature. In most if not all of these scales, the only specific component of communicative competence that is explicitly marked is linguistic, i.e., vocabulary, grammar and, in some cases, pronunciation (Hall & Overfield 1996). Other aspects of communicative competence are covered through the use of such terms as "fluency" and "comprehensibility."

The organization of the communication standards differs rather substantially from that of the Guidelines. The commitment to the attainment of proficiency is not abandoned. However, rather than structuring communicative competence in terms of four separate skill areas, the standards frame communicative development in terms of three general communicative domains. Thus, in keeping with the principles of development that underlie authentic assessment, the tasks we design to measure learners' development must directly correspond to their classroom-based communicative activities, taking into account both global and discrete knowledge and abilities. Clearly, given what we know about communicative competence and development, new forms of assessment and criteria for evaluating student performance in the target language are needed.

In sum, assessment is the crucial link between teaching and learning. It helps teachers and students determine students' progress in meeting their educational goals, and the effectiveness of the means for helping them to do so. The current measurement tools and criteria for evaluating student learning in foreign language classrooms are based on a traditional concept of language and language learning and thus are inadequate. New authentic assessment tools based on the principles underlying the Communication goal are needed.

Implications for Research and Teacher Education

My intent in writing this chapter was to provide an overview of what is currently known about communication and the process of communicative development, and to use this knowledge as a principled basis for proposing a pedagogy of foreign language learning based on the Communication goal and its three standards. Reconceptualizing foreign language learning in this way generates a number of interesting implications for research and foreign language teacher preparation.

Research

Because our communicative development is tied to and mediated by engagement in communicative activities, reaching a full understanding of learner development requires that the communicative environments of our classrooms become the primary source of data on learning. Until recently there has been little if any interest in investigating what actually goes on in foreign language classrooms. What little we have learned has come from university and other adult learning communities (e.g., Brooks 1993; Ohta 1995; Polio & Duff 1994). Consequently, we still know very little of the kinds of communicative environments that comprise K–12 classrooms and how learners' involvement in them mediates their development. Research by Donato, Antonek, and Tucker (1996) on Japanese elementary classrooms and my own investigations on two high school Spanish language classrooms (Hall 1995, in press) notwithstanding, we continue to operate in and make decisions about communicative worlds that are ill-defined. Clearly, much more classroom-based research is needed. As our understanding of these worlds and their relation to individual learner development in the target language grows, we can then give our attention to devising activities through which we can build developmentally rich communicative environments in our classrooms.

A related area worthy of further investigation concerns the communicative activities of significance to groups who are native speakers of the target language. Although part of the goal of learning foreign languages is to be knowledgeable about and able to participate in these communicative events, we actually know very little about them, including, for example, the conventions and norms for their realization, and the roles the events play in the lives of those who use the target language. Thus our ability to construct and assess learners' development in these communicative activities is rather limited. At the very least, we need to add corpus-based approaches to the study of language use to our research agendas. Using large databases of naturally occurring discourse, we can examine and compare patterns of language use found in the daily activities of different native speaking groups. Through such investigations, we may find, as we have through such studies in English (Biber 1988, 1994) that the actual patterns of use often run counter to our expectations, which are usually based on textbook models of language use. Such findings would also be useful in our continued refinements of the concept of communicative competence. Although we have a much better understanding of its theoretical foundation and its constituent elements now than we did in the 1980s, there is still much we do not know. As Celce-Murcia et al. (1995) acknowledge, the model they propose is only "part of an ongoing discussion" (30). Further elaboration of the components and the concept itself is needed.

Also worthy of additional attention are the standards against which learners' communicative performances are judged. Currently, the assumed norm is the "native speaker" of the target language. I have two concerns with this. First, given the variety of groups that speak the languages we typically teach in foreign language classrooms, it is unclear who we consider to be exemplars of native speakers of those languages. Is a prototypical native speaker of Spanish, for example, a citizen of Spain? of Mexico? of Puerto Rico? Do we consider this person to be a man or a woman, an adolescent or an adult, a member of a social elite or someone from the middle class? Although we may not be able to articulate clearly the prototypical features of such a person, our research agendas and the textbooks we are using in our classrooms have (Ramirez & Hall 1990). If we look at these closely, we may find that they are inaccurate, or at least incomplete. We need to begin examining the tacit assumptions about native speakers embedded in our research and classroom practices and use this knowledge to inform, and subsequently transform, the decisions we make about performance standards.

Secondly, it has been argued that the "native speaker" norm we are using to judge our learners' performances is that of a monolingual, someone who speaks only one language (Firth & Wagner 1997), which as Cook (1993) points out, is not a valid point of reference. Rather, those learning another language are becoming bilingual, users of two languages, who differ rather significantly from monolingual language users (Pearson, Fernandez, & Oller 1993). If this is the case, should we not be examining bilingual communicators who are competent in the communicative activities important to our learners in order to develop appropriate norms for performance standards? Recent work by Jiménez, Garcia, and Pearson (1995) on strategies used by successful bilingual readers suggests that we should. At the very least, their work provides a fruitful place to begin looking at ways by which we might reframe our assumptions about communicative norms and our current assessment measures.

Finally, we need to develop ways to assess the process of learning. Current methods for assessing communicative development can only describe whether students have met some set of expectations, and thus they capture only a small aspect of learning. They cannot tell anything about the developmental paths traveled by the students in their journeys. Consequently, we cannot know how and why they arrived where they did. For a fuller understanding, we need different kinds of studies, both in scope and depth, that would help us to better understand the specific conditions of learning and thus to construct viable methods for assessing our learners' development.

Teacher Education

In addition to the need for additional research, we need to look more closely at teacher development. Although the standards were originally addressed to foreign language programs in grades K–12, the successful transformation of these programs will require the involvement of more than just those who teach in them. At the minimum they require the involvement of those in teacher preparation programs and in university language programs. To that end, most language-specific organizations have endorsed the standards for grades K–16. Teacher preparation programs play a crucial role in the development of pedagogical content knowledge (Grossman 1990) of foreign language teachers (Strasheim 1991). Pedagogical content knowledge is the knowledge of how to make the subject matter accessible to students. For foreign language teachers this includes knowledge of theories of communication, communicative competence, and second language acquisition. Also included is knowledge of effective methods and materials for the development of learners' communicative competence in the target language. In a recent analysis of foreign language methods textbooks used in teacher preparation programs (Hall & Overfield 1996), a colleague and I found that although discussions of communication and communicative competence are included in these texts, their treatment is uneven, varying both in terms of quality and quantity. Thus, we concluded that K–12 teachers using these texts were likely to be getting an incomplete and somewhat confusing mixture of ideas and activities. Such confusion could, we argued, negatively affect these teachers' ability to develop communicatively rich environments in their own classrooms. Clearly, additional investigations documenting what actually occurs in foreign language teacher preparation programs are needed to help us create viable means for preparing K–12 teachers to build a pedagogy based on the communication standards.

What happens in foreign language teacher preparation programs is only part of the picture. Because university language programs are the fundamental sites of foreign language development for most K–12 foreign language teachers, what happens in their classrooms in terms of target language knowledge preparation is of great consequence to K–12 teacher development. Not only do they form the foundation of teachers' communicative development in the target language, they also structure what the teachers learn about teaching for communicative development. Currently, the curricular emphasis of many university language programs remains on literature, usually defined as the great literary works of a highly developed country where the target language is the official language (Torres & Trautmann 1997), and taught by professors who rarely have background knowledge in theories and practices of foreign language learning. Moreover, in universities with graduate programs, lower levels of language instruction, the content of which is often organized around grammar, are typically taught by teaching assistants whose background in theories and practices of foreign language learning may be equally limited.[4] Thus, what teachers of elementary, middle, and high schools learn to do in a foreign language and what they learn about "learning" in their university language classes departs, sometimes radically, from what they learn about communication and teaching for communicative development in their teacher preparation programs. Although they may understand and be sympathetic to the concepts underlying the communication standards, those coming from university language programs organized around different educational goals may lack the skills and knowledge needed to communicate effectively. Until the curricula of all university language programs themselves are organized around the communication standards, the successful transformation of K–12 programs is likely to be problematic.

In addition to language and teacher preparation programs with goals that are commensurate with the national standards, teachers need courses and other experiences to help them develop into lifelong foreign language learners. It is ludicrous to expect foreign language teachers to know everything about the various nations and cultures who use the target language. It is equally ludicrous to expect them to be experts in all communicative situations. Few if any of us possess such knowledge and competence in our native languages. We can, however, expect that teachers have a solid understanding of such concepts as community, communication, and communicative development and that they be good explorers themselves. Concepts, ideas, and skills from such fields as anthropology, communication, sociology, ethnographic and other research methods, and technology can provide them with the knowledge and abilities they need to design and conduct their own intellectual and practical explorations as they help their students in theirs. Our ongoing professional development is the only way to ensure the continued vitality of the foreign language learning field.

Conclusions

The principles of communication and communicative competence that underlie the Communication goal and its three standards provide a frame for designing a pedagogy of foreign language learning around involvement in a wide range of meaningful experiences that encompass the diversity of communicative needs of our students. Using the communication standards to reconceptualize programs and curricula has already begun in many places, and interest in building standards-based programs continues to grow. As we move into the twenty-first century our success in reconstructing foreign language education will depend on our continued willingness to seek out new ideas, to ask new questions, and to find new ways of answering them.

NOTES

1. Although the term "mode" is used in National Standards documents, I use the term "domain" here as I think it better captures the premises underlying the Communication Standards.
2. This excerpt is taken from Hall 1995.
3. A recent study on the use of children's literature in a Spanish language high school class is a nice example of one such interpretive activity (Jacobson, Flood, & Lapp 1996).
4. Fortunately, the last decade has seen an increased emphasis on pedagogical training for teaching assistants.

REFERENCES

Bachman, Lyle. 1990. *Fundamental Considerations in Language Testing*. Oxford: Oxford University Press.
Baker, Carolyn. 1992. "Description and Analysis in Classroom Talk and Interaction." *Journal of Classroom Interaction* 27(2):9–14.
Bandura, A. 1977. *Social Learning Theory*. Englewood Cliffs, NJ: Prentice Hall.

Barnes, Douglas. 1992. *From Communication to Curriculum.* Portsmouth, NH: Boynton/Cook.

Berman, Ruth, and Dan Slobin. 1994. *Relating Events in Narratives. A Crosslinguistic Developmental Study.* Hillsdale, NJ: Lawrence Erlbaum.

Bernhardt, Elizabeth. 1993. *Reading Development in a Second Language: Theoretical, Empirical, and Classroom Perspectives.* Norwood, NJ: Ablex Publishing.

Biber, Douglas. 1988. *Variations in Speech and Writing.* Cambridge: Cambridge University Press.

———. 1994. "Corpus-Based Approaches to Issues in Applied Linguistics." *Applied Linguistics* 15(2):169–89.

Blum-Kulka, Shoshana. 1997. *Dinner Talk: Cultural Patterns of Sociability and Socialization in Family Discourse.* Hillsdale, NJ: Lawrence Erlbaum.

Bodrova, E., and D. Leong. 1996. *Tools of the Mind.* Englewood Cliffs, NJ: Prentice Hall.

Bouton, Lawrence. 1994. "Conversational Implicature in the Second Language: Learned Slowly When Not Deliberately Taught." *Journal of Pragmatics* 22:157–67.

Bowers, C. A., and D. Flinders. 1990. *Responsive Teaching: An Ecological Approach to Classroom Patterns of Language, Culture, and Thought.* New York: Teachers College Press.

Brooks, Frank. 1993. "Some Problems and Caveats in Communicative Discourse: Toward a Conceptualization of the Foreign Language Classroom." *Foreign Language Annals* 26(2):233–42.

Brooks, Frank, and Richard Donato. 1994. "Vygotskyan Approaches to Understanding Foreign Language Learner Discourse During Communicative Tasks." *Hispania* 77(2):262–74.

Cabello, Beverly, and Raymond Terrell. 1994. "Making Students Feel Like Family: How Teachers Create Warm and Caring Classroom Climates." *Journal of Classroom Interaction* 29(1):17–23.

Canale, Michael, and Merrill Swain. 1980. "Theoretical Bases of Communicative Approaches to Second Language Teaching and Testing." *Applied Linguistics* 1:1–47.

Carbaugh, Donal. 1996. *Situating Selves: The Communication of Social Identities in American Scenes.* Albany: SUNY Press.

Carey, James. 1989. *Communication as Culture.* Boston, Unwin Hyman.

Carlsen, William S. 1992. "Closing Down the Conversation: Discouraging Student Talk on Unfamiliar Science Content." *Journal of Classroom Interaction* 27(2):15–21.

Carrell, Patricia. 1992. "Awareness of Text Structure: Effects on Recall." *Language Learning* 42(1):1–20.

Cazden, Courtney. 1988. *Classroom Discourse.* Portsmouth, NH: Heinemann.

Celce-Murcia, M., D. Zoltan, and S. Thurrell. 1995. "Communicative Competence: A Pedagogically Motivated Model with Content Specifications." *Issues in Applied Linguistics* 6(2):5–35.

Chang-Wells, G. L., and G. Wells. 1993. "Dynamics of Discourse: Literacy and the Construction of Knowledge," pp. 58–90 in E. Forman, N. Minick, and C. A. Stone, eds., *Contexts for Learning: Sociocultural Dynamics in Children's Development.* New York: Oxford University Press.

Chomsky, Noam. 1965. *Aspects of the Theory of Syntax.* Cambridge: MIT Press.

Cook, Vivian. 1993. *Linguistics and Second Language Acquisition.* New York: St. Martin's Press.

Crookes, Graham, and Susan Gass, eds. 1993a. *Tasks in a Pedagogical Context: Integrating Theory and Practice.* Clevedon: Multilingual Matters.

———, eds. 1993b. *Tasks and Language Learning: Integrating Theory and Practice.* Clevedon: Multilingual Matters.

Detterman, D., and R. Sternberg, eds. 1993. *Transfer on Trial: Intelligence, Cognition and Instruction.* Norwood: Ablex.

Donato, Richard. 1994. "Collective Scaffolding in Second Language Learning." pp. 33–56 in J. P. Lantolf and G. Appel, eds., *Vygotskyan Approaches to Second Language Research*. Norwood, NJ: Ablex.

Donato, Richard, Janis Antonek, and G. Richard Tucker. 1996. "Monitoring and Assessing a Japanese FLES Program: Ambiance and Achievement." *Language Learning* 46(3): 497–528.

Edwards, A. D., and D.P.G. Westgate. 1994. *Investigating Classroom Talk*. London: The Falmer Press.

Edwards, Derek. 1995. "Two to Tango: Script Formulations, Dispositions, and Rhetorical Symmetry in Relationship Troubles Talk." *Research on Language and Social Interaction* 28(4):319–350.

Ellis, Rod. 1992. *Second Language Acquisition and Language Pedagogy*. Clevedon: Multilingual Matters.

Firth, Alan, and Johannes Wagner. 1997. "On Discourse, Communication and (Some) Fundamental Concepts in SLA." *Modern Language Journal* 81(3):277–300.

Forman, Ellice. 1996. "Learning Mathematics as Participation in Classroom Practice: Implications of Sociocultural Theory for Educational Reform," pp. 115–30 in L. Steffe, P. Nesher, P. Cobb, G. A. Goldin, and B. Greer, eds., *Theories of Mathematical Learning*. Hillsdale, NJ: Erlbaum.

Fotos, Sandra. 1994. "Integrating Grammar Instruction and Communicative Language Use Through Grammar Consciousness-Raising Tasks." *TESOL Quarterly* 28(2):323–51.

Fradd, S., and P. L. McGee. 1994. *Instructional Assessment. An Integrative Approach to Evaluating Student Performance*. Reading, MA: Addison-Wesley Publishing Co.

Goldenberg, Claude. 1991. *Instructional Conversations and Their Classroom Application*. Washington, DC: The National Center for Research on Cultural Diversity and Second Language Learning.

Goodwin, M. H. 1990. *He-Said-She-Said: Talk as Social Organization among Black Children*. Bloomington: Indiana University Press.

Grossman, P. 1990. *The Making of a Teacher: Teacher Knowledge and Teacher Education*. New York: Teachers College Press.

Gumperz, John. 1981. "The Linguistic Bases of Communicative Competence." pp. 323–34 in D. Tannen, ed., *Georgetown University Round Table on Languages and Linguistics*. Washington, DC: Georgetown University Press.

———.1992. "Contextualization and Understanding," pp. 229–52 in A. Duranti and C. Goodwin, eds., *Rethinking Context: Language as an Interactive Phenomenon*. Cambridge: Cambridge University Press.

Gutierrez, Kris. 1994. "How Talk, Context, and Script Shape Contexts for Learning: A Cross-Case Comparison of Journal Sharing." *Linguistics and Education* 5:335–65.

Gutierrez, Kris, Betsy Rymes, and Joanne Larson. 1995. "Script, Counterscript and Underlife in the Classroom: James Brown versus Brown v. Board of Education." *Harvard Educational Review* 65(3):445–71.

Hadley, Alice O. (1993). *Teaching Language in Context*. Boston: Heinle and Heinle.

Hall, Edward. 1959. *The Silent Language*. New York: Doubleday.

———. 1983. *The Dance of Life*. New York: Doubleday.

Hall, Joan K. 1995. "'Aw, man, where we goin?': Classroom Interaction and the Development of L2 Interactional Competence." *Issues in Applied Linguistics* 6(2):37–62.

———. In press. "Differential Teacher Attention to Student Utterances: The Construction of Different Opportunities for Learning in the IRF." *Linguistics and Education*.

Hall, Joan K., and Denise Overfield. 1996. "The Pedagogical Treatment of Interactional Competence: A Text Analysis." Paper presented at the Second Language Research Forum, October 1996. University of Arizona, Tucson, AZ.

Halliday, M.A.K. 1994. *An Introduction to Functional Grammar.* London: Edward Arnold.

Heath, Shirley B. 1983. *Ways with Words: Language, Life and Work in Communities and Classrooms.* Cambridge, MA: Cambridge University Press.

Hymes, Dell. 1964. "Formal Discussions of a Conference Paper," in U. Bellugi and R. Brown, eds., *The Acquisition of Language: Monographs of the Society for Research in Child Development.*

———.1972. "On Communicative Competence," in J. B. Price and J. Holmes, eds., *Sociolinguistics.* Harmonsworth: Penguin.

Jacobson, J., J. Flood, and D. Lapp. 1996. "Children's Literature as a Tool for Adolescent Second Language Learning." Paper presented at the National Reading Conference, Charleston, South Carolina.

Jiménez, Robert, Georgia Garcia, and David Pearson. 1996. "The Reading Strategies of Latina/o Students Who Are Successful English Readers: Opportunities and Obstacles." *Reading Research Quarterly* 31:90–112.

Kieffer, Ron, and Mark Faust. 1994. "Portfolio Process and Teacher Change: Elementary, Middle, and Secondary Teachers Reflect on their Experiences with Portfolio Evaluation," in C. Kinzer and D. Leu, eds., *Multidimensional Aspects of Literary Research, Theory and Practice.* National Reading Conference, Inc.

Kowal, M., and M. Swain. 1994. "Using Collaborative Language Production Tasks to Promote Students' Language Awareness." *Language Awareness* 3(2):73–93.

Krashen, Stephen. 1989. *Language Acquisition and Language Education.* New York: Prentice Hall.

———. 1980. *Second Language Acquisition and Second Language Learning.* Oxford: Pergamon Press.

Lee, Carol. 1993. "Signifying as a Scaffold for Literary Interpretation: The Pedagogical Implications of an African American Discourse Genre." *NCTE Research Report No. 26.* Urbana, IL: National Council of Teachers of English.

Lee, Carol. 1995. "A Culturally Based Cognitive Apprenticeship: Teaching African American High School Students Skills in Literary Interpretation." *Reading Research Quarterly* 30:608–30.

Lee, James, and Bill VanPatten. 1995. *Making Communicative Language Teaching Happen.* New York: McGraw Hill.

Lemke, Jay. 1988. "Genres, Semantics, and Classroom Education." *Linguistics and Education* 1(1):81–89.

Leontiev, Alexei A. 1981. *Psychology and the Language Learning Process.* Oxford: Pergamon Press.

Levy, Elena, and Katherine Nelson. 1994. "Words in Discourse: A Dialectical Approach to the Acquisition of Meaning and Use." *Journal of Child Language* 21:367–89.

Light, P., and G. Butterworth, eds. 1993. *Context and Cognition: Ways of Learning and Knowing.* Hillsdale, NJ: Lawrence Erlbaum.

LoCastro, V. 1997. "Pedagogical Intervention and Pragmatic Competence Development." *Applied Language Learning* 8:75–109.

Luckmann, T. 1995. "Interaction Planning and Intersubjective Adjustment of Perspectives by Communicative Genre," pp. 175–86. in E. Goody, ed., *Social Intelligence and Interaction.* Cambridge: Cambridge University Press.

Lyster, Roy. 1994. "The Effect of Functional-Analytic Teaching on Aspects of French Immersion Students' Sociolinguistic Competence." *Applied Linguistics* 15(3):263–87.

McHoul, A. 1990. "The Organization of Repair in Classroom Talk." *Language in Society* 19(3):349–77.

Mehan, Hugh. 1979. *Learning Lessons: Social Organization in the Classroom.* Cambridge, MA: Harvard University Press.

Miller, Suzanne. 1996. "Open-Forum Text Discussion as a Zone of Proximal Development: Shaping Which Habits of Mind?" Paper presented at the 1996 NCTE Vygotsky Centennial: Vygotskian Perspectives on Literacy Research, Chicago, IL.

Ninio, A., and C. Snow. 1996. *Pragmatic Development.* Colorado: Westview Press.

Nystrand, Martin. 1997. *Opening Dialogue.* New York: Teacher's College Press.

Ochs, Elinor. 1988. *Culture and Language Development: Language Acquisition and Language Socialization in a Samoan Village.* Cambridge: Cambridge University Press.

O'Hair, D., G. Friedrich, J. Wienmann, and M. Wienmann. 1995. *Competent Communication.* New York: St. Martin's Press.

Ohta, Amy S. 1995. "Applying Sociocultural Theory to an Analysis of Learner Discourse: Learner-Learner Collaborative Interaction in the Zone of Proximal Development." *Issues in Applied Linguistics* 6:93–121.

O'Malley, J. M., and L.V. Pierce. 1996. *Authentic Assessment for English Language Learners: Practical Approaches for Teachers.* Reading, MA: Addison-Wesley Publishing Co.

Palincsar, A. S., A. Brown, and J. Campione. 1993. "First-Grade Dialogues for Knowledge Acquisition and Use," pp. 43–57. in E. Forman, N. Minick, and C. A. Stone, eds., *Contexts for Learning: Sociocultural Dynamics in Children's Development.* New York: Oxford University Press.

Patthey-Chavez, G. G., L. Clare, and R. Gallimore. 1995. *Creating a Community of Scholarship with Instructional Conversations in a Transitional Bilingual Classroom.* Washington, DC: The National Center for Research on Cultural Diversity and Second Language Learning.

Pearson, B. Z., S. Fernandez, and D. K. Oller. 1993. "Lexical Development in Bilingual Infants and Toddlers: Comparison to Monolingual Norms." *Language Learning* 43(1):93–120.

Philips, Susan. 1983. *The Invisible Culture: Communication in Classroom and Community on the Warm Springs Indian Reservation.* Prospect Heights, IL: Waveland Press.

Pica, Teresa. 1991. "Foreign Language Classrooms: Making Them Research-Ready and Research-able," in Barbara Freed, ed., *Foreign Language Acquisition Research and the Classroom.* Lexington, MA: D.C. Heath.

———. 1994. "Research on Negotiation: What Does It Reveal about Second-Language Learning Conditions, Processes, and Outcomes?" *Language Learning* 44(3):493–527.

Pine, Julian. 1994. "Environmental Correlates of Variation in Lexical Style: Interactional Style and the Structure of Input." Applied Psycholinguistics 15:355–70.

Polio, Charlene, and Patsy Duff. 1994. "Teachers' Language Use in University Foreign Language Classrooms: A Qualitative Analysis of English and Target Language Alternation." *The Modern Language Journal* 78(3):313–26.

Purves, Alan. 1990. *The Scribal Society.* New York: Longman.

Ramirez, Arnulfo. 1995. *Creating Contexts for Second Language Acquisition: Theory and Methods.* New York: Longman.

Ramirez, Arnulfo, and Joan K. Hall. 1990. "Language and Culture in Secondary-Level Spanish Textbooks." *Modern Language Journal* 74:48–65.

Rosenblatt, Louise. 1995/1938. *Literature as Exploration.* New York: Modern Language Association.

Rueda, Robert, Claude Goldenberg, and Ronald Gallimore. 1992. *Rating Instructional Conversations: A Guide.* Washington, DC: The National Center for Research on Cultural Diversity and Second Language Learning.

Schiefflin, Bambi. 1990. *The Give and Take of Everyday Life: Language Socialization of Kaluli Children.* Cambridge: Cambridge University Press.

Schmidt, Richard. 1994. "Deconstructing Consciousness in Search of Useful Definitions for Applied Linguistics." *AILA Review* 11:11–26.

Scholes, Robert. 1989. *Protocols of Reading.* New Haven: Yale University Press.

Scollon, Ron, and Susie Scollon. 1996. *Intercultural Communication.* Cambridge: Cambridge University Press.

Shatz, M., and L. McCloskey. 1984. "Answering Appropriately: A Developmental Perspective on Conversational Knowledge," pp. 19–36 in S. Kuczaj, ed., *Discourse Development: Progress in Cognitive Development Research.* New York: Springer-Verlag.

Shrum, J., and E. Glisan. 1994. *Teacher's Handbook: Contextualized Language Instruction.* Boston: Heinle and Heinle.

Smagorinsky, Peter. 1993. "The Social Environment of the Classroom: A Vygotskian Perspective on Small Group Process." *Communication Education* 42(2):159–71.

Solokov, Jeffrey, and Catherine Snow. 1994. "The Changing Role of Negative Evidence in Theories of Language Development," pp. 38–55. in C. Gallaway and B. Richards, eds., *Input and Interaction in Language Acquisition.* Cambridge: Cambridge University Press.

Stone, A., and E. Forman. 1988. "Cognitive Development in Language-Learning Disabled Adolescents: A Study of Problem-Solving Performance in an Isolation-of-Variables Task." *Learning Disabilities Research* 3(2):107–14.

Strasheim, L. 1991. "Priority: Teacher Education. Preservice and Inservice Teaching Education in the Nineties: The Issue Is Instructional Validity." *Foreign Language Annals* 24:101–07.

Tharp, R. G., and R. Gallimore. 1988. *Rousing Minds to Life: Teaching, Learning, and Schooling in Social Context.* New York: Cambridge University Press.

———. 1991. *The Instructional Conversation: Teaching and Learning in Social Activity.* Washington, DC: National Center for Research on Cultural Diversity and Second Language Learning.

The New London Group. 1996. "A Pedagogy of Multiliteracies: Designing Social Futures." *Harvard Educational Review* 66(1):60–92.

Tomasello, Michael, Ann Cale Kruger, and Hilary Horn Ratner. 1993. "Cultural Learning." *Behavioral and Brain Sciences* 16:495–552.

Tomasello, M., G. Conti-Ramsden, and B. Ewert. 1990. "Young Children's Conversations with their Mothers and Fathers: Differences in Breakdown and Repair." *Journal of Child Language* 17:115–30.

Torres, G., and G. Trautmann. 1997. "The Future of our Profession: Trends and Challenges in the Teaching of College Spanish." *The Beacon* 31(2):9–14.

Toth, Paul. 1997. "The Pragmatics of Foreign Language Classroom Communities." Paper presented at the 1997 meeting of the American Association of Applied Linguistics, Orlando, Florida.

VanPatten, Bill. 1993. "Grammar Teaching for the Acquisition-Rich Classroom." *Foreign Language Annals* 26(4):435–50.

VanPatten, Bill, and Teresa Cadierno. 1993. "Input Processing and Second Language Acquisition: A Role for Instruction." *Modern Language Journal* 77(1):45–57.

Vygotsky, Lev S. 1978. *Mind in Society: The Development of Higher Psychological Processes.* Cambridge, MA: Harvard University Press.

Warren, B., and A. S. Rosebery. 1996. "This Question Is Just Too, Too Easy!": Students' Perspectives on Accountability in Science," pp. 97–125 in L. Schauble and R. Glaser, eds., *Innovations in Learning Environments for Education.* Mahwah, NJ: Erlbaum.

Wells, Gordon. 1993. "Reevaluating the IRE Sequence: a Proposal for the Articulation of Theories of Activity and Discourse for the Analysis of Teaching and Learning in the Classroom." *Linguistics and Education* 5:1–17.

————. 1996. "Using the Tool-Kit of Discourse in the Activity of Learning and Teaching." *Mind, Culture, and Activity* 3(2):1–22.

Wertsch, James. 1991. *Voices of the Mind.* Cambridge, MA: Harvard University Press.

————. 1994. "The Primacy of Mediated Action in Sociocultural Studies." *Mind, Culture, and Activity* 1(4): 202–08.

White, Karen, and Janet Kistner. 1992. "The Influence of Teacher Feedback on Young Children's Peer Preferences and Perceptions." *Developmental Psychology* 28(3):933–60.

3

Planning for and Using the New National Culture Standards[1]

Dale L. Lange

University of Minnesota

A. Introduction

In the recent history of language learning, 1950s to the current moment, the inclusion of culture as an element in the language learning curriculum, in instructional practice, and in assessment of learning cannot be denied. It is a truism in language teaching that language cannot be taught without cultural content. But does this truism really function?

In the period mentioned, there was enormous effort given to the inclusion of culture in the foreign language curriculum and classroom. One of these important contributors is Brooks (1960) who defines culture as both a "sense of refinement . . . accompanied by the creative, selective and eliminative factors that are essential to art," and "the learned and shared elements of communal life" (80). In response to both aspects of the definition, he provides a listing of cultural themes to consider in the teaching of language. These cultural themes allow students to ask the who, what, why, when, and how questions expected in cultural inquiry. Nostrand (1967, 1974; see also Seelye, 1972:58–59) develops a conceptual or "emergent" model of culture. This model, intended for language teachers, contains the essential themes of a language/culture learning curriculum. The model contains some thirty headings under the categories of the Culture, the Society, the Individual, and the Ecology, into which many hundreds of themes are classified. The Nostrand

Dale L. Lange (Ph.D., Minnesota) is professor emeritus of Second Languages and Cultures Education at Minnesota, where he was also associate dean in the College of Education and director of the Center for Advanced Research on Language Acquisition. He edited the ACTFL Annual Bibliography (1968-1972) and the ACTFL Foreign Language Education Series (1970-1972). He was president of ACTFL (1980). Lange has taught at elementary, secondary, undergraduate, and graduate levels. His publications may be found in several volumes of the ACTFL FL Education series and in journals such as the *ADFL Bulletin, Minnesota Language Review, Foreign Language Annals, Modern Language Journal,* and *Unterrichtspraxis*.

1974 publication shows how the themes could be used with experiential and cognitive strategies to develop empathy for another culture.

Others have contributed significantly to the inclusion of culture in the foreign language classroom. Lafayette (1978, 1988) develops principles for the coherence of language and culture in instruction, indicating that language cannot be taught without culture and vice versa. Stern (1982) provides a vision of how four contents or syllabi (the linguistic, the cultural, the communicative, and the language learning) can be integrated so that language and culture would ultimately be learned as one. And Seelye (1984, 1993) creates a system for the teaching of culture from the development of objectives in the generation of a language learning curriculum, to the compilation of strategies for instruction and, finally, to principles for the assessment of cultural learning. Together, the work of these and other individuals offers us extremely rich and thoughtful resources from which to develop cultural learning within the foreign language classroom.

Although these resources and ideas have existed for more than forty years, culture still remains a superficial aspect of language learning in K–12 and post-secondary language programs. It has been talked about, talked around, and has been the subject of workshops, conference presentations, books, and articles in books, such as this one, but it still remains a superficial aspect of language learning programs. As a result, I offer the following statement and subsequent questions: **We do not agree on what culture to teach.** Should the culture taught in secondary schools be that of a literary and artistic nature? Should it be that of social systems such as education, government, and social institutions? Should it be anthropological patterns of human behavior? Should it be of a historical nature? All of these orientations have been either mentioned at some time or other, mixed together without significant justification, or ignored to avoid the inclusion of culture at all in language learning. Because of the resulting confusion, culture may be excluded or included only as an afterthought. In this light, the planning for clear and measurable learning outcomes that include culture in the foreign language curriculum is ignored.

Following on the lack of agreement on the content of culture in the language learning curriculum, and because there is little or no research to prove otherwise, **I say that we do not agree on how to integrate culture and language in teaching and learning.** Some of us tell students what they should know and how they should know it, and assess that knowledge with objective measures. Teaching materials offer generally this same perspective. Others argue that culture is included with the language, making language learning strategies those for teaching culture as well. I mean here that culture must be planned for and taught in an active manner. And as I listen to conference presentations, there is also a kind personal enthusiasm that accompanies proposals for the teaching and learning of culture that may be appealing but that do not resolve the problem. What is important here is that we recognize not only the importance of the inclusion of culture in the language learning curriculum, but also concomitantly we recognize that we need serious discussion, debate, and resolution of how to teach it. Further, research of either a quantitative or qualitative nature on the teaching and learning of culture in language learning is almost nonexistent. We have little to go on except the urgings and suggestions that have been offered above.

At this point, how might we agree on the interrelationship of language and culture in language learning programs? Leadership has emerged from several sources. For example, the National Standards Project (*Standards* 1996) provides five goal areas of Communication, Culture, Connections, Comparisons, and Communities, into which it has categorized eleven standards for language learners (See Lafayette 1996 for a thorough discussion of the National Standards Project). The complete enumeration of the National Standards (Standards 1996) is provided in the opening pages of this book. And both the National Standards Project and the American Association of Teachers of French (AATF) National Commission on Cultural Competence (Singerman 1996) offer standards for the learning of culture. In the National Standards Project, culture appears in two other areas (Cultures and Comparisons) and three specific standards are stated (2.1, 2.2, and 4.2), which are intended to apply and to be adapted to all cultures (and languages):

CULTURES

Standard 2.1: Students demonstrate an understanding of the relationship between the practices and perspectives of the culture studied.

Standard 2.2: Students demonstrate an understanding of the relationship between the products and perspectives of the culture studied.

COMPARISONS

Standard 4.2: Students demonstrate understanding of the concept of culture through comparisons of the cultures studied and their own.

However, one can make the case that culture permeates all of the standards, that it appears in any of the topics related to **Communication,** in any of the disciplines suggested in **Connections,** and in any use of language in **Communities.**

As a very important contribution, the National Standards define culture as practices, products, and perspectives. Such a definition avoids the common, overworked conflict between C and c by interweaving the formal and informal aspects of daily life as one normally lives it in any culture. This simple definition allows for enormous flexibility that honors what teachers bring to the classroom. It also honors the developmental level of learners in that teachers can adapt the outcomes to these levels. This definition permits the use of any document—be it an advertisement, newspaper article, or literary text—for cultural learning where appropriate. At the same time, the definition gives the authors of materials the opportunity to push the curriculum toward important elements of practices, products, and perspectives. Teachers will then have the classroom materials with which to plan a curriculum that will allow students to meet expected outcomes. In this regard, **there is important agreement on what culture to teach.**

Even though it is dangerous to add to what a national group has generated, I would like to add one element to the definition that is crucial for the understanding and teaching of culture. That element is the impermanence of culture; it is constantly in flux and changing. We teachers approach culture as though it were static, that we can know Culture X. It is probably important for us to recognize the limits of this static nature and to understand that the teaching of culture is more related to the process of discovery than it is to static information.

Although somewhat different in approach, the AATF's standards designate four stages of competence in each of two broad categories, the first of which contains two generalized competencies: Empathy, and Ability to Observe and Analyze a Culture. In a second broad category, Knowledge of French-Speaking Societies, the standards relate to five specific areas of the world where French culture is important: France, North America, Sub-Saharan Africa, the Caribbean, and North Africa. In each of these categories four stages of competence (Elementary, Basic Intercultural Skills, Social Competence, and Socio-Professional Capability) are offered. Within each stage for the culture-specific categories, there are competencies listed in the following areas: communication in a cultural context, the value system, social patterns and conventions, social institutions, geography and the environment, history, and literature and the arts. The AATF statement of competencies is highly complex, extremely prescriptive, and very difficult for the classroom teacher to use. It is not clear that the four stages of competence function on a continuum. And there is an overreliance on knowledge in the Knowledge of French-Speaking Societies category. However, regardless of the design, whether that of the National Standards Project or the AATF, the communication to both teachers and students is the same: **From this**

moment, culture and language are inextricably connected. There is more agreement on what culture is and more agreement on what to teach than at any other time. It appears that a direction has been set. What is to be determined is how we will help students arrive at these outcomes.

In my mind, the direction set by both the National Standards Project and the AATF National Culture Commission points directly away from culture as information toward culture as an integrated aspect of language learning. If culture is then integrated into language learning, and if understanding of culture is then an overall goal as announced in both sets of standards, a different kind of learning is required. Just as the Sapir-Whorf hypothesis manifests this relationship, so must the learning of culture/language exhibit this same relationship. As Whorf (1952:5) has indicated,

> The linguistic system . . . of each language is not merely a reproducing instrument for voicing ideas but rather is itself the shaper of ideas, the program and guide for the individual's mental activity for his analysis of impressions, for his synthesis of his mental stock in trade . . . .

And as Sapir (in Mandelbaum 1949:162) has also commented,

> Language is a guide to "social reality" . . . Human beings do not live in the objective world alone, nor alone in the world of social activity as ordinarily understood, but are very much at the mercy of the particular language which has become the medium of expression for their society. It is quite an illusion to imagine that one adjusts to reality essentially without the use of language and that language is merely an incidental means of solving specific problems of communication or reflection.

How do we bring language and culture learning together in the classroom to give the "language" in "language learning" the human and social reality that it deserves, as well as to give students an idea of how their own social reality has been shaped by language?

In a recent book, the sociolinguist Gee (1996) brings the two concepts of acquisition and learning to this discussion. There is an important distinction between the two that gives learning a different focus. Let me set a little background. Gee writes about discourse that is clearly the relationship of language to its social context as in the Sapir and Whorf quotes above. In other words, discourse combines language and culture. For Gee, there is the language and culture of the "home" (primary discourse), and there is the use of language in an outside-the-home, social context or culture (secondary discourse). Any interaction in social places automatically includes us in secondary discourses that "involve behaving, which go beyond the uses of language in our primary discourse no matter what group we belong to" (Gee 1996:142). He also introduces the concepts of *acquisition* and *learning* of language and culture. *Acquisition,* according to Gee, "requires exposure to models in natural, meaningful, and functional settings," (1996:144) and significant time to imitate those models. This explication of the acquisition of language and culture is similar to that of Krashen (1981) wherein he defines acquisition as "a process similar to the way children develop ability in their first language" (1981:10). However, Gee's concept of *learning* of language and culture (discourse) takes on a slightly different meaning from that of Krashen. With Gee, learning becomes a matter of how to explain, analyze, compare, contrast, and evaluate so that such functions can be translated to understand other languages and cultures (discourses). Krashen (1982:10) focuses on learning as knowledge of language rules. And Gee is using learning here in the sense of *transfer.* What we learn and understand from one context can be transferred to other learning, other languages and cultures (other secondary discourses), including one's home language and culture (primary discourse). In Gee's mind, this transfer of learning is called *liberating literacy.* Having this knowledge frees us from ourselves and allows us to examine who we are, how we use language, and how we interact with others in social contexts. Gee's concept of learning will be the subject of further exploration in another part of this chapter.

There are not abundant examples and models of how this kind of learning functions in language and culture learning. However, there are a couple of proposals for explaining this learning, one in foreign language education and one in English as a Second Language (ESL). In foreign language education, one example of how a liberating discourse can integrate language/culture acquisition and learning is that of Crawford-Lange and Lange (1984). In their article on integrating language and culture, they unify language and culture through a process of overlapping steps that allow both acquisition and learning (in Gee's sense of the meanings of those words) to function together. In this process, the foreign language is acquired through experiencing, as well as learning about, its culture in relation to that of the home language and culture. The process allows learners to expand their knowledge of an original statement about a cultural perception through consecutive explorations of different materials related to a theme or topic. In assessment, they display the various aspects of their learning. In an ESL context, Wallerstein (1983) recommends that adult learners create the language and cultural situations to be used in the classroom from their own experience. Similar to Crawford-Lange and Lange, learners find as many possible "sides" (contradictions) to a cultural issue as possible. Their response is then to resolve the contradictions through personal action. Personal action here could mean deciding what is the truth. It could mean both sorting out the truth and acting upon it, such as writing a letter to county authorities about fixing potholes on specific roads even though the county has denied that potholes exist in those places. Both the Crawford-Lange and Lange and the Wallerstein examples demonstrate the potential for using what Gee calls *liberatory literacy* to understand the home culture and other languages and cultures.

The purpose of this chapter is to examine the context for new learning in culture. This task first involves some examination of the new standards for culture. We will examine them to determine if they really allow students new opportunities to learn culture. Because learning should not take place in a vacuum, three theoretical models will be examined for their capacity to inform us what culture/language learning might be, how such learning might be assessed, and how instruction could help such learning. From this investigation, we will proceed to show how curriculum = assessment = learning/teaching. Some suggestions for the examination of culture learning within examples of widely different contexts will be suggested. Finally, recommendations for research will be offered.

B. New National Standards for Culture: Are They Real?

As indicated earlier, both the National Standards Project and the AATF National Commission on Cultural Competence have created new standards for culture learning. While the culture standards for the former are included above, I include a more detailed version of the AATF culture standards in summary form in Appendix A. It is not my intent to explain them further, but to ask an important question about them. In order to ask this question, the reader must know that the new national standards, including those for culture, serve as a model for foreign language or "world" language standards being set for the fifty states as they strive to reinvent public education in the United States. Little of this kind of examination is taking place in community colleges and colleges/universities. But there is interest and some activity as the national AAT organizations (American Association of Teachers of French, American Association of Teachers of German, and American Association of Teachers of Spanish and Portuguese, among others) begin to create language-specific standards for grades K–16. The question is the following: Are these **world-class standards?**

Answering the question is a difficult, although certainly possible task. However, trying to compare these standards with those in other countries would be like comparing apples and oranges. We have seen examples of how such comparisons have been done between the Japanese and American school systems. The controversy from those comparisons has certainly been misleading to say the least (Berliner and Biddle 1995). Not wanting to tackle the international comparison question, I settled on a different question: **How would one get some kind of handle on the quality of the culture standards?** The answer is related to a report I gave (Lange 1997) on my analysis of the National Standards Project standards for culture, the culture standards of AATF, and some thirty-three state documents containing culture standards.

What did I do to answer the question? I thought it would be useful to find a filter through which all of the standards could be strained. Such a filter would then allow a comparison of all national and state standards documents. Actually, two filters were chosen: the taxonomies of cognitive and affective objectives for education, the former by Bloom (1956) and the latter by Krathwohl, Bloom, and Masia (1964). (See Appendix B for a detailed description of cognitive and affective objectives, as well as the relationship between cognitive and affective objectives.)

It is my strong belief that both communication and culture are the core of the standards. Communication is the "how" of the standards and culture is the "what." Thus, culture permeates standards goal areas 2, 3, 4, and 5. In my analysis, the two filters were applied to the sample progress and/or performance indicators at grade 4, 8, and 12 for these four standards categories. The performance indicators were judged as to the category of cognitive or affective outcomes into which each performance indicator fell (Cognitive: knowledge, comprehension, application, analysis, synthesis, and evaluation; Affective: receiving, responding, valuing, organization, characterization). The intensity of the activity was also judged. Was the activity of major intensity or only minor intensity? The same judgments were made for the National Standards document, the AATF document, and the thirty-three state standards documents. In the analysis, there were three categories of states: those that followed the National Standards directly; those that modified the National Standards somewhat; those not at all related to the National Standards. What are the results of this analysis?

For those National Standards specifically designated as culture standards (2.1, 2.2, 4.2), the results are indicated in Figure 1. To interpret this figure and those that follow, the reader needs to know that the **X** means major, intensive activity in the areas of the cognitive and affective objectives, while the **xx** is an indication of only minor activity.

The results of the major analysis for the National Standards for culture indicate strong activity in the areas of knowledge and comprehension in cognitive outcomes and for receiving and responding for affective outcomes. In other words, for Standards goal areas of culture (2.1, 2.2, and 4.2), the analysis of the performance indicators shows major activity in the less complicated categories of both cognitive (knowledge and comprehension) and affective educational outcomes (receiving and responding). The same basic result is achieved in the analysis of secondary culture standards (3.1, 3.2, 5.1, and 5.2), connections and communities.

For the AATF standards, the results are indicated in Figure 2. They show a different picture. In "developing empathy toward other cultures," the major emphasis is on a full range of affective outcomes with less emphasis on cognitive outcomes. For ability to "observe and analyze a culture," the pattern is again different. Major attention is given to cognitive outcomes of knowledge, comprehension, application, and analysis, with minor attention to affective outcomes. Thus, the AATF standards emphasize the more complex categories of affective outcomes for empathy and the more complex categories of cognitive outcomes for observation and analysis of a culture. At the same time, the prescriptive nature of these standards must be kept in mind. The complete picture does not include the area-specific culture outcomes for France, North America, Sub-Saharan Africa, the Caribbean, and North Africa; they were not part of this analysis.

Among the three categories of states, looking at those states that adopted the National Standards for culture as their own shows a similar pattern to that of the National Standards analysis. For these states (Figure 3), the pattern for both cognitive and affective outcomes is basically the same as for the analysis of the National Standards. The outcomes are concentrated at the less complicated categories of cognitive learning (knowledge and comprehension) and the same for affective learning (receiving and responding).

Well, this is interesting, but what does it mean? For the National Standards, the results suggest the need for the development of expanded progress indicators so that the national model truly demonstrates use of more complicated cognitive behaviors such as apply, analyze, synthesize, and evaluate. The same condition holds for the affective domain, which needs expanded progress indicators such as value, conceptualize, organize, and characterize the learner's own values. Note that **both** cognitive and affective behaviors work together, especially in developing an awareness of another culture. (See Appendix B for Cognitive Learning, Affective Learning, and the Relationship of the Two.) In fact, it can be argued that the avoidance of affective learning could be detrimental to culture learning. Affective learning is hardly related to the "values clarification" movement of the 1970s. This issue needs reexamination in the light of what we are attempting with culture learning, namely the understanding and creation of personal meaning in relationship to another culture.

NATIONAL STANDARDS PROJECT— 4,8,12	Cognitive Learning 1 Know	Cognitive Learning 2 Comp	Cognitive Learning 3 Applic	Cognitive Learning 4 Anal	Cognitive Learning 5 Syn	Cognitive Learning 6 Eval	
MAJOR							
2.1 Demonstrate understanding of practices and perspectives	X	X	xx				
2.2 Demonstrate understanding of the relationship of products and services	X	X				xx	
4.2 Demonstrate understanding of culture through comparisons of cultures	X	X	xx	X			
SECONDARY							
3.1 Reinforce and further knowledge of other disciplines	X	X					
3.2 Acquire information and recognize distinctive viewpoints	X	X		X			
5.1 Use language within and beyond the school	X	X	xx	?			
5.2 Show evidence of becoming life-long learners with use	X	X	xx	?			

Affective Learning 1 Receive	Affective Learning 2 Resp	Affective Learning 3 Value	Affective Learning 4 Organ	Affective Learning 5 Char
X	X	xx		
X	X	xx		
X	X	xx	X	
X	X	?		
X	X	xx		
X	X	xx		
X	X	xx		

Figure 1

Emphasis on Cognitive and Affective Learning in National Standards That Apply to Culture

AATF NATIONAL COMMISSION ON CULTURAL COMPETENCE	Cognitive Learning 1 K	Cognitive Learning 2 C	Cognitive Learning 3 Applic	Cognitive Learning 4 Anal	Cognitive Learning 5 Syn	Cognitive Learning 6 Eval	
EMPATHY TOWARD OTHER CULTURES							
Stage 1	XX	XX					
Stage 2	XX	XX	XX				
Stage 3		XX	XX	XX	XX		
Stage 4		XX	XX	XX	XX	XX	
ABILITY TO OBSERVE AND ANALYZE A CULTURE							
Stage 1	X	X					
Stage 2		X	X	XX			
Stage 3		X	X	X			
Stage 4		X	X	X	XX		

OVERALL— CATEGORY I	Cognitive Learning 1 K	Cognitive Learning 2 C	Cognitive Learning 3 Applic	Cognitive Learning 4 Anal	Cognitive Learning 5 Syn	Cognitive Learning 6 Eval	
Culture	X	X	XX	XX	?	XX/?	
Comparisons	X	X	XX	XX	?	?	
Connections	X	X	X	XX	?	?	
Communities	X	X	XX	?	?	?	

Affective Learning 1 Receive	Affective Learning 2 Resp	Affective Learning 3 Value	Affective Learning 4 Organ	Affective Learning 5 Char
X	X			
	X	X		
	X	X	xx	?
			X	X
xx	xx			
	xx	xx		
	xx	xx		
		xx	xx	

Figure 2
Emphasis on Cognitive and Affective Learning in AATF Culture Standards

Affective Learning 1 Receive	Affective Learning 2 Resp	Affective Learning 3 Value	Affective Learning 4 Organ	Affective Learning 5 Char
X	X	xx	?	?
X	X	xx	?	?
X	X	xx	?	?
X	X	xx	?	

Figure 3
Summary of Emphasis on Cognitive and Affective Learning in Thirty-Three State Standards for Culture

The analysis of thirty-three state culture standards in comparison to that of the National Standards shows the same emphasis on the less complicated categories of both the cognitive and affective taxonomies. The study suggests that **if** the emphasis in the progress indicators for these standards is only on cognitive knowledge and comprehension as well as only on affective receiving and responding, **then** students may not necessarily be able to compare, contrast, analyze, synthesize, and evaluate aspects of another culture. In addition, they may not necessarily be able to value, organize values and attitudes, or be known for their own values and attitudes in relation to another culture. For example, if the expected outcome is to compare and contrast some element of culture, will the student be able to so function if her work is only at the level of knowledge and comprehension? These results indicate that the development of cultural awareness both cognitively and affectively is still an issue that requires significant exploration.

As a result of this analysis, what can we say about the National Standards for culture and the AATF Culture Commission culture standards? The AATF standards and their described levels for cultural empathy, analysis, and specific culture knowledge lack certain credibility and applicability to the classroom. They also appear to be highly complex, and the means of assessment appear to be extremely difficult. None of the thirty-three states had incorporated these standards into a set of state standards. It will be important to see how they are used in the future as states expand from generic standards to language-specific curriculum.

The National Standards for culture have been used as a major model in the development of state standards for culture. The National Standards are credible, flexible, and useful. They project high expectations. However, the National Standards, as well as the culture standards for states that have adopted them, are problematic. The performance indicators ask for relatively uncomplicated performances, while the standards themselves project more complicated performances. This problem will need to be remedied. It will be interesting to see how it is resolved.

C. Theoretical Models: What Guides Learning, Teaching, and Assessment?

The framework of expectations for learning in the form of national standards informs learners of what is anticipated of them as well as guides teachers in arranging the curriculum, assessing student learning, and conducting instruction. The importance of this and other frameworks cannot be underestimated **IF** we expect learners to achieve high standards in culture learning. The lack of planning for culture learning has contributed to lack of success in culture learning. Lack of curricular organization, deficient or nonexistent assessments, and unfocused learning strategies essentially promote the unsuccessful inclusion of culture with language learning. In other words, the requirements of student learning, approaches to assessment, and use of learning strategies must connect with what students are learning.

In order to overcome these deficiencies, culture learning must be placed in a context where the appropriate planning can take place. Frameworks for learning can help that planning. There are two frameworks that we will consider here: one for educational development, the other for the development of cultural sensitivity. Other models will be briefly considered as well. The framework for educational development is that of Egan (1979). The framework for the development of cultural sensitivity is that of the Bennetts, which is explored in J. Bennett (1993), M. J. Bennett (1993), and Bennett, Bennett, and Allen (1996). Egan's model of educational development and the Bennetts' model of cultural sensitivity development are important because both are based on the precepts of continuity, progression, and expansion of competence. Once a point or stage of competence has been reached, it does not have to be repeated. In other words, when a learner reaches Egan's romantic stage (see Figure 4), that stage is not repeated, nor does she regress as she progresses toward the philosophic stage. The same concept functions with the minimization and acceptance stages in the Bennett model (Figure 7). In this way, these two models are dynamic and interact with the maturational levels of learners. The models also provide direction for teachers as they prepare the interaction of learner qualities and the learning curriculum. The other models are those of Byram (1989; Byram, Morgan, et al. 1994), and Kramsch (1993). These models are more static in nature, but also require our consideration.

Educational Development. Since narrative is so important to language development and because narrative automatically includes culture as defined here, the work of Egan (1979) is important to consider. Theoretical underpinnings of the importance of narrative in human learning can also be found in Bruner (1990). Egan's four stages of development give meaning to expression in language through a link to the educational growth that learners possess at a particular stage (Figure 5). The framework provides for the link between the maturational level of the learner and the appropriate curriculum, the most suitable assessments, and the most applicable learning and teaching strategies. As a result, the adaptation of curriculum, assessment, and instruction to student characteristics, needs, and interests can and should be anticipated. In this context, the primacy of the learner's development **and** the continuance of that development become crucial to the learning of language

Mythic (Approximate ages 4/5 to 9/10 years)	1. Mythic thinking provides absolute accounts of why things are as they are, and fixes the meaning of events to sacred models. 2. Myth stories and children lack a sense of otherness, e.g., concepts of historical time, physical regularities, logical relationships, causality, and geographical space. 3. Mythical thinking lacks a clear sense of the world as autonomous and objective. The child's world is made full of meaning by those things the child knows best: love, hate, joy, fear, good, bad. 4. Myth is articulated on binary oppositions such as big/little, love/hate, security/fear, etc.
Romantic (Approximate ages 8/9 to 14/15 years)	The move from the mythic to the romantic stage is noticed in the development of "otherness" and the development of historical time, geographical space, physical regularities, logical relationships, and causality, which come from experience of the outside world. It is in this framework that children develop their sense of distinct identity.
Philosophic (Approximate ages 14/15 to 19/20 years)	The move from the romantic to the philosophic stage strengthens the realization that all the important bits and pieces of experience and knowledge are interconnected parts of a general unit. The major defining characteristic then is the search for the truth about human psychology, for the laws of historical development, for the truth about how societies function—the general laws whereby the world works.
Ironic (Approximate ages 19/20 through adulthood)	The reason for the transition from the philosophic to the ironic stage is that students' appreciation of the general schemes cannot fully accommodate all the particulars and that no general scheme can adequately reflect the richness and complexity of reality. General schemes are seen as useful but not true. There is reference and recognition of the "other" in this stage.

Figure 4

Egan's Stages of Educational Development

Taken from Egan, Kieran. 1979. *Educational Development.* New York: Oxford University Press.

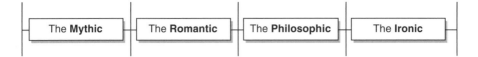

Figure 5
Egan's Educational Development Model*
*Based on Egan, Kieran. 1979. *Educational Development.* New York: Oxford University Press.

and culture. This primacy allows for the alignment of standards, assessment, and instruction. Consequently, planning for the culture learning of children, adolescents, and adults operates within a knowledge base rather than by guess or by individual teacher preference.[2] Others have used Egan's work in foreign language education. Byrnes (1990) uses Egan's developmental model as the basis for articulation in foreign languages, and Pesola (1995) develops a model for the creation of curriculum in foreign languages in the elementary school with Egan's educational developmental model as a core element.

Cultural Sensitivity. While Egan provides us with an understanding of educational development, J. Bennett (1993) and M. J. Bennett (1993) supply us with a perception of the development of cultural sensitivity. That development is outlined in a set of six stages, which lead a person to evolve from an ethnocentric perspective to one that is ethnorelative. This model was very carefully outlined in a presentation (Bennett, Bennett, and Allen 1996) at a University of Minnesota conference entitled "Culture at the Core: Transforming the Second Language Curriculum." As a means of indicating how instruction might be associated with the six stages, I am also providing the direction that such instruction would take with each stage. The six stages of the model are classified under two rubrics: ethnocentric (denial, defense, and minimization) and ethnorelative (acceptance, adaptation, and integration).

The **Ethnocentric Stages** are defined as follows: **Denial of difference** is the inability of the individual to recognize cultural differences because the constructs to which the differences refer are not part of the individual's repertoire; thus, the differences are denied. "As long as we speak the same language, there's no problem."

In this context, the Bennetts (J. Bennett 1993; M. J. Bennett 1993; M. J. Bennett, J. Bennett, and Allen 1996) suggest the importance of support, trust, friendliness, and cooperation in the classroom for learners as they begin to process their ability to gather appropriate cultural information; explore aspects of values, beliefs, and behavior; and recognize, but not judge, differences. Some of the content includes objective or formal culture (art, music, literature, theater, dance), heroes, holidays, and selected values, beliefs, and behaviors. Cultural contrasts are to be avoided here.

Defense against difference operates when the individual sees differences but evaluates them negatively through overt stereotyping. "How stupid to say 'grandmother' in that way? Our way is better!"

Within the focus on difference, learners develop skills of patience and tolerance. Difference is managed through attention to commonalities, as well as some existing distinctions within the in-group—in this case, within the class—or even broader distinctions within one's own culture. Attention is given to the mediation of conflict and to team building through the promotion of cooperative activities that center on shared needs and goals between the in-group and the out-group. Some cultural contrasts may be useful.

In the **Minimization of difference,** the individual sees superficial cultural differences but wants to minimize those differences by suggesting that "deep down, we are all the same, no matter where we are from."

The appropriate intercultural skills to be cultivated in this stage are listening, general cultural knowledge, knowledge of one's own culture, ability to perceive others with accuracy, and the maintenance of a nonjudgmental posture. These skills are enhanced through contact with cultural informants, opportunities to seek difference, emphasis on one's own cultural awareness, expansion of curiosity from in-group to out-group, and examination of cultural contexts when cultures are similar. Excessive use of cultural contrasts should be avoided.

The **Ethnorelative Stages** are described as follows: In the **Acceptance of difference** stage, individuals appreciate cultural difference and acknowledge that other cultures provide alternative resolutions to human existence. "The more difference the better! More difference equals more creative ideas!" In this stage, individuals can understand cultural phenomena within a context and elaborate on them.

In this stage, learners refine categories of cultural contrast as they make cultural difference the focus of their processes. They handle issues of cultural relativity, "distinguishing them from those of a moral or ethical relativity." The skills that learners work with at this stage, beyond culture-specific knowledge, are knowledge of and sensitivity toward cultural context, respect for the values and beliefs of others, and the tolerance of ambiguity.

In **Adaptation to difference,** individuals have the ability to see through the eyes of the "other," and to develop the communication skills necessary to communicate with the "other." "The more I understand this culture, the better I get at the language."

In the adaptation stage, the learner is learning how to take risks, solve problems, be flexible, adapt socially, and adapt to different communication patterns. The strategies for learning such behavior are carried out through the use of informants, case studies, and research strategies. Topics for consideration are humor, cultural deviance, and examples of difference.

In the final stage, **Integration of difference,** individuals find themselves in the process of creating an adaptable identity, not based on any one culture, which allows them to evaluate situations from a "multiple" perspective and communicate constructively with the "other." "Whatever the situation, I can usually look at it from a variety of cultural points of view." This latter stage would probably be difficult to attain in the classroom.

In this stage, the learner addresses the self as the process. "Am I able to interact culturally with others? Do I know how I will behave culturally? Can I act flexibly? Can I adapt my person to this or that role, still be true to my own cultural values, but still function in another culture?" This examination takes place within a framework of ethical and multicultural behavior as learners cross cultures.

One of the very important contributions of this model is the balance between content and process as expressed in Figure 6 (J. Bennett 1993). Content is what is to be learned (cultural patterns such as friendship, respect, heroes, holidays, and the like); process is what is done with content in the classroom (how to arouse curiosity, the identification of skills to deal with difference, the promotion of cooperative activities, preparation of learners to

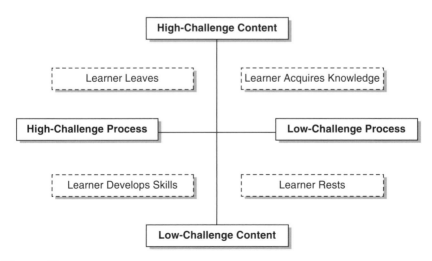

Figure 6
The Bennett Model

Figure 7
The Bennett Model*
*M. J. Bennett. 1993. The Intercultural Communication Institute

function autonomously using research strategies). A low-challenge process could be the memorization of facts and information when the learner has easy access to the information. A high-process challenge might be the use of research techniques when the learner is not clear on what research techniques are. On the other hand, low-challenge content is content that is already familiar, while high-challenge content is information that is largely unknown to the learner, depending on the stage in which the learner finds himself or herself, for example, certain values and beliefs when one is just beginning to learn about another culture. What is important here is that the learner be challenged in a positive way so that the learner is supported in what he or she is learning.

If there is both low-challenge process and low-challenge content, the learner "rests" or is provided no challenge. If there is both high-challenge process and high-challenge content, there probably is also no learning because the challenge is too high. It is in the criss-cross between high-challenge content and low-challenge process or between high-challenge process and low-challenge content that the learner will develop both skills and knowledge. In other words, a useful example in thinking through this balance is to locate where the high-challenge topic of stereotypes might be approached through a low-challenge process. The evening news or the front page of the newspaper may illustrate how overgeneralizations come about and may be a useful example in thinking through this balance.

The contribution of the Bennett model is a description of the *development* of cultural sensitivity. We can observe development take place and, in that process, determine how to plan for, teach toward, and evaluate learners within that environment.[3] The sample of instructional strategies and learning content give a notion of the kinds of behaviors to fit each developmental level. For example, from this discussion we are aware that the use of comparison is a strategy to be avoided in **Denial of difference;** it has some use in **Defense against difference;** and, in **Minimization of difference,** overuse of contrasts is a concern.

Both the Egan and the Bennett developmental models serve as umbrella frameworks as we give consideration to the inclusion of culture in the second-language classroom. They provide us with decision-making capacity that is interactive with the needs of learners at various stages, thereby giving teachers, curriculum developers, and assessors appropriate guidance.

Other Models. Two other major statements on the inclusion of culture in the foreign- or second-language classroom are important to mention here (Kramsch 1993; Byram 1989; Byram, Morgan, et al.1994). However, they lack the interactivity demonstrated between learners, their development, and their competence with either educational development or the development of cultural sensitivity that the Egan and Bennett models provide. Yet both Kramsch and Byram do offer different and important perspectives on how language and culture are integrated.

In her approach to this integration at the college/university level, Kramsch elaborates a dialectic or critical dialog between the need for students to use language *and* the context(s) within which that language is found. Those broadly conceived contexts are the culture of text, including texts of an oral and a written nature; the responses of other students to such text; or the culture of the classroom itself, the teacher → student → teacher relationship. In this dialectic, learning language is not aimed at the learning of listening, reading, speaking, and writing *per se,* but at the interrelationship of speakers and hearers, writers and readers, instructors, or any combination thereof, with the object of the dialectic, which is cultural context, or "text." In this way, Kramsch has integrated language and culture, for the core issue here is the *cultural context.*

An important concept in this dialectic is that of subjectivity in the form of intersubjectivity, intertextuality, and interculturality. The intersubjectivity among speakers in the classroom, including teachers, brings an awareness of multiple voices, different experience, and the diversity of race, gender, sexual orientation, and the like to the dialog. The result is the creation of multiple layers of meaning brought to the discussion, which require understanding and which are used to interpret the context.

Particularly in the teaching of literature, the voices of readers and the intended voice(s) of the text may not be the same. This intertextuality allows the reader to interact with the author's intended text. And when many readers exchange meaning with the text, the exchange offers a variability of interpretations, perceptions, and experiences to the dialogue with the text. As a result, the learner's world is opened to a variety of attitudes and values that make literature and culture inseparable (175).

The concept of interculturality recognizes the subjectivity of both the home and other cultures. Individual experiences and perceptions can easily fracture the stereotypes that are created through the passing down of information. In this context, culture and language can be taught and learned through an interpersonal process, by an examination of difference, and as a cross-disciplinary examination of issues and language. The emphasis on the individual in the processing of literature, the connection of literature to the social sciences, and the examination of differences in language and culture are what Giroux (1992) calls "border crossing." It is a pedagogy that "points to the need for conditions that allow students to write, speak, and listen in a language in which meaning becomes multiaccentual and dispersed and resists permanent closure" (Giroux 1992:29). Traditional pedagogy recognizes the teacher as the master of the subject and the giver of knowledge. However, as we allow learners to focus on the perspectives, practices, and products of others, the learners will have and will want to voice their own perspectives. In this regard, they will have crossed the border between given information to the area of personal participation. Once that border has been crossed, it is the students who are recognized as the creators of their own learning. The result is the opening of learning to difference, many voices, and a negotiation of meaning in the variety of texts and contexts wherein learning takes place. It is the essence of what might be called critical language pedagogy (Kramsch 1993:244–47). In language programs, such border crossing makes language and culture inextricably intertwined. And it provides the basis for a personal understanding of culture that cannot be given through transmitted information. (See Crawford and McLaren [1998] for further discussion of this issue.)

Based on a model of critical pedagogy and discourse analysis, Kramsch's orientation to the integration of language and culture fails to attract major attention of teachers in a way similar to that of Crawford-Lange and Lange in foreign languages (1984) and Wallerstein (1983) for ESL. Teachers are not comfortable with these ideas. They have not been prepared to teach in ways that are so centered on the learner; they have not been prepared to listen to the meaning of the voices; they are not necessarily prepared to negotiate or help negotiate meaning. Their focus has been on themselves as teachers. Teachers feel that they must have full control of language/culture learning; they must give meaning to what is taught; they must provide the information or feel guilty if they cannot. However, if culture learning is to create meaning for learners to be heard, and to develop cultural sensitivity, then the learning focus must shift from the teacher giving instruction to the learner's needs. Here, the wise counsel of Freire (1989, 1996), who recommends the creation of an atmosphere of questioning and exploration for learners, could be helpful to teachers. And the need for changes in teacher education to accommodate the learner's perspective have been anticipated by Lange (1990), Tedick, et al. (1993), and Tedick and Walker (1996).

Byram (1989) and Byram, Morgan, et al. (1994) arrive at his model through an extensive consideration of the literature on language and culture and their relationship to the social sciences. As a result of this survey, Byram bases his argument on language as both an object and a medium of study. In other words, the learning of language is a means to "learning about the people and culture associated with it" (Byram 1989:51). In this regard, like Kramsch, Byram sees the interrelationship of language and culture as a natural one. Yet, that interrelationship is somewhat different. Byram sees culture as actualized by the group and is not as concerned with individual perceptions or meaning. For him, culture is already marked through identities and boundaries. He argues that the full integration of language and culture comes in advanced classes with the examination (description, analysis) of literature—not only in the unique representation of the culture by the author, but also as the author represents that culture in general—as well as through experience. The integration of language and culture at the advanced level suggests that younger learners, because they can only express themselves in the foreign language in simple ways, use the native language (for our purposes English) to describe and analyze culture, including C_1 (Culture 1 = native culture) as well as C_2 (Culture 2 = taught culture). Gradually, they work toward the expression of the analysis and the contrasts in the foreign language.

Byram's model is presented as a circle divided into four quarters, containing the following elements: 1. *Language Learning:* a communicative, "skill"-oriented foreign language focus. 2. *Language Awareness:* a sociolinguistic, knowledge-oriented, comparative focus, in the L_1. 3. *Cultural Awareness:* a knowledge-oriented comparative $[C_1–C_2]$ focus in the L_1 (See Triandis, et al. 1972). 4. *Cultural Experience:* a knowledge-oriented foreign culture focus in the FL (see Figure 8).

This model allows the use of the native language for comparative analysis of one's own and other cultural meanings. It combines the learning of a foreign language with an experiencing of foreign cultural phenomena in four recurring phases:

Phase 1.   Communicative skills acquisition, which is

Phase 2.   enhanced through language awareness, an idea similar to that of Stern's linguistic syllabus (1982).

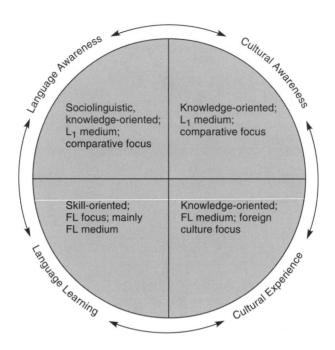

Figure 8
Byram's Language/Culture Learning Model

Phase 3.   The study of language phases 1 and 2 is combined with the study of culture in an L_1 comparative mode, in which the home and foreign cultures are described, analyzed, and compared; and,

Phase 4.   the direct experience of some aspects of the C_2 is accomplished from the viewpoint and within the perspective of the foreign peer group in L_2.

There is both a flow and a balance among elements in this model. It is not intended that the model be linear; it is circular, as indicated by the arrows on the outside. Yet it is a model that is disconnected from the educational development of learners, whether secondary or post-secondary.

The importance of the Byram contribution is that it includes the *contrast of cultural knowledge* as an important content in the learning of both C_1 and C_2. Contrast serves as the basis for experiential work. Cultural experiences are incorporated into language and cultural learning *after* the contrast has been understood. These experiences could be through educational visits, home stays, family trips, and the like. Yet not all cultural experiences require living or traveling in or to the foreign culture. They can be achieved in a *section biculturelle* of a language course, where content is taught through the foreign language.

Further elaboration of the model is evidenced in Byram, Morgan et al. (1994). The theory behind the model includes the especially important issues of empathy, attitudes, and moral development as applied to the classroom. In this publication, the authors discuss the use of comparison as a method, explore the implications of comparison in teacher development, display nine case studies of cultural learning according to principles of the model, and make recommendations for assessment. In this process, they provide a detailed understanding of the model.

Conclusion. The discussion in this section, while somewhat theoretical, provides the reader with frameworks that situate language/culture learning. Those settings include the educational development of a person from childhood through adult learning, the development of cultural sensitivity, and two perspectives on the interrelationship of language and culture. For each of these frameworks, objections can be found. It can be argued that the Egan framework must be translated into a foreign language and that the concept of narrative is too unfamiliar as a basic teaching and learning strategy. A similar objection can be raised with the work of the Bennetts, namely that it comes from the intercultural training literature and does not integrate language with it. Although Kramsch focuses on the integration of language and culture, her ideas may work at the college level but not in elementary and secondary schools. And Byram's ideas function well in a British context. The issue here is not the objections, but rather the importance of frameworks in guiding the development of cultural competence of learners in foreign language programs. Without frameworks to guide teaching and learning, classroom activities consist of the use of isolated worksheets and independent activities that have no coherent purpose. The frameworks provided here are included for their importance, reflection, and use.

The next three sections of this article deal with curricular organization, assessment, and instruction, in that order. The purposes for this treatment are (1) to provide an organization for the culture learning curriculum; (2) to tie assessment to curriculum, particularly to the outcomes and the tasks associated with outcomes; (3) to show the association of assessment to instruction. I am again referring to the relationship of curriculum = assessment = instruction. Such an approach comes from the work of Wiggins (1993, 1998). Its major intent is to directly link assessment to instruction for student outcomes. Such an approach is different because it allows the teacher to teach directly to the outcomes and to the "test." We will see how this works.

D. Curricular Organization: Orientations, Structure, Standards, and Design

Orientations. Much of the foreign language literature on curriculum has been based on a technical orientation of curriculum, instruction, and assessment derived from the scientific nature of the area of study. It has also been directed to some degree by the curriculum literature in English as a Second Language (ESL). In his description of the foreign language curriculum crisis, Lange (1990) outlines four categories of curricular inquiry: the scientific-technical, the connective, the practical, and the critical or emancipatory.

The *scientific-technical curriculum* is a linear, objective, and scientific-technical approach to curriculum in which the breakdown of elements to be learned is based on a scientific analysis of the field of study. For language, this scientific analysis comes through the science of linguistics. This analysis guides learning decisions from a broad mission statement to goals, objectives, specification of content and tasks, ordering of content and tasks, choice of learning materials, designation of instruction, and selection of assessments (Banathy and Lange 1972 in foreign languages; Brown 1995 in ESL).

The connection between a scientific-technical and a communicative approach to curriculum and program development is labeled *connective inquiry.* It allows for the development of language proficiency as a means of discovering and expressing the individual's personal meaning, but within a scientific-technical framework (See Dubin and Olshtain 1986; Johnson 1982; Nunan 1989; Yalden 1987; all for ESL). As a result, the processes of scientific-technical curriculum are applied to the development of the ability to communicate personal meaning, i.e., discourse rules are the basis for competence in language use.

Practical curriculum inquiry does not refer to the practical, everyday concerns for teaching language. Instead, it is "a quest for meaning and comprehension of the world as individuals strive to grasp an awareness of their own worth and identification" (Lange 1990:91). This highly personal orientation to curriculum recognizes the individual's knowledge and experience as central to an understanding of herself, the group, and society as a whole. Stevick (1976) is the best representative of this curriculum type.

Finally, *emancipatory inquiry* brings unity to reflection and action within a social, economic, and political context. In this context and in this unity, individuals and groups reflect on their society and act on it to correct social inequities and to support fairness, justice, and emancipation for all persons regardless of race, creed, age, gender, sexual orientation, or social class. Friere (1996) is the best general example of this inquiry, while Crawford-Lange and Lange (1984) and Kramsch (1993) are foreign language examples and Wallerstein (1983) is one for ESL.

The importance of this discussion is that, although there are some distinctions in the different curricular orientations, these orientations overlap. If there is concentration on any one, single orientation, student abilities will be limited to that orientation. In the current learning climate, it is also clear that the most prevalent curriculum disposition is the scientific-technical. In this climate, if students are limited to the scientific elements of language (phonology, morphology, syntax, and discourse rules) in the four language modalities, they will be able to function mainly with those elements. However, if the orientation is toward overlapping curricular directions (connective, practical, or emancipatory), then learners will be capable of communication of personal meaning and of understanding their relationship to a broader culture, and they will gain an ability to express and act upon the need to better the human condition. In addition, when culture is integrated with language learning, it is my firm belief that curriculum is directed beyond the pure scientific-technical orientation. In other words, the organization of a curriculum that includes culture will automatically relate to connective, practical, and emancipatory curriculum perspectives.

Structure. If curriculum is not linear or purely related to the scientific aspects of language, thereby including culture as defined by the National Standards, the structure of curriculum will not be linear either. In this context, I propose that curriculum be recursive and thematic (Lange 1996). What does that mean? Simply stated, it means that culture learning will be organized around cultural themes, and that these themes will recur throughout the curriculum. Once a theme has been introduced at the developmental level that is appropriate for learners (see Egan 1979, or Figure 4 as an education developmental framework), it can be repeated in another developmental level with appropriate expansion of experience and necessary complexity of concept. Some general themes to consider are the following: family and relatives; relationships, such as friendships; transportation; education; manners; role of food preparation and consumption; work; play and recreation; the neighborhood; health; money.

If, for example, the theme of family is chosen, it might be treated at the Egan mythic level in the following manner:

> Learners might listen to a story about a family of goats traveling through the mountains to get to the other side to find food and water, where the mother and father protect "kids" from the wolves who want to capture and eat the "kids." Learners might tell their own simple stories about a trip they have taken with their own families.

In the above example, the story deals with the theme of family and the subthemes of family as a protection in providing security from the fear that children normally have of elements outside themselves and of the value of the comfort and security of the family. Stories like this one and "Little Red Riding Hood" demonstrate the importance of family as a sacred model, where the focus of the listener is on self, where meaning is on things that the child knows, such as love, fear, and security.

At the Egan romantic stage (See Figure 4), the story would certainly change significantly. Here, the story and activities could be set in the foreign culture and involve logical family relationships through the development of a family tree. The story might involve some elements of the past, be set in different geographical places, and demonstrate how the family evolved. Such stories direct learners to concerns outside themselves, which include an emphasis on family (but one that seeks origins of family members from the past in terms of name, place, and time). Learners could then develop a portion of their own family tree.

When the learners reach the Egan philosophic stage (See Figure 4), their energy would be directed to a deeper level of comprehension. They would be involved in understanding the psychology of family through literature that deals with family in a social sense through the reading of authentic materials on family in newspapers, magazines, and journals, as well as stories, poetry, and extracts from novels that demonstrate how families function. Comparisons of family functioning could be made between one's own culture and other cultures.

In the Egan ironic stage (See Figure 4), learners would recognize the stories about family in the previous stages as contributing to their knowledge about family. However, at this stage they would recognize that those stories were their own truth, their own perceptions. In this stage, they would free themselves to play with the mythic, romantic, and philosophic stages as a means of creating an imaginary story about family. Such stories could certainly be extended to the creation of stories about families in other cultures. It is for the teacher to provide the necessary knowledge and information for learners to include in this creation.

The several stages of the Bennett model could also be given this same treatment. The point of the above example is to show that a curricular organization can be tied to an educational framework. There are other means by which a recursive curriculum in the foreign language classroom can be structured, as in the following examples:

- By year: Here, similar thematic material would provide expansion of the learners' perceptions, knowledge, and understanding.

- By semester: Similar themes could recur, which could expand on previously acquired knowledge and perceptions. Such a structure would be particularly useful in the modular, four-period school day that has become so popular in block scheduling in the United States in recent years.

• By specific design: curriculum or text materials could establish principles upon which themes would reappear and be expanded. Another variation: Several connected themes could be interwoven in text materials to expand on learners' perceptions and knowledge.

The most important aspect of these examples is to demonstrate that the recursive curriculum expands learners' knowledge and comprehension as they progress through their educational development. Few foreign language culture programs are organized in this manner. If we intend to take advantage of learner development, time, or learner curiosity about other cultures, the proposal for a recursive curriculum needs serious consideration.

Standards. Within a recursive framework, standards for performance can characterize curriculum. The National Standards (1996) provide both goals and standards for culture in both Culture and Comparisons goals categories (See *SFLL* 1996:9, or statements of those standards at the beginning of this article). The standards set both content and a general level of performance. In essence, students are to *demonstrate an understanding* of the **practices, products, and perspectives** of the culture being studied, as well as *demonstrate an understanding* of the **concept of culture** *through comparisons* of the culture studied *and* their own. Practices, products, and perspectives, and the concept of culture are the content. **Understand, demonstrate, compare** are the performances that are enunciated in the standards. These words can have more concrete meaning. For example, *understand* means "to see, grasp, accept, digest, interpret, and learn." It is not a concept that lends itself to easy exemplification. But it is a particular human trait. And it represents both cognitive and affective learning. *Demonstrate* means "to show, describe, explain, illustrate, make clear," and even "teach." *Compare* means "to liken, contrast, relate, match, equal," and "associate," among other things. These contents and these performances are the general achievements expected from the National Standards. Within the iterative, recursive curriculum structure, we need to see how the performances can be achieved within the very general designated content.

Design. For this discussion, I have drawn heavily on the presentation "Understanding by Design," by Grant P. Wiggins and Everett Kline, given at the ACTFL Collaborative Seminar, January 22, 1998, in Yonkers, New York (Wiggins and Kline 1998). How do we design a curriculum that allows our students to meet the standards? The general principle is easily stated, but is not necessarily easy to carry out. The principle has three parts: (1) determine the performance or standard that all students have to meet for a program or unit of learning; (2) determine how that performance is to be assessed; and (3) determine what lessons or activities derive from the performance tasks. Another way of stating the question is through three simple questions: What are the desired results for learning (standards or targeted achievements)? What evidence of results will be accepted (assessments)? What activities and experiences contribute to the desired evidence and results (instruction)? These three questions are the basis for what is conceptually or theoretically labeled "backward curriculum design" (Wiggins 1998). This label is used to designate a curriculum based on student performance rather than on content. A backward curriculum design asks some other key questions that help us understand better what the term means as we prepare programs, courses, and lessons:

- Toward what standards and tasks does the content point, as a means to an end?
- Do the proposed final tasks require the key understandings, knowledge, and skills at the heart of the syllabus?
- Are there sufficient rehearsal and refinement opportunities built in?
- Are there lessons to provide enabling knowledge and skill?

This design leads us away from the "traditional" approach to curriculum design that is the acceptance of a text as *the* curriculum. With the acceptance of a text as *the* curriculum comes the concept of "coverage." Instead of focusing on student performance, we teachers announce how many chapters of the book we are covering in a month, a semester, or a school year. In the context of "covering," assessment is mostly a series of tests to determine if learners have "learned" the covered material. However, in this "backwards design logic," the targeted performance and the assessment drive the curriculum that is then enabled by instruction. It is neither the content nor the instruction that determines what is learned; it is the learners' performance that is the key to learning. The teacher is no longer a "coverer" of material, but a coach who mentors learners toward the designated performance. This curriculum differs from the traditional one, and the role of coach may be difficult for some to assume. Continuing teacher development to focus on these aspects will be important as a vehicle for change.

As we think about this concept of curriculum design for culture, let me work through an example to demonstrate one person's understanding of how such a design comes about. In this example, I am going to choose a key word from the above discussion of the National Standards for culture, namely *understanding*. I am going to link that word to the "demonstration of an understanding of practices." And, within the "demonstration of an understanding of practices," I am going to choose a more specific "practice" within which to create my example, namely "understanding friendships."[4] In this context, the example will be a general one and not tied to any particular culture.

The design tasks are three in number. My *first* task is to state the specific standard or performances I want students to complete as a means of giving evidence that they have met the standard. In the case of the culture standards, this requires determining the specific learner performances related to the understanding of the relationship between practices and perspectives, products and perspectives, and the understanding of the concept of culture through comparisons between C1 and C2. The questions that need answering in order to design a curriculum and determine standards are the following:

- What practices in this culture should students learn?
- What perspectives will they have of these practices?
- Upon learning more about these practices, how will these perspectives change?
- What products should students learn about?
- What perspectives will students have of these products?
- Upon learning more about these products, how will these perspectives change?
- How are these practices, products, and perspectives related?

Answers to these questions give details to the local culture curriculum. Further decisions need to be made as to how the answers to the questions are distributed throughout the curriculum.

My *second* task is to state specifically the knowledge and skills that learners need in order to provide evidence that they fulfill the performance. The quality of the learners' performance is another aspect that needs attention. Questions that need to be answered in this regard are the following:

- What knowledge and skills are important for learning the practices, products, and perspectives of another culture?
- What knowledge and skills will lead learners to give us authentic performances?

- To what tasks will we have learners respond?
- To what prompts will we have learners respond?
- What authentic performances will give us evidence that learners meet the standards?
- How will we document the quality of the performances to know that the standards have been met?

My *third* design task is that of arranging instruction so that learning tasks contribute to the desired performances. The basic purpose of instruction is to guide learner progress toward the desired performances through activities that will help reach those performances, to give feedback on learner progress, and to judge the learners' readiness to meet established standards. Answers to the following questions and to those decided by the reader will inform instructional strategies:

- How do we guide learners toward determined performances?
- What learner strategies relate to the determined performances?
- Which of our multiple intelligences help expand learner functioning with any performance? (See Gardner 1993a; Gardner 1993b; Gahala and Lange 1997)
- By what processes do we give learners feedback on progress toward meeting the standards?
- What kinds of assessments contribute to giving learners feedback leading up to determined performances?

Let me provide an example with "Understanding Friendships." This theme is different from the more common topics of food, music, and dance. It is also an abstract theme that requires more than surface knowledge. It combines both thought and feelings. In working through this example, I have found the topic difficult because I have had to create the example as it relates to curriculum, assessment, and instruction. Note that language is not dealt with in these examples. The complexity of cultural issues is a sufficient challenge. The reader might want to consult Crawford-Lange and Lange (1984) on this matter. Note also that I have kept the example in the "home culture" to allow the example to be as comprehensible as possible. Yet even with these apologies it is my intent to push us beyond the usual topics. Without examples in new and different areas of culture, it is not possible to move away from the familiar and help learners grow as a result.

Example of Standard and Evidence. With this example, I have already determined that the theme of "friendship" fits into the National Standard 2.1, "demonstrate an understanding of the relationship between the practices and perspectives of the culture studied." And I have determined the evidence that I would need to know to show how the theme could be assessed. The theme in the form of a classroom standard is stated below, as well as the categories of evidence: knowledge, skills, attitudes, processes, and experience (See Pratt, 1994:65–101, particularly 74–93).

Standard: Explain your understanding of friendship in this culture.

Evidence: Student responses to prompts or academic tasks, activities, papers, simulations, and authentic tasks generate evidence. Some of those responses come from activities related to the following that have been categorized into knowledge, skills, attitudes, processes, and experiences. The importance of the evidence as a contribution to the learner's developing competence with the standard (critical, important, or desirable) has also been indicated. Most of the following activities would be classified as prompts or academic activities.

Knowledge

• Obtain basic information on friendship *in your own* culture. (Critical)
• Obtain basic information on friendship *in the other* culture. (Critical)
• Outline and sort information for both cultures. (Important)

Skills

• Define friendship in *your* culture. (Critical)
• Define friendship in the *other* culture. (Critical)
• Explain how kids in *your* culture make friends. (Critical)
• Explain how kids in the *other* culture make friends. (Critical)
• Dramatize friendship in *your* culture. (Desirable)
• Dramatize friendship in the *other* culture. (Desirable)

Attitudes

• Recognize differences in friendship patterns. (Critical)
• Seek further information on friendship voluntarily. (Important)
• Help others understand differences in friendship. (Critical)
• Plan to respect differences in friendship. (Critical)

Process

• Distinguish friendship in the *other* culture from your *own.* (Critical)

- Compare/contrast being friends in the *other* culture with your *own*. (Critical)

Experience

- Create/imagine/develop a situation between you and a person in the other culture in which you would become friends. (Critical—Here is the authentic task that is like or simulates real life.)

Knowledge, Skills, and Activities: In the "backward" design of curriculum and instruction for performance assessment, Wiggins and Kline (1998) show how the designation of standards leads to assessment evidence. A couple of more detailed steps in this design for instruction/assessment are also necessary, such as determining the *enabling knowledge and skills* necessary for basic understanding of any concept and *enabling and engaging activities* to help the students meet the standard.

In our example of "friendship," the enabling knowledge and skills would be associated with activities regarding some very basic questions that individual learners would answer for themselves (Who is a friend to you? How do you know a friend? When is a friend a friend? When is a friend not a friend?). In this instance, knowledge and skills are stated in response to the questions and other activities. The first activity could be an outline of the knowledge obtained from answering the questions. And each student creates a definition from the outline—his or her definition. From the definition, learners explain, according to their experience, how friendships are made. That explanation can be actualized in a dramatic presentation of how friendships are made. Here are the *knowledge and skills* "needed" for this example:

- What is friendship to me?
- What questions did we answer about friendship?
- What words did you use? What words did you need to learn?
- How did you define "friend"?
- Explain what a friend is.
- With a partner, show us what a friend is.

Responses to the first three activities could be assessed through observation of the group. A list of responses, words used, and words that need to be learned could be established. The "needed" words could then be pursued in further learning and the used words could be reentered later. The responses could be directed toward the creation of the definition of a friend.

Some process skills are also appropriate to the learning about friendship, as indicated in the following questions:

- What is the structure of a definition like "friendship"? Is there only one?
- What tool(s) can we use to explain "friendship"?
- How do we know when we have explained a concept like "friendship"?

The process activities connected with these questions are the basis on which definitions, explanations, and dramatic performances could be improved. These more cognitive and strategic activities also provide a basis on which performances can be strengthened. Evidence can be associated with these activities as well in evaluating the improvement of the definitions, explanations, and dramatizations of friendship in the other culture.

Enabling and engaging activities consist of both prompts and authentic tasks, which draw upon basic knowledge and skills to challenge learners to perform in more sophisticated ways that allow them to demonstrate their competence in relationship to the standard. Although prompts are more often associated with academic problems, they are intended to prepare learners for authentic tasks. Prompts also tell the learner what is required and what she or he is supposed to do. Examples of prompts within our continuing cultural example would be the following: Prepare an oral presentation that describes the differences/similarities between friendship in a nation or community and that of Culture X. For this presentation, gather information on teenage friendship in Culture X, summarize and evaluate that information, and present your summary and evaluation to the group in your class that is working on friendship among adults.

Authentic tasks provide an authentic challenge to the learner that is based in real life. It may be in a real or simulated context. It answers the following question: "Is this the kind of problem adults face in the 'real world'?" If not, then the problem is a prompt or a quiz (Wiggins and Kline 1998). What would be an authentic task for our culture example? I would argue that the experience category in the outline of evidence for meeting the standard, **Explain your understanding of friendship in the culture,** "Create/imagine/develop a situation between you and a person in the other culture in which you would become friends," meets the requirement as a simulation of a real-life personal situation.

E. Assessments

If we examine the current state of culture learning in our classrooms, we find a lack of standards. We find assessment that is meager. What assessment there is of culture learning may be focused on facts and information, which are "tested" by objective means. However, the National Standards Project clearly outlines what is to be learned and brings language and culture into a natural alliance. And with sample progress indicators the project also provides us with directions for the assessment of culture/language learning. As a result of setting standards for culture, we are obliged to map out our intentions, to indicate what students are to learn and perform as well as how we will assess them. For the learning of culture, this is an enormous step forward. Since the emphasis is now on learners and their performance, we will need to think beyond the narrow focus of tests. That is our next step. Let me provide some background.

Background. Until recently in the history of testing and assessment, much of the work has been associated only with testing. Testing is associated with the creation of standardized tests, which use a multiple-choice format for national and even local classroom tests to examine knowledge and information. Assessment is associated with more complicated performances and more complex learning, which are examined through rubrics that inform the learner about how well his or her performance matches a previously stated standard. Lado (1961) was the first person to seriously pay attention to the testing of language. Although his work dealt with English as a Second Language, he did use examples in other languages. His main orientation was the testing of listening, reading, writing, and speaking. Lado also focused on the qualities of tests, such as reliability and validity, and on issues relating to the construction and analysis of items, since most of his work concerned standardized tests. The testing of culture was mentioned, but received limited attention.

In the decades that have followed, major publications on language testing have generally continued this orientation. A sampling of those publications suggests three basic categories of work on testing, with some attention to assessment: (1) major focus on the qualities of tests; (2) major focus on the evaluation of language and language skills; and (3) major orientation toward proficiency that mixes testing and assessment. In the first category, the literature concerns itself mainly with testing and its various features, including item creation, item analysis, item discrimination, reliability, validity, use of machines with testing, and research on testing (Bachman 1990; Henning 1987; Oller and Perkins 1978; Oller and Perkins 1980; Spolsky 1978 and 1979). In this category, culture as defined by the National Standards Project is not included, although reference to the sociolinguistic context is mentioned in several references. While the sociolinguistic context is important for communication as defined by the National Standards Project, it does not provide the content of culture perspectives, products, and practices. The second category, evaluation of language and language skills, is represented by Valette (1977). In this work, the concentration is on classroom tests: types of tests, how to prepare them, and how to analyze results. However, the major contribution centers on tests for the four modalities of listening, reading, writing, and speaking, and on literature. By far, the emphasis is on the four modalities. A very short chapter on culture gives emphasis on culture largely as information, and shows some interrelationship between language and its social uses. The item types represented are largely objective in nature.

In the third category, there is a mixture of testing and assessment. This mixture results from a carryover of the generally strong tradition of testing in American educational culture. And it happens because of a relatively new direction in language teaching, namely, that for language proficiency or communicative competence.[5] This trend resulted in a translation of the Foreign Service Oral Proficiency Interview for the academic world through a project of the Educational Testing Service and the American Council on the Teaching of Foreign Languages (Byrnes and Canale 1987). This same project led to the development of proficiency guidelines in listening, reading, speaking, and writing. While originally there were guidelines for culture in the American Council on the Teaching of Foreign Languages Provisional Proficiency Guidelines, those guidelines were subsequently eliminated because they were unwieldy. The literature represented in this category (Jones and Spolsky 1975; Lowe and Stansfield 1988; Omaggio 1983) examines some of the technical issues of the oral proficiency interview, explores the translation of the oral interview as a model for classroom testing for other modalities, and relates some of the problems and research issues that need addressing in order to make this new direction a viable one. Again, in this literature, culture is referred to in the "sociolinguistic" sense, but not as a content. Beyond this literature, there are three references in foreign languages that are particularly oriented toward assessment (Cohen 1994; Genesee and Upshur 1996; Shohamy and Walton 1992).

What Is Assessment? In his introduction to *Approaches to Language Testing,* Spolsky (1978) argues that language testing finds itself in a postpositivistic, postscientific state that concentrates on the creative aspects of language and that is directed toward the individual's understanding of varieties of language and their use in a variety of contexts. To me this suggests that the concept of testing has to be broadened beyond a narrow, scientific orientation to assessment and has to include culture. Even though some twenty years have passed since Spolsky's statement, the narrow focus of testing still mainly exists and culture is hardly included. In my own reaction to testing priorities at the 1990 ACTFL Priorities Conference (Lange 1990), I argued for the use of assessment in language learning. I suggested that assessment includes

> observation of production (taped and written samples) which are reviewed holistically; triangulated examination of responses to oral, written, and cultural texts; connected use of more than one modality to receive and express meaning of events, people, institutions, and relationships which concern the individual; collaborative use of language in situations where the second culture (C2) context is made problematic (in some dissonance with that of the native culture C1), and reacted to by more than one person . . . outcomes associated with personal understanding and expression (Lange 1990:404).

Wiggins (1993), who is not a foreign language specialist but whose thinking and work in assessment must be considered, more fully elaborates the concept of assessment. But what do we mean when we talk about assessment?

According to Richards, Platt, and Weber (1985), assessment is "the measurement of the ability of a person. For example, assessment of the comprehension of an immigrant child may be necessary to discover if the child is able to follow a course of study in a school" (18). In general terms, this definition points to what the student is actually capable of doing with the process of comprehension. Madaus and Kelleghan (1992) confirm this definition when they state that assessment "may be defined as an activity designed to show what a person knows or can do. Thus, it is concerned with the appraisal of individuals. As we shall see, assessment in the classroom is based largely on a teacher's observations of students as they go about their normal learning activities" (120). Madaus and Kelleghan discuss the range of assessments that can occur, from oral examinations to the use of the essay exam to multiple-choice questions, which are used particularly in standardized exams (124–25). In foreign languages, the American Council on the Teaching of Foreign Languages Oral Proficiency Interview is an example of an assessment of oral competence that is judged against a set of guidelines (Met and Galloway, 1992.) Concomitant guidelines for listening, reading, and writing have been developed for the purpose of assessing those modalities in similar ways (ACTFL Proficiency Guidelines 1987). The University of Minnesota has developed proficiency assessments in speaking, reading, and writing based on the oral interview procedure and the guidelines for speaking, reading, and writing (CARLA 1997). These are examples of assessments in foreign languages that point specifically to "what the learner can do." Yet, we must remember that there is still a healthy discussion and some confusion between testing and assessment. In this chapter, we are concentrating mainly on performance assessment, which is defined as "our ability to perform [creatively] with knowledge" (Wiggins 1993:209 ff.).

Wiggins (1993) provides deep background to the concept of assessment. In his discussion, Wiggins is not friendly to the kind of standardized testing that occurs on a one-time basis to determine one's capabilities, such as IQ tests, the National Assessment of Education Progress (NAEP), or even classroom tests. Wiggins is concerned about lack of feedback on such tests, the use of standardized procedures in examining competence, and issues of reliability and validity of the measures. Yet, the concept of assessment is not without its own problems of validity and reliability. Liskin-Gasparro (1996) reviews some of the issues that arise with both the reliability and validity of assessments in her article on the assessment of standards.

For what reasons and how do we give tests? According to Wiggins (1993:38–46), we give them (1) for information; (2) for transmission of knowledge only; (3) to examine a standardized knowledge; (4) with distrust of students in mind; (5) for objective knowledge, when knowledge is never neutral; (6) for student control over knowledge first before creative use; (7) for largely utilitarian knowledge; (8) without incentives to reach expectations. Such reasons and manners concentrate on a less thoughtful "education," or on learning that is mainly information-focused. A "more thoughtful assessment system" provides resolution to the tensions created with the current system of testing.

Assessment Postulates. A more thoughtful assessment system assumes that

1. Learners are asked to justify their understanding of their learning and skill. Assessments should provide the opportunity for the assessor, through questions, probes, and cues, to understand what learners' abilities are and how the learners are misleading themselves. In this context, learners are rewarded for self-corrections.

2. Because students are novice learners, they are given access to models of how the subject of study functions and opportunity to work with real problems in the subject. There is no secret to how assessment works, since learners are given sample tests or assessments in advance of any assessment event. Students know how and why they are being assessed. In this context, Wiggins says, "All assessment should be thought of as 'formative'" (Wiggins 1993:51).

3. Learners know that the assessment system is based on "known, clear, public, non-arbitrary standards and criteria" (Wiggins 1993:51). There is nothing mysterious about the assessment system. And also it is not used as a reward or punishment system.

4. Self-assessment is key to an "authentic" education. Learners apply the "known, clear, public, non-arbitrary standards and criteria" to their own performances. Such opportunity allows learners to be their own best critics and prepares them for self-judgments that will have to be made in adult life.

5. Learners are engaged in the field in which they perform; they are not bystanders.

6. Learners develop confidence and the ability to express themselves as they read, understand, function with, and resolve authentic problems in a particular field. Confidence in learning does not arrive overnight; neither does ability to express one's self in the language of a field. Working with authentic problems of a field, expressing perceptions, and receiving probing feedback generates sophisticated learning.

7. Learners understand that their comprehension of the field is best assessed when their answers are probed. A field is not understood through one question, but through extensive series of questions. Probing questions begin at the commencement of learning in any new field and continue, hence the importance of the recursive curriculum concept.

8. Learners learn that ideas, theories, and systems are not fixed. They can and should be challenged. A critical aspect of all human endeavor (practices, products, perceptions, ideas, theories, and systems) engages these endeavors in dialog with potential action to resolve inconsistencies, generate new perspectives, and create new knowledge.

9. Through the assessment of others, as well as self-assessment, learners' intellectual honesty, personal character, and attitudes about knowledge and learning distinguish what they know and what they do not know.

Extensive discussion of these postulates is available in Wiggins (1993:46–69). They are the key issues that form the major discussion in the book. Here, they provide a context in which we can question our own assessment practices.

Implications for Culture Learners and Cultural Assessment. Briefly, when these postulates are applied to learning with understanding (cf. Wiggins 1998) and the relationship of that learning to assessment, there are significant implications for all. In particular with culture, the standards focus on *understanding*. And, in this context, understanding is *not* a vague concept.

Both learning and the assessment of understanding can be very precise. These postulates have the following implications for any understanding but also apply specifically to the National Culture Standards (See Wiggins and Kline 1998):

- Understanding means the student can apply, predict, adapt, demonstrate, avoid misconceptions, verify, defend, critique, make qualified and precise judgments, and make connections with other ideas and facts. These expectations go well beyond information and establish important expectations for understanding, one of the major arguments for culture learning.

- The learner can answer key questions: What? Why? How? Whose? Which? When? Where? What if? So what? These questions reveal the core of cultural understanding. *What* is only the first question.

- While the accuracy of knowledge per se is important, assessment focuses more on the ability of the learner to verify and critique information and ideas. Process is crucial in the development of understanding another culture. Facts and information are only one basis for such understanding.

- Interaction of teacher and learner in assessment provides evidence of progress to both in learning and furnishes the teacher with the opportunity to detect important learning errors. Ongoing teacher-learner interaction in processing cultural knowledge and understanding shows how process is being applied and where misconceptions may arise.

- Assessment is anchored in authentic and contextualized problems as opposed to highly focused tests of information. In order to promote deep cultural understanding, culture is presented in the form of authentic problems that have several resolutions. The example of "organization of adolescent sports programs in French culture" in Crawford-Lange and Lange (1984) and the many examples in Wallerstein (1983) indicate that problems in a process context yield sophisticated cultural understanding, whereas information out of context in our usual tests does not.

- The use of rubrics and recurring tasks across time gives learners an understanding of the sophistication of their learning. In developing cultural understanding, the importance of the growth of that understanding cannot be underestimated. Use of a recursive curriculum, authentic performances within that curriculum, and assessment strategies (similar rubrics) demonstrate growth in learner cultural understanding.

These are some of the implications from the discussion on assessment that give us pause to think not only about assessment but also about curriculum and instruction related to cultural understanding.

Rubrics. While the postulates and their implications give us a broad context within which to work, they are only guidelines to carry out assessments. They establish a more ethical attitude toward students, an attitude that allows students to understand what is to be learned as well as how well it is to be learned in an atmosphere that honors student learning. In this context, assessment actually occurs in the interaction of student performance as evidence to be judged against a standard. That judgment comes through the application of a rubric to the performance.

What is a rubric? A rubric is "a guideline for scoring that consists of descriptors of each level of performance on a scale. The scale is applied to elements of the performance that have been determined in advance [as contributing significantly to the performance and thereby to meeting the standard]" (Gahala and Lange, 1996). Consequently, to create rubrics in the context of assessment that are intended to give feedback to the student, several principles apply:

- Use numerical and/or descriptive categories: 4-3-2-1-0 or Very Good to Excellent, Good, Acceptable, Weak, Unacceptable; or a three-point scale (3-2-1-0 for no response—Excellent, Acceptable, or Weak) or on a continuum of Naive-Sophisticated or Novice-Expert. Scales larger than 5 levels become difficult to define; three levels with a "no response" or 0 category may be more manageable.
- Define categories to reflect learning that is deep and insightful and that recognize differences among learners.
- Determine descriptors after the task has been determined but *before* it has been performed.
- Involve learners in the development of the categories within the rubric so that they understand fully how they are being assessed.
- Provide opportunity for outsiders to view and critique assessments to make sure they are authentic.

I am using the assessment postulates, their implications for culture learning, and the principles for the development of rubrics in the development of an example of assessment of the standard, **"Explain your understanding of friendship in this culture."**

Assessment Example. One way of assessing this standard is to allow ongoing, formative assessment through a number of activities. However, for demonstration purposes, I would like to take a specific example of one form of evidence already mentioned above for this example.

You will remember our example had several categories leading to the fulfillment of this standard: knowledge, skills attitudes, processes, and experience(s). For the assessment example, as well as for instruction, I have chosen to focus on, "Explain how kids in your culture make friends."

Since the class will be divided into groups, the first assessment task to be developed jointly with students is the assessment of group functioning, something they do regularly with us. The assessment and the rubric look something like the one presented in Figure 9.

Class _____   Date _____ / _____ / _____

Group Members _____

Task _____

In our group:

	Strongly Disagree				Strongly Agree
• Everyone was on task.	1	2	3	4	5
• Everyone helped complete the task.	1	2	3	4	5
• We helped each other.	1	2	3	4	5
• We are proud of the product we created.	1	2	3	4	5

What we did best was _____

What we could have done better is _____

We needed help and still need help on _____

Next time we should _____

Student Signatures

Teacher Comments: _____

_____

_____

_____

_____

Teacher Signature

Student Reactions: _____

Figure 9
Cooperative Group Task Assessment

The second assessment (see instruction example in Section F below) is that for the creation of a definition. The task is an individual one that involves reflection, discovery, and feelings that learners record in their journals, feelings diaries, and/or personal histories. In this class, we have used similar criteria for assessment as with other tasks of this kind that have been negotiated with learners. The assessment of the definition has been added to the usual assessment form (Figure 10).

Criteria for Journaling

	Strongly Disagree $\longrightarrow$			Strongly Agree
• I expressed my feelings completely.	1	2	3	4	5
• I gave appropriate examples to reflect my feelings.	1	2	3	4	5
• My feelings represent my behavior.	1	2	3	4	5
• I learned new things about myself.	1	2	3	4	5

Summarize here what you have learned about yourself in reflecting about friendship.

Important Points:

1.

2. (etc.)

On another sheet of paper, use that summary to answer the question, *What is a friend?*

Criteria for Assessing the Definition of a Friend

3. Exceptional

The definition is based on reflections, discoveries, and feelings from a journal, a feelings diary, and/or a personal history with several elaborations indicating a fully developed and perceptive understanding of what you define as a friend. The writing of the definition is carefully constructed to reflect your experience and your meaning.

2. Acceptable

The definition is based on reflections, discoveries, and feelings from a journal, a feelings diary, and/or a personal history. The definition is written with minimal examples to express your personal meaning of friendship and it shows only an adequate reflection of your understanding of what you define as a friend. The writing of the definition is sufficient in reflecting your experience and your meaning.

1. Poor

While the definition is based on a journal, a feelings diary, and/or a personal history, the examples mentioned have not been developed in the definition to show an understanding of what you define as a friend. The writing lacks clarity and reflects misunderstanding of your experience and its relationship to your meaning.

Figure 10

Assessment of Journaling and Definition of a Friend

The third assessment (see instruction example in Section F below) is for a group presentation to "explain what a friend is in your culture." This task involves the development of a group product as well as a verbal explanation of that product (see Figure 11).

As you will see in Section F, the same items that have been developed for assessment are also the subject of instruction. The purpose is to show consistency between standard, assessment, and instruction.

---

5. Exceptional

The group presents a fully developed definition of friendship, indicating how the knowledge and examples of individual group-member definitions of friendship are represented in the group's one clearly articulated definition. The representation of the group product (mime and dance, collage, story) demonstrates a high degree of clarity between the product and the definition, thereby representing a mature and confident understanding of friendship in our culture.

4. Accomplished

The group presents a carefully developed definition of friendship, indicating some of the knowledge and examples from group-member definitions that are articulated with care. The representation of the group product (mime and dance, collage, story) demonstrates careful attention to the relationship of product and definition, thereby representing a very useful understanding of friendship in our culture.

3. Adequate

The group presents a somewhat developed definition of friendship. The illustration of knowledge and examples of group-member definitions, though relatively few, show that the group considered their importance in the definition. Although the relationship of the product to the definition is visible in the presentation of the group product (mime and dance, collage, story), the presentation lacks clarity.

2. Limited

The group presents a definition of friendship. The examples and knowledge from individual group members are limited. While the explanation of friendship is given by the group (mime and dance, collage, story), it is not clear how the knowledge and examples of the definition are related to it.

1. Inferior

The group presents a definition of friendship. There is little or no cohesion to the definition although knowledge and examples of individual group members are presented. The explanation of friendship (mime and dance, collage, story) is so limited that its message is hardly understood and has little or no relationship to the definition presented.

Figure 11
Group Presentation—Explain What a Friend Is

F. Instruction

As I am working with the concept of assessment as the engine for curriculum development and instruction, I am having my own struggles with this concept. In some of my own work (Banathy and Lange 1972), I have seen curriculum as that engine, and assessment has always been a derivative of curriculum. Yet I also know the importance of efficiency and effectiveness, and of the reduction of knowledge to serve those purposes (See Lange 1990b; Giroux 1988). In other words, if goals and objectives are set to learn the dates of the major holidays in French culture, that knowledge is what students will learn. What will be left out is any understanding of what the holidays are about, why they are important, how they came to be, the value they have within French culture, or how they relate to holidays in U.S. culture. And certainly the scientific-technical-rational curriculum does not ask the question, To what end is this learning important? It only asks, What can you reproduce?

The role of instruction in a fully rationalized curriculum is to present the learner with the knowledge that is to be reproduced in manageable steps. The learning tasks required within the breakdown of this knowledge tend to be predictive of the learning outcome and prescriptive of the learning process. As a result, in language teaching we have seen a variety of "rational methods" that have proven restrictive of student learning. It is important to at least name a few here that fall into the category of rational-scientific-technical: Direct Method (Coleman 1929), Audio-lingual (Lado 1964), Individualized Instruction (Strasheim 1972[6]), and Total Physical Response (Asher 1977).

Other language teaching methods, such as communicative language teaching (Richards and Rodgers 1986) and proficiency oriented language learning (Omaggio-Hadley 1993), fall into a bridge category between the rational-scientific-technical and more humanistic approaches to language instruction, the practical and the emancipatory (Lange 1990b). They can be characterized in a set of contrasts of communicative and rational-scientific-technical instructional principles (Finocchiaro and Brumfit 1983). I am providing only a few important contrasts:

Communicative	**Rational-Scientific-Technical**
1. Meaning is paramount.	1. Attends to structure and form.
2. The ability to use the linguistic system effectively and appropriately.	2. Linguistic competence is the desired goal.

Communicative	Rational-Scientific-Technical.
3. Drilling may occur, but peripherally.	3. Drilling is a central technique.
4. Students are expected to interact with other people, either in the flesh, through pair and group work, or in their writings.	4. Students are expected to interact with the language system, embodied in machines or controlled materials.

It is only in communicative language teaching that culture becomes a player (Omaggio-Hadley 1993), but where it is in practice, it remains an afterthought with few real designated outcomes. However, culture plays a larger role in humanistic learning. It is here that learner choice becomes more important (See Stevick 1980 for a discussion of Counseling Learning, The Silent Way, and Suggestopedia). In emancipatory learning (Crawford-Lange and Lange 1984), culture is the content. Here, the purpose for language study is highly individual and learner choice is optimal. It is also where the learner asks the questions: (1) **Why is this culture important;** (2) **How can I use language to act upon cultural knowledge?**

The Role of Instruction. In any approach to the development of communicative ability, the focus must be on the individual learner's need to become a competent user of the language because each arrives at the process of language and culture learning with a unique background and experiences. As a result, instruction adapts to individual learners to meet mutually agreed-upon outcomes. The attention to the learner is not just for the learning of language; it applies to the learning of culture through language just as well. Here, in the context of National Standards for Cultures, the practices and products of another culture are given meaning through language, and perceptions are created and communicated through language. For the learner, the expectation is to perceive and communicate meaning and understanding of the products and practices of others. For the teacher, the expectation is to guide learners toward that goal and to assess their competence. The goal for each is the same, but the role is different. While the role of both is an active one, the teacher is no longer "saddled" with the need to produce the outcome where there is attention on student performance. That is the learner's role.

It is the teacher's responsibility to guide the learner through the needed performances with the prompts and tasks that reflect the standard. Here is where instructional guidance and assessment come together: where knowledge is connected to receive, respond, value, organize, and characterize (see Appendix B); where learning requires application, analysis, synthesis, and evaluation in addition to knowledge and comprehension (see Appendix B); and where assessment in the learning framework provides honest feedback and authenticity of task to bring learners to a fuller understanding of the culture about which they are learning.

In my view, the broader educational scene, discussed in Section C above, including theoretical considerations of education development and theoretical models for culture, applies equally well to instruction as it does to curriculum. The design for curriculum, assessment, and instruction—the "backward design" of Wiggins (1998) that I have used as a major frame in this chapter—is especially important because of attention to learner performance rather than a focus on teacher behavior. In this way, curriculum, assessment, and instruction are based on learner performance in a different kind of program internal articulation: curriculum = assessment = instruction. This internal articulation avoids isolated and self-contained cultural instructional strategies that have been part of culture teaching: culture capsules (Miller and Bishop 1979; Miller, Drayton, and Lyon 1979; and Miller and Loiseau 1974), culture clusters (Meade and Morain 1973), and cultural incidents and assimilators (Fiedler, Mitchell, and Triandis 1971). These instructional strategies emphasize information and facts about another culture with little stress on understanding, the matter featured in the new National Standards. Facts and information are simply not enough. Certainly such instructional tools could be useful if they are used in connection with more sophisticated performances other than reporting information, such as gathering more information and applying critical operations to that information through analysis, synthesis, and evaluation.

Instruction, like curriculum, is related to some comprehensive theoretical principles of learning (e.g., Egan's in Figures 4 and 5), or instruction with the new cultural standards is connected to some theory of culture learning like that of the Bennetts (Figures 6 and 7). I believe very strongly that theory is related to practice and practice generates theory. Under the umbrella of curriculum = assessment = instruction, we must be constantly aware of how these three relate so that student performances linked to cultural understanding reach expected standards. Two relatively new books on the teaching of culture include a variety of activities for culture learning (Seelye 1996; Fantini 1997). While both of these publications are very useful in generating ideas, it is still important that any teacher integrate the actual or derived ideas into the curriculum = assessment = instruction framework for understanding culture, which includes not only presentation of information but the more critical operations, as indicated above. We must not recreate the past focus on information and random activity, when the future holds so much promise through the new National Standards.

An Ethic of Instruction. The learner is primary to any learning in the approach that Wiggins (1993, 1998) has outlined. In instruction/assessment, the ethic related to this context is summarized in the following statements:

- Learners are honored for their knowledge, their processes, and their mistakes.
- Learners absorb and practice with the knowledge and skills that they use in the learning activities and also the assessments within which they are assessed.
- Learners are involved in the development of activities and choice of learning strategies as a result of learner differences (Breen 1987).
- Learners are given honest, immediate, and appropriate feedback in both learning and assessment conditions.
- Learners know the means of assessment and the rubrics applied to them in advance of both instruction and assessment.
- Learners individually apply both the means of assessment and appropriate rubrics to their own learning.

These statements outline the basic relationship between learner and teacher. They suggest an environment where the learner is respected, honored, and treated as a valuable human being, as is the teacher. This environment empowers the interaction of language with culture and culture with language in an atmosphere where quality teaching and quality learning can occur.

Instruction as Guidance. In our quest for the one magic solution to teaching foreign languages, the Holy Grail as Higgs (1984) called it, a variety of options have been explored. I have mentioned some of them above (Lange 1990c). None of those options hit the mark as the single "magic bullet." As a result, we have turned to an eclectic approach to instruction, applying what we think is appropriate mostly from either logic or experience. And, to some degree, the research on learning strategies in foreign language learning and acquisition has received important attention and inclusion in our eclecticism (Oxford 1990).

With the development of national standards for foreign languages, including culture, an eclectic, somewhat haphazard global approach to instruction is appropriate. If the curriculum is planned around standards and performance evidence presented by learners, then instruction is no longer targeted completely at the whole group, but is much more related to the needs and talents of individual learners. Here, more individual attention to and interaction with learners are required so that they can process the knowledge and skills that contribute to performances. As a result, the situation calls for an important shift in instruction from major focus on the large group controlled by the teacher to extensive teacher involvement with individual learning controlled by learners.

OK, you say, but if instruction is not telling, giving, or drilling cultural information, then what is it? Clearly, the new direction in culture learning is on learner performance with products, practices, and perspectives. We have already established that fact. The new direction strongly places learning within the abilities, attitudes, and capacities of learners themselves. Because it is my perception that the Wiggins frame of curriculum = assessment = instruction speaks specifically to guiding individual learners to perform, I believe a link to that guidance is found in the work of Howard Gardner (1993a; 1993b; 1995) in multiple intelligences.

What are multiple intelligences? In Gardner's explanation of multiple intelligences (1993a), he mentions two very important prerequisites for an intelligence: (1) a set of skills to "resolve genuine problems or difficulties"; and (2) a set of skills for "finding or creating problems" (Gardner 1993a:61). Through a delimiting process, Gardner arrives at multiple intelligences as a set of core processes or abilities that can be observed as brain functions. These unique functions can be developed and expanded. He originally determined seven intelligences (1993a) and has since argued for the emergence of an eighth (1995). The seven-plus intelligences are categorized in the following ways:

Personal Intelligences

Intrapersonal/Introspective—Self Smart
Interpersonal/Social—People Smart

Expressive Intelligences

Bodily/Kinesthetic—Body Smart
Visual/Spatial—Picture Smart
Musical/Rhythmic—Music Smart

Academic Intelligences

Logical/Mathematical—Logic Smart
Verbal/Linguistic—Word Smart

Emerging

Naturalist—Nature Smart

According to Gardner, everybody has this array of intelligences. Because schooling and language learning concentrate on the academic intelligences, they are the ones that most people assume accompany learning. However, if we reflect on the matter carefully, we recognize that we can involve the personal, expressive, and emerging intelligences as we involve learners with new standards for cultural learning. In some way, culture learning involves all of these capacities. Yet it is important to comprehend that the multiple intelligences are not learning styles. They are capacities that are expanded through active use. They provide pathways for learning for different individuals. They provide understanding of complex individuals with whom we teachers can work better. But they are also not labels and should not be used to categorize individuals. And multiple intelligences interact with each other in interesting ways. Not all are used with any one learning task, but they can be intermingled. Most importantly, they allow us to guide students to take responsibility for their own learning.

Example of Guidance with Multiple Intelligences. As we help learners work through the matter of "friendship," in our example of the standard, **Explain your understanding of friendship in this culture,** multiple intelligences can help us guide learners as they process the tasks. In the **Knowledge and Skill Activities** in Section C above, several activities progressed toward the tasks, "How do you define a friend?" and "Explain what a friend is in your culture." In getting to this point, learners have had to draw on their own **intrapersonal/introspective intelligence** (self smart) to reflect on, to discover, and to feel what a friend is. We have guided them to express such reflection, discovery, and emotions through activities such as autobiographical journals, feelings diaries, and personal history, on which we have given them feedback.

Now, in cooperative groups, where they have used their **interpersonal/ interactive intelligence** (people smart), we have asked students to share their reflections, self-discoveries, and feelings about friends. And through their E-mail addresses, they have gotten a wider range of information from learners in other schools. As a result, they have begun to consolidate the information they have pursued individually. We have asked the learner to form different groups, where they will use different talents to arrive at a definition of friendship. Once that definition has been finished, we will ask them to explain their definition in a group presentation to the entire class.

Two groups have chosen to represent their understanding of friendship through combination of mime and dance, using their **bodily/kinesthetic intelligence** (body smart). In this process, they will use their **verbal/ linguistic intelligence** (word smart) to describe how the mime and dance express the knowledge they have shared and how they define friendship. Their explanation of friendship will come through both body movement and verbal expression.

Two other groups are expressing their knowledge through two separate collages, electing to use their **visual/spatial intelligence** (picture smart) to indicate how they would define friendship. They too will be using their verbal/linguistic intelligence to explain how the making of the collage represents their collective knowledge and their definition. These groups will use a collage and a verbal explanation of their collage to explain their understanding of friendship.

Finally, two groups are using their **verbal/linguistic intelligence** (word smart) and their **logical/mathematical intelligence** (logic smart) to read stories of friendship, look up "friendship" in dictionaries and encyclopedias, to interview others, and to write in their journals, feelings diaries, and personal histories. From this activity, they will write a story about friendship and present it to the class as a written document, representing their view of friendship. And they will give their own definition of friendship.

While the groups are doing their work, it is obviously our responsibility to provide them with the needed materials and make sure that electronic equipment such as computers functions. It is also our obligation to attend to the needs of individuals as they work through the problems by answering questions, giving feedback to assumptions, asking questions, and serving as a sounding board. We are providing the kind of atmosphere where learners work with each other, yet in different ways according to their talents, to resolve problems that are highly related to the standard that they are working on and the assessments that contribute to that standard.

When each group finishes its explanation of friendship, we will open each group's presentation to probing questions from other groups and from the teacher(s). The following kinds of questions might be asked:

- Why did you choose to represent your explanation in this way?
- What role did the personal reflection of individual learners play in the development of the explanation?
- What did you learn from your presentation?
- What do you still need to know?
- How will you pursue what you still need to know?

Assessment will be accomplished with the rubric developed in Section E above. Before we use this rubric, teachers will give learners input so that they can make necessary changes from that input. Once the rubric has been applied, we will give the groups feedback on what has been done well and what needs improvement. The opportunity to redo any aspect of the definition or presentation will also be afforded.

This example is brief and partial, but it demonstrates the use of multiple intelligences in instruction, where teachers guide learners to use their talents in achieving a classroom task to develop a definition and to explain it. It also shows the close relationship of classroom tasks and their assessment. This relationship allows constant feedback to learners on their progress. In their workshops on the use of multiple intelligences in both language and culture learning, Gahala and Lange (1997) have developed some materials that show how activities to promote learning with the multiple intelligences generally relate to assessments with those same intelligences. That relationship is summarized for each intelligence in Appendix C.

Obviously, the next step in reading the standard, **Explain your understanding of friendship in this culture,** could be a similar process whereby learners develop a definition of friendship in the culture that they are studying. Here, they would be more limited and be required to use much more of the language they are learning as well. Learners would go to teen magazines to read articles on friendship. Interviews in class with native speakers from the area could focus on "What is a friend?" E-mail with pen pals could ask questions about what it means to be a friend in the other culture. Beyond the development and explanation of a definition of friendship in the other culture, a further step would be the comparison of definitions, leading ultimately to the development of situations where learners would imagine how friends are made in the other culture—the authentic performance.

G. Research and Research Needs

Even though the National Standards (*SFLL* 1996) are barely a couple of years old, now is the time to think about and plan the necessary research to examine the use of these standards in learning contexts. The basic model for setting standards, developing evidence, and relating learning to assessment in the Wiggins model (1993 and 1998) opens research in language/culture learning beyond that of a reductionary, quantitative direction that is limited to the usual forms of standardized and objective testing. Learner performances bring teachers, learners, and researchers together to examine the processes by which learners reach those performances, as well as the nature of the performances themselves. With this background in mind, I would like to examine three contexts, in addition to the usual public schools, where research on culture/language learning might take place. These three contexts are somewhat familiar to us: block-scheduled schools, charter schools, and immersion schools. I argue for other contexts because learning from those environments that are different can inform those that are more familiar.

Research Contexts. As always in American education, certain innovations take the spotlight from time to time. One of the more recent innovations is *block scheduling,* or the four-period day. In foreign language education, there is only one study that I know of that examines this structure. Freeman and Maruyama (1998) examine the achievement of students in writing over a three-year period in block-scheduled schools in contrast with students in seven-period-day schools. Using the ACTFL Guidelines (Byrnes 1987) for writing, they basically found no differences in student writing "proficiency" between the four- and the seven-period day. While this finding is important for language learning in school because it may indicate that the same work can be achieved in one semester of ninety minutes per day in a subject as in fifty minutes per day for a full year, these findings are not necessarily relevant here. Yet the context is. With the new National Standards in place, the four-period day allows a time frame in which learners can simulate cultural experiences in the language, as well as other performance activities that bring language and culture together. In this milieu, research on both the language and culture performances would give learners, teachers, and researchers the appropriate conditions to examine how products, practices, and perceptions are being addressed in learning, assessment, and teaching.

Another context in which research on learning culture/language in a setting where the National Standards could take precedence would be in charter schools (Nathan 1996). Charter schools are entrepreneurial educational institutions that have been established by teachers and funded through local school districts. They are intended to improve the learning of students. Many of these schools participate as a challenge to public schools in school reform. Some entrepreneurial foreign language teachers would have to bargain with a school district to develop a school that placed language/culture learning with National Standards as the priority for improving education in foreign languages. Such a school might function in either a four- or six-year mode to give some longevity to learning. Results with language/culture learning in such a context provide a way of testing out the standards and their effectiveness in such a context. It is my personal belief that new directions need to be examined carefully. An entrepreneurial school that also had some business support would be an excellent place to examine the performance of learners with the new standards and different kinds of assessments. The ever popular magnet schools (Estes, Levine, and Waldrip 1990) for foreign languages might be useful venues for the same purpose.

Finally, the very popularity of foreign language immersion schools in the United States (Curtain and Pesola 1988; Met and Galloway 1992) suggests that such programs would provide a likely milieu for long-term research on language/culture learning with the National Standards. With the proviso that the immersion schools would continue into secondary education, such research would be important in providing long-term results. In other words, there would be no break in learning, so that the immersion program is connected to middle/secondary education and learning can continue through the secondary school. The long "sequence" of language/culture learning is necessary for the research to be useable and for the long-range effect of language/culture learning to be evaluated. The immersion school/middle-secondary school connection is also the place where the interaction of the National Standards with educational development (Egan 1970) can be explored. Dual language immersion programs might be another venue for similar examination (see Valdés 1997).

In any of these contexts—whether the usual school environment, schools that are block scheduled, charter or magnet schools, single- or dual-immersion schools—teachers, administrators, parents, and researchers *must* recognize that they are heavily involved in language planning. While these settings provide excellent possibilities for the insertion of National Standards and the evaluation of learners' performances in language/culture with those standards, these same settings involve learners and the results of their learning in how they will use language in their adult lives and how they will participate in U.S. society beyond school. What value is placed on competence in a language other than English in U.S. society? How important is it to understand another culture as a means to understand one's own? Are these values that apply across the entire culture or are they important only for a certain segment of our society? As a result, extremely careful thought must take place in all situations where languages other than English are included in the school curriculum (see Valdés 1997).[7]

Research Questions. In stating the kinds of research questions that are appropriate to address, I will enumerate only those that deal with culture and with the culture standards. For me, these questions group themselves in the following ways:

Curriculum Content

• What knowledge and skills are needed to create learning in the practices, products, and perceptions in and of another culture?

• Which practices (patterns of social interaction) and products (books, tools, foods, laws, music, games, literature, etc.) of a culture will be included?

• How will perceptions developed within a culture be made known, and how will the learner's perceptions also be encouraged?

- How will instructional materials handle these same issues?
- How will a recursive curriculum structure be developed so that learners will revisit and expand on initially learned cultural themes?
- How do practices, products, and perceptions fit with the educational development of the learner? If one were to use Egan (1979) as an example, what kinds of content would fit which level of educational development?
- Is comparison a content or a cognitive learning strategy?
- When and how will similarities, differences and comparisons among the cultures studied be introduced to learners? Is there a relationship to educational development?
- What tasks and prompts lead to the development of competence for learners as they work toward authentic performances in learning another culture?
- How is authentic performance connected with understanding practices, products, and perspectives?

Assessment

- What types of evidence and in what combinations demonstrate that learners are competent in understanding another culture?
- What is the role of objective tests, quizzes, and standardized measures in the assessment of student performance on their understanding of another culture?
- What rubric structures best assess the tasks, prompts, and authentic performances in understanding another culture?
- By what means can the validity of tasks, prompts, and authentic performances in assessing an understanding of another culture be established?
- By what means can we verify the reliability by which an understanding of another culture is assessed?
- Wiggins (1998) writes extensively about the role of the portfolio and anthology as means of representing student learning in relationship to a standard. How does the presentation of several means of evidence represent and assess understanding of another culture?
- When is the foreign language used in assessment of an understanding of another culture, and when is it not used?

Instruction

- Since culture/language learning is oriented to a group and the individual, are knowledge and skills structured in any way for a particular task, prompt, or authentic performance for the development of understanding culture?
- What does it mean to guide learners toward performance with tasks, prompts, and authentic performances?
- Which feedback processes are the most useful to learners for understanding another culture?
- What learning strategies (Oxford 1989) from language learning apply to understanding another culture?
- How does educational development (Egan 1979) affect the choice of learning strategies (Oxford 1990) for understanding another culture?
- Which of the several intelligences (Gardner 1993a; 1993b), in which combinations, are involved, and to what tasks do they apply in the development of cultural understanding?
- What is the interrelationship of educational development (Egan 1979) in using the several intelligences to develop understanding of another culture?
- What is the instructional role of comparison in cultural understanding?

H. Summary and Conclusions

In these several pages, we have examined a number of issues related to planning and using culture standards. The topics have explored the long tradition of concern for the inclusion of culture in foreign language education programs. Yet even today culture seems to be superficially included in the form of songs, food, and games. With new national standards for foreign language learning, there is excitement about new possibilities for the inclusion of culture in language learning. In fact, the new standards put culture at the core of foreign language learning as a major content. Yet there is also concern that the new standards may continue to focus on less-than-sophisticated outcomes. In that regard, at least one model of general education development and several models of culture learning were reviewed to demonstrate the need for the connection of culture learning to a broader vision. To help with the organization of learning for new standards based on performance, some detailed attention was given to three basic elements involved in learning. In this context, we examined the development of curriculum, including standards statements, needed knowledge and skills, and evidence to meet the new culture standards. The assessment associated with the curriculum focused on a judgment of tasks, prompts, and real-world performances to provide corroboration of learner competence in understanding another culture. And for instruction, we investigated the active use of our multiple intelligences to give learners the means of applying some of their innate talents to the development of cultural understanding. Finally, a number of research issues have been raised that serve as a basis for developing a greater comprehension of how curriculum, assessment, and instruction work together to help meet new standards, in this case for cultural understanding.

Even though some forty years or more of struggle have passed in trying to integrate language and culture in the foreign language classroom, I remain optimistic. The attention given to new standards, the place of culture in those standards, the emphasis on performance instead of coverage, new approaches to assessment, and potential new directions for research in culture learning support that optimism. It will take time, energy, and collaboration to find culture learning integrated into language programs. Let's see what the next twenty years brings.

NOTES

1. This chapter is dedicated to the memory of H. Ned Seelye, who died in late 1997. Ned provided inspiration, important ideas, goodwill, and laughter when we all needed them. His presence in person and in print has energized those who knew him in both ways. His counsel will be greatly missed as we integrate culture in a better-planned approach to language learning.

2. The discussion of Egan's educational development is based on one of a similar nature in an article published in the *ADFL Bulletin.* See **References,** Lange (1997).

3. The discussion of Bennett's "development of cultural sensitivity" is based on one of a similar nature in a forthcoming book by the Center for Applied Linguistics (see **References,** Lange [Forthcoming] for complete citation) and from Janet Bennett (1993) and her part of the Bennett, Bennett, and Allen (1996) presentation.

4. This example is based on a discussion with Rebecca Kline and Lynn Sandstedt, who were table partners with me during the "Understanding by Design" presentation by Grant P. Wiggins and Everett Kline at the ACTFL Collaborative Seminar, January 22, 1998, in Yonkers, New York.

5. It is not my intent to enter into the controversy between the concept of proficiency as developed within the context of the American Council on the Teaching of Foreign Languages and communicative competence as stated by Savignon (1983) and Canale and Swain (1980), since my focus is on the issue of culture.

6. Lorraine Strasheim distinguishes between individualized pacing and personalized instruction as two very different aspects of individualized instruction. The former is teacher-dominated and controlled; the latter allows the student to construct her own education. Individualized instruction here is used in the sense of individualized pacing.

7. It is not my intent to discourage experimentation with the National Standards in any of these places. I believe very strongly that the inclusion of a culture/language other than English in the curriculum of any schooling situation needs hard and careful study in recognition of the long-term benefits and problems of such study. This is especially true of any type of immersion program, where students begin in elementary education and continue through high school. And it is particularly true of dual immersion programs, where minority and majority learners are working toward culture/language competency in each other's cultures/languages. Have we looked into the future to understand what the long-term effect of such learning actually is, as well as its effect on society's understanding of the contribution of language/culture to the education of the learner?

REFERENCES

Asher, James J. 1982. *Learning Another Language Through Actions: The Complete Teacher's Guide Book.* 2nd ed. Los Gatos, CA: Sky Oaks Productions.

Bachman, Lyle F. 1990. *Fundamental Considerations in Language Testing.* Oxford: Oxford University Press.

Banathy, Bela, and Dale L. Lange. 1972. *A Design for Foreign Language Curriculum.* Lexington, MA: D. C. Heath.

Bennett, Janet. 1993. "Cultural Marginality: Identity Issues in Intercultural Training, pp. 109–35 in R. Michael Paige, ed., *Education for the Intercultural Experience.* Yarmouth, ME: Intercultural Press.

Bennett, Milton J. 1993. "Towards Ethnorelativism: A Developmental Model of Intercultural Sensitivity," pp. 21–71 in R. Michael Paige, ed., *Education for the Intercultural Experience.* Yarmouth, ME: Intercultural Press.

Bennett, Milton J., Janet Bennett, and Wendy Allen. 1996. "Culture in the Second Language Classroom: A Conceptual Overview." Presentation at a conference at the Center for Advanced Research on Language Acquisition (CARLA), sponsored by the National Foreign Language Center at the University of Minnesota, entitled "Culture as the Core: Transforming the Language Curriculum," May 2.

Berliner, David C., and Bruce J. Biddle. 1995. *The Manufactured Crisis: Myths, Frauds, and the Attack on America's Public Schools.* Reading, MA: Addison-Wesley.

Bloom, Benjamin S., ed. 1956. *Taxonomy of Educational Objectives: The Classification of Educational Goals, Handbook I: Cognitive Domain.* New York: David McKay.

Breen, Michael. 1987. "Learner Contributions to Task Design," pp. 23–46 in Christopher N. Candlin and Dermot Murphy, eds., *Language Learning Tasks.* Lancaster Papers in English Language Education, Vol. 7. Englewood Cliffs, NJ: Prentice Hall International.

Brooks, Nelson. 1960. *Language and Language Learning: Theory and Practice.* A-LM ed. New York: Harcourt Brace & World.

Brown, James D. 1995. *The Elements of Language Curriculum: A Systematic Approach to Program Development.* Boston: Heinle & Heinle.

Bruner, Jerome. 1990. *Acts of Meaning.* Cambridge, MA: Harvard University Press.

Byrnes, Heidi. 1990. "Priority: Curriculum Articulation: Addressing Curriculum Articulation in the Nineties: A Proposal." *Foreign Language Annals* 23:281–92.

———— and Michael Canale, eds. 1987. *Defining and Developing Proficiency: Guidelines, Implementations, and Concepts.* The American Council on the Teaching of Foreign Languages Foreign Language Education Series. Lincolnwood, IL: National Textbook.

————, James Child, Nina Levinson, Pardee Lowe Jr., Seiichi Makino, Irene Thompson, and A. Ronald Walton. 1987. "ACTFL Proficiency Guidelines, 1986," pp. 15–24 in Heidi Byrnes and Michael Canale, eds., *Defining and Developing Proficiency: Guidelines, Implementations, and Concepts.* The American Council on the Teaching of Foreign Languages Foreign Language Education Series. Lincolnwood, IL: National Textbook.

Byram, Michael. 1989. *Cultural Studies in Foreign Language Education.* Philadelphia: Multilingual Matters.

———— and Carol Morgan et al. 1994. *Teaching and Learning Language and Culture.* Philadelphia: Multilingual Matters.

Canale, Michael, and Merrill Swain. 1980. "Theoretical Bases of Communicative Approaches to Second Language Teaching and Testing." *Applied Linguistics* 1:1–47.

CARLA (Center for Advanced Research in Language Acquisition). 1997. *MLIP: The Minnesota Language Proficiency Assessments.* Minneapolis: CARLA. (E-mail: mlpa@tc.umn.edu)

Cohen, Andrew D. 1994. *Assessing Language Ability in the Classroom.* 2nd ed. Boston: Heinle & Heinle.

Coleman, Algernon. 1929. *The Teaching of Modern Languages in the United States.* New York: Macmillan.

Crawford-Lange, Linda M., and Dale L. Lange. 1984. "Doing the Unthinkable in the Second-Language Classroom: A Process for the Integration of Language and Culture," pp. 139–77 in Theodore V. Higgs, ed., *Teaching for Proficiency, the Organizing Principle.* The American Council on the Teaching of Foreign Languages Foreign Language Education Series. Lincolnwood, IL: National Textbook.

———— and Peter McLaren. 1998. "A Critical Perspective on Culture in the Second Language Classroom." Presentation given at the 1991 Symposium, "Interdisciplinary Perspectives on Culture Learning in the Second Language Curriculum," held at the University of Minnesota in May. [To be published in 1998 in Dale L. Lange, Carol Klee, and R. Michael Paige, eds., *Interdisciplinary Perspectives on Culture in the Second Language Curriculum.* Minneapolis: Center for Advanced Research on Language Acquisition (CARLA). The CARLA address is: Suite 111, UTEC, 1313 5th Street S. E., Minneapolis, MN 55414.]

Curtain, Helena Anderson, and Carol A. Pesola. 1988. *Languages and Children—Making the Match: Foreign Language Instruction in the Elementary School.* Reading, MA: Addison-Wesley.

Dubin, Fraida, and Elite Olshtain. 1986. *Course Design: Developing Programs and Materials for Language Learning.* Cambridge: Cambridge University Press.

Egan, Kieran. 1979. *Educational Development.* New York: Oxford University Press.

Estes, Nolan, Daniel U. Levine, and Donald R. Waldrip. 1990. *Magnet Schools: Recent Developments and Perspectives.* Austin, TX: Morgan.

Fantini, Alvino E., ed. 1997. *New Ways in Teaching Culture.* Alexandria, VA: Teachers of English to Speakers of Other Languages.

Fiedler, Fred E., Terence Mitchell, and Harry C. Triandis. 1971. "The Culture Assimilator: An Approach to Cross-Cultural Training." *Journal of Applied Psychology* 55:95–102.

Finocchiaro, Mary, and Christopher Brumfit. 1983. *The Functional-Notional Approach: From Theory to Practice.* New York: Oxford University Press.

Freeman, Carol, and Geoffrey Maruyama. 1998. Write-up of Anoka Hennepin Foreign Language CRT Data. Unpublished manuscript. Minneapolis: Center for Applied Research and Educational Improvement, College of Education, University of Minnesota, Minneapolis, MN 55455.

Friere, Paulo. 1996. *Pedagogy of Hope: Reliving Pedagogy of the Oppressed.* New York: Continuum.

———— and Antonio Faundez. 1989. *Learning to Question: A Pedagogy of Liberation.* New York: Continuum.

Gahala, Estella M., and Dale L. Lange. 1996. "Toward Classroom Assessment of Oral Performance for New Foreign Language Standards." Presentation at the Southwest Conference on Language Teaching, Albuquerque, NM, April 11.

———. 1997. "Multiple Intelligences: Multiple Ways to Help Students Learn Foreign Languages." *Northeast Conference on the Teaching of Foreign Languages Newsletter* 41:29–34.

Gardner, Howard. 1993a. *Frames of Mind: The Theory of Multiple Intelligences.* 2nd ed. New York: Basic Books.

———. 1993b. *Multiple Intelligences: The Theory in Practice.* 2nd ed. New York: Basic Books.

———. 1995. "Reflections on Multiple Intelligences: Myths and Messages." *Phi Delta Kappan* 77: 200–02, 206–09.

Gee, James P. 1996. *Social Linguistics and Literacies: Ideology in Discourses.* London: Taylor and Francis.

Genesee, Fred, and John A. Upshur. 1996. *Classroom-Based Evaluation in Second Language Education.* Cambridge: Cambridge University Press.

Giroux, Henry A. 1992. *Border Crossings: Cultural Workers and the Politics of Education.* London: Routledge, Chapman, and Hall.

———. 1988. *Teachers as Intellectuals: Toward a Critical Pedagogy of Learning.* Granby, MA: Bergin & Garvey.

Henning, Grant. 1987. *A Guide to Language Testing: Development, Evaluation, Research.* Cambridge, MA: Newbury House.

Higgs, Theodore V. 1984. "Introduction: Language Teaching and the Quest for the Holy Grail," pp. 1–9 in Theodore V. Higgs, ed., *Teaching for Proficiency, the Organizing Principle.* The American Council on the Teaching of Foreign Languages Foreign Language Education Series. Lincolnwood, IL: National Textbook.

Jones, Randall L., and Bernard Spolsky. 1975. *Testing Language Proficiency.* Washington, D.C.: Center for Applied Linguistics.

Johnson, Keith. 1982. *Communicative Syllabus Design and Methodology.* Oxford: Oxford University Press.

Kramsch, Claire. 1993. *Context and Culture in Language Teaching.* Oxford: Oxford University Press.

Krashen, Stephen D. 1981. *Second Language Acquisition and Second Language Learning.* Oxford: Pergamon Press.

———. 1982. *Principles and Practice in Second Language Acquisition.* Oxford: Pergamon Press.

Krathwohl, David R., Benjamin S. Bloom, and Bertram H. Masia. 1964. *Taxonomy of Educational Objectives: The Classification of Educational Goals, Handbook II: Affective Domain.* New York: David McKay.

Lado, Robert. 1964. *Language Teaching: A Scientific Approach.* New York: McGraw-Hill.

———. 1961. *Language Testing: The Construction and Use of Foreign Language Tests.* London: Longmans.

Lafayette, Robert C. 1988. "Integrating the Teaching of Culture in the Foreign Language Classroom," pp. 47–62 in Alan J. Singerman, ed., *Toward a New Integration of Language and Culture.* Reports of the Northeast Conference on the Teaching of Foreign Languages. Middlebury, VT: The Northeast Conference.

———, ed. 1996. *National Standards: A Catalyst for Reform.* The American Council on the Teaching of Foreign Languages Foreign Language Education Series. Lincolnwood, IL: National Textbook.

———. 1978. *Teaching Culture: Strategies and Techniques.* Language in Education: Theory and Practice Series, No. 11. Washington, DC: Center for Applied Linguistics.

Lange, Dale L. 1990a. "A Blueprint for a Teacher Development Program," pp. 245–68 in Jack C. Richards and David Nunan, eds., *Second Language Teacher Education.* Cambridge: Cambridge University Press.

———. 1997. "Collaboration on National and State Standards for Culture: Is There Alignment?" Presentation at the Northeast Conference on the Teaching of Foreign Languages, New York City, April 5.

————. 1996. "Implications of Theory and Research on Teaching Culture in Second Language Programs." Presentation at a conference at the Center for Advanced Research on Language Acquisition (CARLA), sponsored by the National Foreign Language Center at the University of Minnesota, entitled "Culture as the Core: Transforming the Language Curriculum," May 2.

————. 1997. "Models of Articulation: Struggles and Successes." *ADFL Bulletin* 2:31–42.

————. 1990b. "Priority Issues in the Assessment of Communicative Language Abilities." *Foreign Language Annals* 23:403–07.

————. 1990c. "Sketching the Crisis and Exploring Different Perspectives in Foreign Language Curriculum," pp. 77–109 in Diane W. Birckbichler, ed., *New Perspectives and New Directions in Foreign Language Education.* The American Council on the Teaching of Foreign Languages Foreign Language Education Series. Lincolnwood, IL: National Textbook.

————. 1998, Forthcoming. "The Teaching of Culture: A Module," in Grace S. Burkhart, ed., *Modules to Assist Teaching Assistants in First and Second Year Foreign Language Courses* (tentative title). Washington, DC: Center for Applied Linguistics.

Liskin-Gasparro, Judith. 1996. "Assessment: From Content Standards to Student Performance," pp. 169–96 in Robert C. Lafayette, ed., *National Standards: A Catalyst for Reform.* The American Council on the Teaching of Foreign Languages Foreign Language Education Series. Lincolnwood, IL: National Textbook.

Lowe, Pardee, Jr., and Charles W. Stansfield, eds. 1988. *Second Language Proficiency Assessment: Current Issues.* Englewood Cliffs, NJ: Prentice Hall.

Madaus, George F., and Thomas Kellaghan. 1992. "Curriculum Evaluation and Assessment," pp. 119–54 in Philip W. Jackson, ed., *Handbook of Research on Curriculum.* New York: Macmillan.

Mandelbaum, David G., ed. 1949. *Selected Writings of Edward Sapir.* Berkeley and Los Angeles: University of California Press.

Meade, Betsy, and Genelle Morain. 1973. "The Culture Cluster." *Foreign Language Annals* 6:331–38.

Met, Myriam, and Vicki Galloway. 1992. "Research in Foreign Language Curriculum," pp. 852–90 in Phillip W. Jackson, ed., *Handbook of Research on Curriculum.* New York: Macmillan.

Miller, J. Dale, Russell H. Bishop. 1979. *USA-Mexico Culture Capsules.* Rowley, MA: Newbury House [Boston: Heinle & Heinle].

————, John Drayton, and Ted Lyon. 1979. *USA-Hispanic South American Culture Capsules.* Rowley, MA: Newbury House [Boston: Heinle & Heinle].

———— and Maurice Loiseau. 1974. *USA-France Culture Capsules.* Rowley, MA: Newbury House [Boston: Heinle & Heinle].

Nathan, Joe. 1996. *Charter Schools: Creating Hope and Opportunity for American Education.* San Francisco: Jossey-Bass.

Nostrand, Howard L., ed. 1967. *Background Data for the Teaching of French. Part A. La culture et la société françaises au XXe siècle.* Seattle: University of Washington.

————. 1974. "Empathy for a Second Culture: Motivations and Techniques," pp. 263–327 in Gilbert A. Jarvis, ed., *Responding to New Realities.* American Council on the Teaching of Foreign Languages Foreign Language Education Series. Lincolnwood, IL: National Textbook.

Nunan, David. 1989. *Designing Tasks for the Communicative Classroom.* Cambridge: Cambridge University Press.

Oller, John W., Jr., and Kyle Perkins. 1978. *Language in Education: Testing the Tests.* Rowley, MA: Newbury House.

————, eds. 1980. *Research in Language Testing.* Rowley, MA: Newbury House. Omaggio, Alice C. 1983. *Proficiency-Oriented Classroom Testing.* Washington, DC: Center for Applied Linguistics.

Omaggio Hadley, Alice C. 1993. *Teaching Language in Context.* 2nd ed. Boston: Heinle & Heinle.

Oxford, Rebecca L. 1990. *Language Learning Strategies: What Every Teacher Should Know.* New York: Newbury House.

Pesola, Carol A. 1995. "Background, Design and Evaluation of a Conceptual Framework for FLES (Foreign Languages in the Elementary School) Curriculum." Ph.D. diss., University of Minnesota.

Pratt, David. 1994. *Curriculum Planning: A Handbook for Professionals.* Fort Worth: Harcourt Brace College Publishers.

Richards, Jack, John Platt, and Heidi Weber. 1985. *Longman Dictionary of Applied Linguistics.* London: Longman.

——— and Theodore S. Rodgers. 1986. *Approaches and Method in Language Teaching: A Description and Analysis.* Cambridge: Cambridge University Press.

Savignon, Sandra J. 1983. *Communicative Competence: Theory and Classroom Practice.* Reading, MA: Addison-Wesley.

Seelye, H. Ned. 1972. "Analysis and Teaching of the Cross-Cultural Context," pp. 37–81 in Emma M. Birkmaier, ed., *Foreign Language Education: An Overview.* American Council on the Teaching of Foreign Languages Foreign Language Education Series. Lincolnwood, IL: National Textbook. [Formerly published as *The Britannica Review of Foreign Language Education,* Volume 1. Chicago: Encyclopaedia Britannica, 1968.]

———, ed. 1996. *Experiential Activities for Intercultural Learning.* Volume 1. Yarmouth, ME: Intercultural Press.

———. 1993. *Teaching Culture: Strategies for Intercultural Communication.* 2nd ed. Lincolnwood, IL: National Textbook. (1st edition; 1984)

Shohamy, Elana, and A. Ronald Walton, eds. 1992. *Language Assessment for Feedback: Testing and Other Strategies.* Dubuque, IA: Kendall/Hunt.

Singerman, Alan J., ed. 1996. *Acquiring Cross-cultural Competence: Four Stages for Students of French.* American Association of Teachers of French National Commission on Cultural Competence. Lincolnwood, IL: National Textbook.

Spolsky, Bernard, ed. 1979. *Approaches to Language Testing.* Advances in Language Testing, Series: 2. Washington, DC: Center for Applied Linguistics.

———, ed. 1978. *Some Major Tests.* Advances in Language Testing, Series: 1. Washington, DC: Center for Applied Linguistics.

Standards for Foreign Language Learning: Preparing for the 21st Century. 1996. Yonkers, NY: National Standards in Foreign Language Education Project.

Stern, H. H. 1982. "Toward a Multidimensional Foreign Language Curriculum," pp. 120–46 in Robert G. Mead, Jr., ed., *Foreign Languages: Key Links in the Chain of Learning.* Reports of the Northeast Conference on the Teaching of Foreign Languages. Middlebury, VT: The Northeast Conference.

Stevick, Earl W. 1976. *Memory, Meaning, and Method: Some Psychological Perspectives on Language Learning.* Rowley, MA: Newbury House.

———. 1980. *Teaching Languages: A Way and Ways.* Rowley, MA: Newbury House.

Tedick, Diane J., and Constance L. Walker. 1996. "R(T)eaching All Students: Necessary Changes in Teacher Education," pp. 187–220 in Barbara H. Wing, ed., *Foreign Languages for All: Challenges and Choices.* Reports of the Northeast Conference on the Teaching of Foreign Languages. Lincolnwood, IL: National Textbook.

———. Dale L. Lange, R. Michael Paige, and Helen L. Jorstad. 1993. "Second Language Education in Tomorrow's Schools," pp. 43–75 in Gail Guntermann, ed., *Developing Language Teachers for a Changing World.* American Council on the Teaching of Foreign Languages Foreign Language Education Series. Lincolnwood, IL: National Textbook.

Triandis, Harry C. 1972. *The Analysis of Subjective Culture*. New York: Wiley.

Valdés, Guadalupe. 1997. "Dual-Language Immersion Programs: A Cautionary Note Concerning the Education of Language-Minority Students." *Harvard Educational Review* 77:391–429.

Valette, Rebecca M. 1977. *Modern Language Testing*. New York: Harcourt Brace Jovanovich.

Wallerstein, Nina. 1983. *Language and Culture in Conflict: Problem-Posing in the ESL Classroom*. Reading, MA: Addison-Wesley.

Wiggins, Grant P. 1993. *Assessing Student Performance: Exploring the Purpose and Limits of Testing*. San Francisco: Jossey-Bass.

———. 1998. *Educative Assessment: Designing Assessments to Inform and Improve Student Performance*. San Francisco: Jossey-Bass.

——— and Everett Kline. 1998. "Understanding by Design." Presentation at the Collaborative Seminar, January 22–23 at the Headquarters of the American Council on the Teaching of Foreign Languages, Yonkers, NY.

Whorf, Benjamin L. 1952. *Collected Papers on Metalinguistics*. Washington, DC: Department of State, Foreign Service Institute.

Yalden, Janice. 1987. *Principles of Course Design for Language Teaching*. Cambridge: Cambridge University Press.

Appendix A

AATF Culture Standards

Understanding Culture

A. Empathy Toward Other Cultures

Indicators of Competence

Upon completing Stage 1, the learner:

- Is curious about similarities and differences between the home culture and the target culture.
- Shows willingness to understand the differences encountered.

Upon completing Stage 2, the learner:

- Is tolerant of differences between the home and target cultures.
- Is open and accepting of different peoples.
- Recognizes the depth and complexity of cultural differences.
- Shows an active interest in the search for understanding of the target culture.

Upon completing Stage 3, the learner:

- Is aware of the problem of accepting the norms of another culture while maintaining one's own values and identity.
- Shows fair-mindedness and tolerance in trying to solve an embarrassing situation or a cross-cultural conflict.
- Can adjust behavior and conversation according to the situational context and to the expectations of participants.

Upon completing Stage 4, the learner:

- Recognizes the importance of understanding manifestations of the target culture in terms of its own context.

- Is aware of his or her own cultural perspective and of how this perspective influences one's perception of phenomena.
- Can act and react in a culturally appropriate way while being aware of his or her "otherness."

B. Ability to Observe and Analyze a Culture

Indicators of Competence

Upon completing Stage 1, the learner:

- Can give examples of the relationship between language and culture (e.g., different forms of oral address, depending on social relations and situation).
- Can identify a few characteristics of the target culture as cultural patterns (e.g., businesses and government offices in France may close for as long as two hours at lunch time).
- Can identify a few common cultural differences between home and target cultures (e.g., the presentation of American and French meals).
- Can identify some commonly held images of the target culture as stereotypes (e.g., "the French drink wine with their meals").

Upon completing Stage 2, the learner:

- Can demonstrate understanding that cultural values, patterns, and institutions cannot be used to predict the behavior of all individuals (e.g., not all French people avoid creating relations with their neighbors to preserve their privacy).
- Can give examples of an observer's own cultural biases interfering with understanding of the target culture (e.g., being embarrassed by kissing on the cheek between female friends in France).
- Can give an example of how cultures change over time (e.g., in some workplaces in France the noon mealtime has been shortened considerably).
- Can discuss ways in which cultural norms and values are transmitted (e.g., the role of parents as models and teachers of values).
- Can give examples of one culture influencing another (e.g., the popularity of American-style fast-food restaurants in France).

Upon completing Stage 3, the learner:

- Can give examples of social behaviors that express the target culture's underlying value system (e.g., the reluctance of French people to invite casual acquaintances into their homes is an expression of their concept of friendship, their value of privacy, and their general distrust of outsiders).
- Can describe and explain important elements of major institutions in the target culture (e.g., can describe the baccalauréat exam and its importance in the French educational system).
- Can interpret social phenomena within the context of the target culture (e.g., understands how the frequent recourse to public demonstrations in France is related to administrative centralization).
- Can describe several instances of major change within the target culture (e.g., fewer and fewer French people attend religious services regularly).
- Can describe some major forces that influence culture and cultural change (e.g., the role of technology: the Minitel, television, etc.).
- Recognizes that a culture is not uniform and can identify the principal subcultures of the target culture (e.g., the increasing importance of Moslem culture in France).

Upon completing Stage 4, the learner:

- Can critique phenomena of the target culture with a minimum of bias (e.g., can discuss the various political parties in France objectively, whether on the "left" or on the "right").
- Can interpret social phenomena at several levels of generalization (e.g., can discuss the development of the role of women in the world, in France in general, and in a given French social class).
- Can describe the multifaceted character of sociocultural phenomena (e.g., the historical, social, religious, economic, and political dimensions of the growing North African population in France).

Knowledge of French-Speaking Societies

- FRANCE
- NORTH AMERICA
- SUB-SAHARAN AFRICA
- THE CARIBBEAN
- NORTH AFRICA

Within each of these areas, culture is broken into seven categories of cultural knowledge:

- Communication in Cultural Context
- The Value System
- Social Patterns and Conventions
- Social Institutions
- Geography and the Environment
- History
- Literature and the Arts

Each of the areas of competence is blocked into four levels, as indicated in *Understanding Culture.* They apply to the *Knowledge of French-Speaking Countries* as well. Those four levels are:

- Stage 1: Elementary
- Stage 2: Basic Intercultural Skills
- Stage 3: Social Competence
- Stage 4. Socioprofessional Capability

The AATF Culture Standards are available from National Textbook, 4255 West Touhy Avenue, Lincolnwood, IL 60646-1975. The full citation is as follows:

> Singerman, Alan J., ed. *Acquiring Cross-Cultural Competence: Four Stages for Students of French.* American Association of Teachers of French National Commission on Cultural Competence. Lincolnwood, IL: National Textbook, 1996.

Cognitive Learning, Affective Learning, And The Relationship of Cognitive and Affective Learning

Cognitive Learning

Cognitive Learning is . . . The learner . . .

1. KNOWLEDGE

Terminology; Facts—Acquires cultural meaning of words; recalls important cultural facts.

Conventions; Trends and Sequences; Categories; Criteria; and *Methodology*—Knows culture's rules for general behavior; knows forces that shape cultural behavior; knows categories of cultural behavior; knows criteria for the evaluation of cultural behavior; knows methods for the study of cultural behavior.

Principles and Generalizations; and *Theories and Structures*—Knows important principles of cultural difference; recalls major theories of cultural difference.

2. COMPREHENSION

Translation; Interpretation; and *Extrapolation*—Comprehends cultural behavior in context; states its potential meaning to others; indicates its future consequences.

3. APPLICATION (Problem solving)

Employs principles of cultural behavior from own culture to understand a new one.

4. ANALYSIS (Breakdown into constituent parts)

Elements; Relationships; and *Principles*—Distinguishes facts of cultural behavior from generalized statements about cultural behavior; checks consistency of hypotheses about cultural behavior with information; recognizes the bias of "the other" in a description of cultural behavior.

5. SYNTHESIS (Putting elements together to form a new whole)

Create a Unique Communication; Develop a Plan; and *Derive Abstract Relations*—Writes a definitive description of cultural behavior for "X" culture; proposes ways of researching cultural behavior; formulates a theory about learning cultural behavior.

6. EVALUATION (Making judgments about the value of ideas, works, solutions, methods, materials, etc.)

Judgments on Internal Evidence; and *Judgments on External Evidence*—Indicates fallacies in arguments in publications about cultural behavior; compares major theories about cultural behavior.

Affective Learning

In . . . , the individual develops . . . Or she or he . . .

1. Receiving

   Awareness—Recognizes cultural differences

   Willingness to Receive—Tolerates differences

   Selected Attention—Becomes sensitive to differences

2. Responding

   Compliance—Forces self to see difference

   Willingness—Seeks information voluntarily

   Enjoys Response—Finds pleasure in information

3. Valuing

   Acceptance—Increases recognition of difference

   Preference—Helps others understand difference

   Commitment—Accepts difference as part of life

4. Organization

Conceptualization of a Value—Identifies the characteristics of difference

Organization of a Value System—Plans to respect difference in dealing with other cultures

5. Characterization by a Value or Value Complex

Predisposition to Act—Willingness to revise attitudes on difference with new evidence

Acting on a Value System—Develops consistent behavior related to cultural difference

The Relationship Between Cognitive and Affective Learning

Cognitive	Affective
1. Recalls and recognizes *knowledge*	1. *Receives* knowledge and attends to it
2. *Comprehends* knowledge	2. *Responds* on request; takes satisfaction in responding
3. *Applies* knowledge comprehended	3. *Values* activity; responds voluntarily
4. *Analyzes* knowledge; and	4. *Conceptualizes* values responded to
5. *Synthesizes* it in new ways	
6. *Evaluates* knowledge to judge value	5. *Organizes* values into systems and a single system, which
	6. *Characterizes* an individual

Multiple Intelligences Activities and Assessments

Personal Intelligences

Intrapersonal Intelligence: Understanding Oneself

"Self Smart"

ACTIVITIES TO PROMOTE LEARNING

reflection	goal setting	visualization
metacognition	self-discovery	imagery
surveys	problem solving	independent tasks
journals	open-ended	independent learning times
relaxation	expression	family heritage
personal graphics	autobiography	

("me" collage or T-shirt, mood cube, cultural heritage poster, etc.)

ENVIRONMENT

time to think/give and get positive feedback

gallery of student work/identification of one's strengths

ASSESSMENTS (PSYCHOLOGICALLY BASED INSTRUMENTS)

Personal application scenarios, autobiographical reporting, metacognitive surveys and questionnaires, higher-order questions and answers, feelings diaries and logs, personal projection, personal history, personal priorities and goals

Interpersonal Intelligence: Individuals in Social Groups

"People Smart"

ACTIVITIES TO PROMOTE LEARNING

cooperative tasks (think-pair-share, round robin, jigsaw, etc.)

technology: E-mail, CD-ROM, Internet

rating scales

creative group tasks (mobiles, collages, songs, poems, comic strips, story books, etc.)

ENVIRONMENT

instructional variety / learning centers

cooperative guidelines / social skills instruction

collaborative problem solving

management tactics for cooperative groups

debriefing / learning that is fun

ASSESSMENTS (RELATIONALLY BASED ASSESSMENTS)

group jigsaws, think-pair-share, explaining to or teaching another, giving and receiving feedback, interviews, people searches, questionnaires, empathetic processing, random group quizzes, assess your teammates

Expressive Intelligences

Bodily/Kinesthetic Intelligence: Skillful Control of Bodily Motions

"Body Smart"

ACTIVITIES TO PROMOTE LEARNING

active learning	projects	interviews
(mime, TPR,	simulations	role-playing
manipulatives,	field trips	creative movement
games, sports,	whole body learning	
creating things)		

ENVIRONMENT

creative dramatics ("pretend," "what if . . .")

hands-on environment (not worksheets and lectures)

whole body movements in exercise or stretch breaks

learning that is fun

ASSESSMENTS (PERFORMANCE-BASED INSTRUMENTS)

charades, mimes, TPR, dramatizations, dance, impersonations, human tableaux, invention projects, physical routines and games, demonstrations, illustrations using body language and gestures

Visual/Spatial Intelligence: Accurate Comprehension of the Visual World

"Picture Smart"

ACTIVITIES TO PROMOTE LEARNING

visuals	graphic organizers	
(photos,	(outlines, charts, matrices, grids, webs,	
paintings,	clusters, time lines, sequence charts, maps,	
drawings,	Venn diagrams, etc.)	
illustrations)	video	
props	demonstrations	imagery
manipulatives	role-play	sketches
overhead	chalkboard	color coding systems
sculpting	constructing	active imagination

ENVIRONMENT

classroom walls that stimulate by color, design, and pattern, but not a bombardment of the senses

verbal instructions that appeal to vision (see, visualize, imagine, picture this . . .) and learning that is fun

ASSESSMENTS (IMAGE-BASED INSTRUMENTS)

video recording, photography, flowcharts, graphs, murals, montages, collages, graphic representations, mind maps, manipulative demonstrations, visual illustration

---

Musical/Rhythmic Intelligence: Musical Abilities

"Music Smart"

ACTIVITIES TO PROMOTE LEARNING

songs	dances	mnemonics
raps	cheers	poems

song, movement, or dance to illustrate ideas or concepts

ENVIRONMENT

sound tapes to prepare the mind for learning, reviewing, imaging, creating, relaxing, energizing, awareness, etc.

choral readings (poems, stories, popular songs)

theme music

learning that is fun

ASSESSMENT (AUDITORY-BASED ASSESSMENTS)

creating concept songs and raps, illustrating with sound, linking music and rhythm with concepts, discerning rhythmic patterns

Academic Intelligences

Logical/Mathematical Intelligence: Scientific and Reasoning Ability, Mathematical Ability

"Logic Smart"

ACTIVITIES TO PROMOTE LEARNING

graphic organizers (see list under Visual / Spatial)

cognitive organizers (lists, summaries, outlines, comparisons,

contrasts, metaphors, analogies, paradigms, categories,

patterns, relationships)

problem solving	experiments	challenge tasks
research projects	manipulatives (puzzles, board games, etc.)	

ENVIRONMENT

well-ordered and sequenced lesson design

clear lesson objectives and connections among parts of lesson

instruction that demonstrates, models, provides guided practice,

checks understanding, and evaluates

authentic applications and learning that is fun

ASSESSMENTS (COGNITIVE PATTERN-BASED ASSESSMENTS)

higher-order reasoning, logic and rationality exercises, mental menus and formulas, deductive reasoning, inductive reasoning, logical analysis and critique, cognitive and graphic organizers

---

Verbal/Linguistic Intelligence: Uses of Language

"Word Smart"

ACTIVITIES TO PROMOTE LEARNING

personal expression (opinions, reactions, experiences)

speakers	interviews	peer teaching
field trips	debate	discussion
role-play	dramatization	simulation

reading (outcome prediction, dramatic reading, seek and organize information, etc.)

writing (logs, journals, student-made books, webs or clusters to brainstorm ideas, etc.)

ENVIRONMENT

posted directions for classroom procedures, helpful hints, etc.

gallery or displays of students' work

classroom library (books, magazines, tapes, etc.)

technology (tape recorders, radio, computers, VCR, television, CD-ROM, Internet, WWW, etc.)

learning that is fun

ASSESSMENT (LANGUAGE-BASED INSTRUMENTS)

vocabulary quizzes, written essays, recall of verbal information, audio recordings, poetry writing, linguistic humor, formal speech, cognitive debates, listening and reporting, learning logs and journals

Emerging Intelligence

Naturalist Intelligence: See Deeply into the Nature of Living Things

"Nature Smart"

ACTIVITIES TO PROMOTE LEARNING

data collection	data analysis	logs
demonstration	awareness projects	video
research projects	reports	charts
identification of flora and fauna		

ENVIRONMENT

outdoors	horticultural gardens	zoos
farms	parks	forests
wildlife preserves	ecological models	

ASSESSMENTS (NATURE-BASED ASSESSMENTS)

observation of phenomena, recognition of events and conditions, identification of elements, classification of materials and events, problem solving, demonstration of findings.

Environmental/ecological issues are a rich context for multidisciplinary studies that utilize all the intelligences.

4

Making Connections*

Myriam Met
Montgomery County (Maryland) Public Schools

Foreign language learning should be an integral part of every student's schooling. Not only can and should all students benefit from learning another language, but all students should have opportunities to see how language use is rooted in and linked to most of what we learn. Goal 3 of the National Standards addresses this important aspect of language learning with its emphasis on connections to other disciplines and the use of the foreign language to acquire information.

A Rationale for the Connections Goal

The two standards under the Connections goal state:

Standard 3.1: *Students reinforce and further their knowledge of other disciplines through the foreign language.*

Standard 3.2: *Students acquire information and recognize the distinctive viewpoints that are only available through the foreign language and its cultures.*

The Connections goal fits well with trends in many areas of the curriculum. Across the educational landscape, notions of integrated curriculum and interdisciplinary instruction are increasingly prevalent. In many schools, teachers plan integrated thematic units that draw on multiple subject areas. Some teachers work independently; others work collaboratively in teams.

Myriam Met (Ed.D., University of Cincinnati) is foreign language coordinator, K-12, for the Montgomery County (Maryland) Public Schools. She has trained teachers, developed curriculum and instructional materials, and has written for professional publications on the topic of content-based instruction in grades K-12.

* I am indebted to Rick Donato and Paul Sandrock whose comments on an earlier draft of this chapter were invaluable. Any errors or misinterpretations of research are, of course, my responsibility.

Integrating content from across disciplines helps students see the connections among all that they are learning in all aspects of the curriculum. It also reflects the growing belief that much of school learning should parallel the demands of authentic, real-life tasks, in which problems are rarely solved by drawing on knowledge or skills from only one domain—there are few pure science problems in real life. Rather, in real life students will need to use knowledge, understandings, and skills acquired from many areas to carry out the demands of their personal lives, their jobs, and their civic responsibilities. Similarly, foreign language will be a tool for students to use to acquire information or to carry out tasks in the real world beyond the classroom.

Theoretical Basis for the Connections Standards

Current research suggests that the human brain is programmed to make meaning from experience. This wired-in orientation to seeking connections between the known and the unknown has some natural implications for how schools can facilitate student learning (Caine and Caine 1991; Jensen 1998). Constructivist theory, a conceptualization of learning that has recently driven educational reform in many disciplines, holds that learners construct their own understandings by giving meaning to information and experience. Learners achieve this by linking new knowledge to what they already know, thus making meaning out of each new experience. Moreover, learning will be deeper and more powerful if learners can see the relationships among the parts of learning and the whole—the broader context of their knowledge and experience (Brooks and Brooks 1993; Caine and Caine 1991; Hawkins and Graham 1994). These relationships are stored in networks in the brain, so that understandings are linked to one another not only within networks but also through the links between and among the networks themselves.

This view is in contrast to more traditional approaches in which learning was conceptualized as the accumulation of bits of knowledge, which eventually led to an understanding of the whole. From a constructivist perspective, learners will benefit from understanding the relationship of the whole to its parts from the start. Making connections among the various areas of the school curriculum will help students see the interrelationships among them and strengthen learning in each. Students learn more quickly and retain learning longer when they see how new information and/or experiences relate to what they already know and how the parts of learning relate to a broader context—in this case, the total school curriculum. The more students know, the more hooks onto which they can peg new learning.

Background knowledge, stored as relationships among information and understandings in the brain, is the context for new learning and plays an important role. The role of context in learning may be compared in some ways to doing a jigsaw puzzle. Looking at the picture on the box of a jigsaw puzzle makes the puzzle easier to complete—it gives an idea of where certain pieces might go and how sections of the puzzle relate to one another. Context in learning, and background knowledge, can be likened to the "big picture." Context aids learning just as completing the border of the jigsaw puzzle facilitates puzzle completion. Imagine working a 1,000-piece puzzle and picking just one piece out of the box. In deciding where that piece might go, we might look at the picture to match the piece's color to it. We might also look at which sections have been completed to see how the individual piece fits with other pieces. Imagine how much more difficult it would be to complete the puzzle if one began by selecting several pieces at random from the box and worked the puzzle around those pieces, without ever looking at the picture on the box or completing the puzzle frame first. From the learner's perspective, the bits of information acquired in various subjects can be equally difficult to mesh together into deep conceptual understanding. From the instructional perspective, puzzle completion strategies may be analogous to how teachers can promote learning. Teachers can provide appropriate opportunities for students to make connections between material to be learned in one discipline and that in another (helping students see how the sections of the puzzle connect with one another, how one piece of information relates to other pieces that have a good "fit" in terms of shape, color, etc.).

Another implication of the role of context in constructivist theory is that learning is enhanced when it is authentically linked to meaning and purpose. Context is found in real-life tasks, and real-life tasks always have a meaning and a purpose. Authentic experiences and situations require learners to put knowledge to purposeful use, whether it is using the formula for the area of a rectangle to determine how much carpeting to buy or using known vocabulary, grammar rules, and cultural knowledge to communicate effectively with a native speaker of another language. In the real life of schools and beyond, language is an essential tool for learning and acquiring information. Using language for content learning and to acquire information is therefore a real-life task. Thus, the theoretical basis for authentic tasks that drives curriculum reform across disciplines also provides a strong conceptual rationale for making connections to other disciplines and using language to acquire information in foreign language education.

Further evidence for integrating language and content is provided by depth-of-processing and discourse comprehension processing research. Grabe and Stoller (1997) cite studies that show that "the presentation of coherent and meaningful information leads to deeper processing, and that deeper informational processing results in better learning" (10). They also cite studies that demonstrate that "more coherently presented information, in terms of thematically organized material, is easier to remember and leads to improved learning" (11).

Connections from a Communicative Perspective

For almost two decades second- and foreign-language educators have emphasized communication as the primary focus of instruction. The terms "communicative language teaching" and "proficiency-based instruction" share a common focus: to prepare learners to use language to communicate effectively in a variety of contexts and settings through classroom experiences that simulate real-world language tasks and uses. Instructional approaches that derive from this focus include opportunities for students to communicate about topics of interest to them. Much of language learning in entry-level classes involves having students talk about familiar topics. Often, students spend much of class time interacting with peers as they describe their personal characteristics, family, leisure-time pursuits, and so on. Clearly, these are topics that will allow language learners to function in an authentic situation outside the classroom, albeit in a limited way, after only a short period of study. Communicative language teaching, in contrast to its predecessors, should seriously reduce the number of former students who querulously claim that they can do nothing in the language after two years of study.

Communicative language teaching and learning are consistent with constructivist approaches. The growth of such holistic approaches (as opposed to structural/analytic approaches) can be seen in the increasing prevalence of communicative language teaching, and the commensurate decline of grammar-driven language programs. As noted earlier, communicative language teaching has among its premises that the purpose of learning a language is to use it in authentic spoken or written interactions—"authentic" being defined as real-life interactions that involve real-life meanings exchanged for real-life purposes. Certainly, in schools, using language to learn content (that is, talking about things other than language itself) has real purposes and involves real meanings.

In both constructivist theory and communicative language teaching, meaning and context play a critical role. Students are most likely to be successful learners if the tasks they engage in require attention to meaning. Grammar is more likely to be understood when we see how the rules affect meaning, and vocabulary is more likely to be successfully learned in context. Ryan (1994) argues cogently that the interpretation and construction of meaning are context-dependent, and that meaning and context are thus vital to the acquisition of communicative competence. Decontextualized drill and practice in which form, but not meaning, is the focus may be less helpful to learners than communicative tasks that require attention to meaning. In decontextualized drill and practice, students manipulate vocabulary and grammar to improve their knowledge of vocabulary and to perfect the production of forms and rules, with little or no attention to meaning. In contrast, in content-based instruction, students use vocabulary and grammar to interpret or convey ideas and concepts. In content-based instruction meaning is always the focus of instruction, learning experiences, and tasks. Students need to communicate with the teacher, one another, or texts, in order to access or apply content. Integrating language and content, therefore, is not just consistent with communicative language teaching; it is likely to promote the development of communicative competence.

Not only does content give learners something meaningful and purposeful to talk/write about, it also expands the range of topics about which learners can communicate. If the goal of proficiency-based instruction/ communicative language teaching is to prepare students to communicate on topics beyond the classroom setting, learners will need a wide repertoire of language. While it may be useful to be able to talk about oneself (one's interests, family, or personal characteristics), at some point students have to go beyond talking about themselves and talk about the world of ideas. Indeed, in some cultures it may even be inappropriate to be so conversationally egocentric, and students will need to be able to talk about more than themselves if they wish to establish and maintain social relationships with native speakers. Making connections to other disciplines will give students the language tools they need.

Using language to acquire information is also a natural extension of communicative approaches to language teaching. If communicative approaches aim to prepare students to communicate their own ideas about topics of interest to them, it stands to reason that not all learners will want to talk about the same thing. This means more than simply allowing students to develop a personalized vocabulary (e.g., allowing some students to learn to say "in-line skating" because it is their favorite sport, while requiring everyone to learn the names of five common pastimes). It also means that the topics students will want to talk about will reflect personal interests, whether academic or not. Some students may be interested in medieval history, others in the martial arts, still others in contemporary cinema or the World Federation of Wrestling. Addressing the diverse interests of learners and preparing them to communicate about them will promote language learning.

Current Trends in Interdisciplinary Instruction

Given the strong theoretical basis for making connections between and among disciplines, it should not be surprising that curriculum integration has been a trend in both general education and in foreign language education for some time.

Interdisciplinary Instruction and Curriculum Reform

In general education, both elementary and middle school curriculum reform have seen increasing emphasis on integrated instruction. In elementary schools, thematic instruction is common. Because in elementary schools one teacher usually teaches all subjects to students, coordinating learning outcomes from many subjects is easier than when several teachers must collaborate. For teachers who spend the whole day with the same students, bells do not suggest the mental breaks between disciplines that may characterize high schools. In an integrated elementary school program, students may be learning about how industrial waste can cause pollution in local waterways (science). They may acquire knowledge about the legislative process (social studies) as they determine how to restrict the disposal of toxic chemicals, and they may write to their local state representatives to state their views on pending legislation (language arts). Clearly, making connections between foreign languages and the curriculum is in keeping with curriculum trends at the elementary school level.

Curriculum restructuring at the middle school level has also seen growing emphasis on thematic, integrated instruction. Many middle schools are organized into teams, and each team is likely to have one teacher from each of several disciplines. Most commonly, a middle school teaching team has representation from reading/language arts, social studies, science, and mathematics, although other configurations are found as well. Often, teams will plan interdisciplinary units in which a theme (such as *Water, Change,* or *Aviation*) serves as the focal point for instruction in each subject (see Jacobs 1989; Messick and Reynolds 1992; Palmer 1991; and Vars 1987 for further discussion and additional examples). Consonant with a constructivist viewpoint, these interdisciplinary approaches provide an organizing principle as well as authentic, meaningful experiences to drive student learning. In fact, it has been suggested that the middle school curriculum be designed around the real-life issues and problems that students need and want to solve (Beane 1992). Integrating foreign languages and content at the middle school fits with the basic tenet of middle schools: it brings languages into the "core" curriculum and language teachers into the heart of the school's program.

In high schools, current reform efforts also include interdisciplinary approaches. For example, the culminating exhibitions favored as a graduation requirement in the Coalition for Essential Schools require students to demonstrate learning across disciplines (Sizer 1992). Of course, interdisciplinary instruction in high schools is not limited to current models. As long as thirty years ago, some high schools scheduled students into linked English and social studies or math/science classes that were taught by collaboration teacher teams.

Teaching Language through Content and Content through Language

Within the language teaching profession, content-based instruction has become increasingly popular at all levels of instruction (Snow 1998). In elementary schools, content plays an important role in language teaching. Immersion programs, in which content learning is central, grew from one elementary school in the United States in 1974 to over 165 in 28 states and the District of Columbia by 1997 (Center for Applied Linguistics 1997). The professional literature, as well as anecdotal reports from elementary school foreign language teachers, indicates an important role for content in many nonimmersion programs as well (Curtain and Pesola 1994). Content-based ESL is also found in elementary settings (Cantoni-Harvey 1987; Crandall and Tucker 1990; Snow 1998).

At the postsecondary level, interest in integrating content and language has been evidenced by a growing number of programs that fall under the rubric of Foreign Language Across the Curriculum (FLAC). In these programs, students may take courses taught in a foreign language, or courses in which collaboration between instructors in language and other courses involves students in using language to learn or reinforce learning in other disciplines (Allen, Anderson, and Narvaez 1992; Brinton, Snow, and Wesche 1989; Jurasek 1998; Krueger and Ryan 1993; Snow and Brinton 1997; Straight 1994). In a parallel vein, many postsecondary English for Academic Purposes programs are designed for nonnative speakers of English to allow them to gain skills in both course content at their institution and the language needed for academic successes (Carson, Taylor, and Fredella 1997; Snow 1997).

The range of programs that integrate language and content learning may be described by a continuum as shown in Figure 1 (see Met 1998 for a more detailed discussion).

At one end of the continuum are *content-driven language programs*. In these programs, language is a vehicle for teaching content, with primary importance given to student mastery of content. Immersion programs, in which the school curriculum is taught through the medium of another language, are an example of content-driven programs At the other end of the continuum are *language-driven programs*. In language-driven programs, language outcomes are the primary goal of instruction, content serves as a vehicle for communicative language use, and student mastery of language, not content, is the driving force. In fact, in language-driven programs teachers are not accountable for ensuring that students master content objectives, nor are students usually evaluated in terms of content learning. Along the continuum between the extremes lie a variety of models for integrating content and language. For example, courses in which a content course is taught in conjunction with a language course may place equal value on content learning and language outcomes. In contrast, mastery of content may be of little importance to those teachers who draw on activities from various subjects primarily to help students acquire language.

The continuum can be useful in interpreting many terms that describe models of content and language integration. Sheltered courses in postsecondary Foreign Language Across the Curriculum (FLAC) programs, as described by Brinton, Snow, and Wesche (1989), lie close to the content-driven end of the continuum in that the main course objective is content—content taught using language and instructional strategies that make content accessible to learners. In the adjunct model of FLAC, a content teacher and a language teacher collaborate in the integration of language and content. Students are held accountable for developing language proficiency and for

Content-Driven   **Language-Driven**

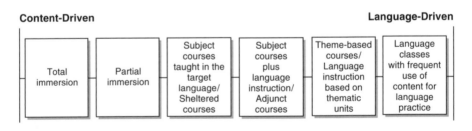

Figure 1
Content-Based Language Teaching: A Continuum of Content and Language Integration

course content (Brinton, Snow, and Wesche 1989). The adjunct model lies at the center of the continuum, placing equal value on language and content learning, and with decisions about what is taught driven by both content and language objectives. The terms "content-enriched" and "content-related" instruction are used by Curtain and Pesola (1994) to refer to two distinct points on the continuum, one at the midpoint and the other at the language-driven end, as exemplified by the following definitions:

> Some FLES programs are "content-enriched," which means that some subject content is taught in the foreign language . . . Content-enriched FLES differs from other forms of FLES in that there is a focus on subject content instruction rather than on language instruction alone. (35)
>
> Content-related programs reinforce the curriculum and may or may not use content directly associated with the grade level of students. (149)

The first definition applies to programs in which some content is taught in the foreign language instead of in English and students are expected to learn both language and content. The second definition applies to programs that use content as a means of improving students' language proficiency, but content learning may not be a primary focus of instruction. Content-related programs use content to enhance language learning, but mastery of content is probably not the goal of instruction nor the responsibility of the language teacher.

Theme-based courses or courses built around a series of thematic units are closer to the language-driven end of the continuum, in that content serves as an organizing principle to give coherence to language to be learned and around which instructional materials are selected. At the extreme end of the continuum are language courses in which a variety of contents or themes are used to provide language practice for predetermined language units/objectives.

Knowing where a program lies on the continuum can be useful in making curriculum decisions. If a program is content-driven, or lies on that end of the continuum, instruction must be designed to ensure opportunities for content learning. And language outcomes may be shaped by the content taught. For example, if students learn science through the target language, then the vocabulary students learn may be scientific terminology; the language functions they acquire may be tied to the discourse style of science, and the kinds of texts they encounter may be limited to expository (vs. narrative) types. In content-driven programs where language outcomes are also important, adjunct language instruction (whether a separate class or as part of content instruction) may need to be provided in order to ensure student access to a broad range of language not likely to be encountered in content learning, such as social language or writing personal correspondence.

In language-driven programs, curriculum decisions are shaped by the outcomes for language learning, and content serves as a handmaiden to language learning. That is, decisions about which content to use, and which learning experiences to select from the range of possible content teaching activities used in that discipline, will be based on what students should be able to do with language. One may choose not to teach about the parts of a flower simply because knowing how to talk about stamens and pistils does not further the communicative goals of the language program. On the other hand, using a science lesson focused on the concept that some objects will float in water and others will not may be an excellent vehicle for practicing vocabulary related to fruits and communicating about future events.

Clearly, there are many extant models of content and language integration to draw upon in aligning current language programs so that students may use language to make connections to other disciplines and to acquire new information. In all likelihood the vast majority of foreign language teachers will be operating from the perspective of a language-driven program. That is, foreign language teachers will be seeking ways in which content can promote language learning and facilitate student acquisition of course outcomes, as well as meeting local, state, and national standards. Current language teachers will find that the current program models in which they work need not be abandoned or restructured. Rather, a new perspective on the role of content can help to reconceptualize the relationship between language learning and other disciplines.

Standard 3.1: Connect with Other Disciplines

Aligning curriculum and instruction to the National Standards will mean that students in foreign language classes will make connections with what they are learning in other classes. Readers who review the benchmarks under Standard 3.1 will observe that at every grade level there is reference to the material students are learning in other subjects and in other classes. The notion of making authentic connections with subject matter in other classes has important implications for language teachers.

Content and the School Curriculum

Many teachers have long considered the content of language courses to be language (e.g., vocabulary, grammar) and culture. Traditionally, there has been a corpus of vocabulary common to most beginning level courses (colors, numbers, days of the week, house/home, clothing, etc.) and a common, sequenced syllabus of grammar. If the standards and schools suggest that connections be made to other disciplines, then "content" needs to go beyond the traditional course content of language instruction. That is, while one might argue that using language to teach "content" might be teaching the structure of the language or culture, content generally goes beyond these to include subject matter from other areas of the curriculum.

For students in K–12 settings, the definition of "content" may be determined by the school curriculum. Two arguments are made here for direct, synchronous links to other classes (that is, the content drawn from other subjects will be grade-level appropriate). One argument has already been offered: constructivist theory suggests that learning is strengthened when students see the connections among what they learn in the various disciplines of the curriculum. Students who study the scientific criteria for distinguishing fruits from vegetables are more likely to learn both science and language well as they make those classifications in a language class.

The other argument is that, from the viewpoint of current trends in K–12 schools, interdisciplinary connections mean making links between what is being learned currently in one class or subject and what is learned in another. Teachers and administrators who teach subjects other than foreign languages hold defined expectations of integrated curriculum. They expect language instruction—like mathematics, science, or reading—to be related to the themes or problems students are working on across disciplines. That means that language educators may be expected to relate the "content" of the content-based language program to what students are expected to study at that grade level. Further, in grades K–5 (where there never seems to be enough time to cover all the mandated curriculum), content-based FLES programs have been introduced as a way of enriching the curriculum without taking time away from the school curriculum. That is, content-based programs can teach or provide practice in aspects of the mandated curriculum. (For example, if students make bar graphs in language class to represent the number of different types of pets owned by the class, they have reinforced concepts from the mathematics curriculum.) Teachers and administrators reasonably expect that the language teacher will draw content from the school's curriculum for that grade level. In these settings, then, content is defined as the content of the mandated curriculum for disciplines other than foreign language.

To participate in schoolwide approaches to curriculum integration does not require that language teachers take responsibility for teaching new concepts in other subjects. The language classroom can be the place where concepts from other disciplines are reinforced and practiced; language instruction can provide review of important information, skills, and concepts taught in a recent unit. Sandrock (personal communication) has suggested that in the language classroom, review of material from the school curriculum that was learned at an earlier grade but incompletely understood or simply forgotten, can lay the groundwork for new instruction that builds on that material to be taught by subject-matter teachers.

Direct ties to the subject content of other disciplines may be easier to make in K–8 settings, and at the postsecondary level. In elementary and middle schools, where teachers usually share responsibility for a group of students, collaborative planning for an integrated language/content approach is facilitated. Similarly, in the adjunct course model often found in postsecondary FLAC programs, content and language instructors work collaboratively. Shared responsibility for a common group of students facilitates planning and implementing integrated language/content models. In contrast, in high schools, where two academic teachers may not share many students over the course of the school day, the language teacher will more likely take sole responsibility for providing opportunities for students to make connections to other disciplines.

Content Is Cognitively Engaging and Demanding

Integrating language and content strengthens the position of foreign languages in schools and universities by promoting academic rigor while simultaneously teaching a demanding set of language skills and understandings. Academic rigor means that content connections must be meaningful and authentic, not trivial. While there are good arguments for making direct links to grade-appropriate content, some teachers will want to draw on subject matter taught at other grade levels in the school curriculum. That subject matter must be intellectually engaging and demanding for students. For example, while simple arithmetic operations such as $2 + 2 = 4$ are indeed in the school curriculum, carrying them out in the foreign language classroom does not represent a valid connection at every grade level. In the early elementary grades, practicing simple arithmetic operations in a foreign language can, indeed, be a legitimate connection between language and content, but it might be a very questionable connection at grade 9. Thus, deciding at which point content connections are (or are not) meaningful and legitimate is important. The question of "what is content" is even more complex in considering the abstract and complex nature of concepts adolescents are expected to learn in relationship to the limited language repertoire they have available to them.

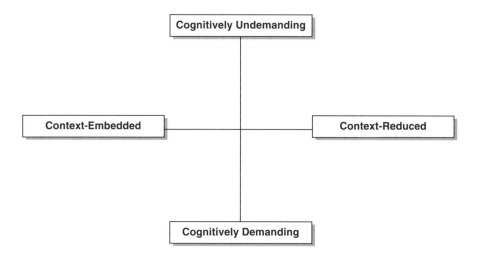

Figure 2

Range of Contextual Support and Degree of Cognitive Involvement
in Communicative Activities

Source: Cummins, James. 1981. "The Role of Primary Language Development in Promoting Educational Success
for Language Minority Students," in *Schooling and Language Minority Students: A Theoretical Framework.* Los
Angeles: California State University at Los Angeles.

Cummins (1981) has suggested a useful model for thinking about the
relationship between content and the language it requires, as shown in
Figure 2.

The intersecting axes describe two important aspects of content and
language learning. On the one axis, content is seen to range from cognitively demanding to cognitively undemanding. For young children, adding
2 + 2 = 4 is cognitively demanding; for adolescents it is cognitively undemanding. On the other axis, Cummins describes contexts for content
learning ranging from context-reduced to context-embedded. In context-
reduced tasks, there are few external cues to support meaning and learning
beyond the language itself. Reading about the functions of the digestive
system is a context-reduced task. In contrast, context-embedded tasks have
multiple cues to meaning beyond language itself. Such cues may be visuals
(e.g., pictures, videos, diagrams), body language, hands-on experiences, and
even knowing the context or background knowledge. Listening to a lecture
about the functions of the digestive system as the lecturer points to visual
displays and diagrams is a context-embedded learning task.

Cummins's grid is helpful in thinking about the integration of language
and content in Standard 3.1. Cognitively undemanding tasks are unlikely to

engage the interest of learners, and consequently unlikely to provoke the motivation or perseverance needed for task completion and thus learning. Therefore, "content" should be cognitively engaging and demanding for the learner. In addition, the instructional experiences teachers plan should reflect consideration of learners' language proficiency, so that abstract concepts are presented in highly context-embedded formats to learners with limited language proficiency. As learners' proficiency increases, the need for embedding multiple cues to meaning may diminish, and instructional experiences may move along the axis toward more context-reduced tasks.

What Is Content?

The definition of content proposed here rests on the principles discussed thus far. "Content" is drawn from the subjects students are studying in the school curriculum. It allows for meaningful connections that help students integrate information, skills, and concepts into the broader context of knowledge. Content is cognitively demanding—it has to be more than a "no-brainer"—and it demands a level of learner engagement with the material. It is suggested here, then, that *"content" in content-based programs represents material that is cognitively engaging and demanding for the learner, and it is material that extends beyond the target language or target culture.*

Models of Interdisciplinary Instruction

How teachers plan to make connections with other disciplines will depend on a number of factors. Most language teachers in the United States work in a language-driven program model, in which their primary focus is on language outcomes. In high schools, where most language teachers work, opportunities for collaborating with other teachers may be fewer than in elementary or middle schools. Regardless of the setting, teachers in language-driven programs can make authentic connections to other disciplines. Because their primary focus will be on enhancing language learning through content, teachers will most likely be choosing content and learning experiences from other subjects that work well for promoting language outcomes. Jacobs (1989) has suggested a continuum for curriculum integration, as shown in Figure 3.

An important feature of this continuum is that each approach that lies along the continuum is a legitimate one for interdisciplinary instruction. Foreign language teachers may find it helpful to know that included in Jacobs's continuum of interdisciplinary instruction is the individual teacher, who reaches out to other subject areas, incorporating relevant connections into his

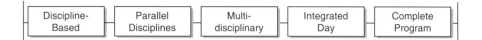

Figure 3

Continuum of Options for Content Design

Source: Heidi Hayes Jacobs, ed. 1989. *Interdisciplinary Curriculum Design and Implementation*. Alexandria, VA: Association for Supervision and Curriculum Development.

or her own instructional program. Thus, while collaboration among one or more teachers may be a desirable way to ensure strong connections among disciplines, individual teachers can effectively provide interdisciplinary instruction as well. Foreign language teachers who work in schools where collaboration is not feasible can still make connections; teachers who work in schools where thematic units are common will find additional rich opportunities for connections as well.

Planning for Connections

Different disciplines provide differing opportunities to exploit for language growth. Ultimately, the connections made should help students become more-proficient language learners. Connections should not be made for their own sake, but rather teachers will need to seek out legitimate avenues that result in student acquisition of language course objectives. Not all content at each grade level will provide the same rich resource for language development. Students who discuss the parts of simple machines may not have the same opportunities for acquiring high-frequency vocabulary or for engaging in extended discourse as those who describe the kinds of goods and services available in their local community. Describing the life cycle of butterflies may be less useful for language development than describing the migratory patterns of Monarch butterflies.

Connections may also be different at different levels of schooling. FLES teachers will find many obvious connections between the language and school curricula, in part because the school curriculum and language curriculum coincide in the early grades (e.g., learning the numbers; naming colors; identifying days, weeks, months, etc.). Other connections will depend on the language proficiency of the learner, the opportunities for context-embedded experiences, and the students themselves. Older students, particu-larly those at the secondary to postsecondary level where teachers often do not share students, may pursue connections to other subjects independently. That is, individual students may decide when they are ready to make connections to other subjects through independent projects. Similarly, students with special interests and greater autonomy as learners may make connections through independent study. In this way, connections to other disciplines will be made by individual students—not planned as a whole-class activity by the teacher—and may be made at the times most appropriate to the needs and interests of the students themselves (Sandrock, personal communication).

It is also important to note that with time, students in middle and high schools will be able to handle more sophisticated and complex language tasks than those that may initially be included in language instruction. As standards increasingly guide language program development, students will start language learning earlier and function at higher levels of proficiency at middle school and high school than is currently the case. The range of possible connections to other disciplines.and the range of learning experiences students engage in are likely to expand significantly.

While connecting to other disciplines from a topical or thematic perspective has been a primary focus of language/content integration, it may be helpful to also consider connections that involve learning processes and strategies. If learning how to learn is an important aspect of education, then it may also be useful to connect the strategies students gain in one area of the curriculum with their application in another (Met 1995; 1994; Met et al. 1983). Research into language learning strategies has identified numerous ways in which students can be empowered to be autonomous, self-directed learners (Chamot and Kupper 1989; O'Malley and Chamot 1990; Oxford 1990). Many of these strategies cross disciplinary boundaries. For example, reading strategies such as calling on prior knowledge, using context clues to deduce the meanings of unknown words, and monitoring oneself to ensure comprehension of text are important in both the English and foreign language classroom. Similarly, prewriting activities such as brainstorming and using graphic organizers are common to both subjects. Other strategies and skills that are common to many disciplines include hypothesizing, observing, and collecting and analyzing information/data—all useful for students encountering new cultural situations, whether directly or indirectly through the media.

Connections to other disciplines can be both thematic and skills-based. Teaching content in a foreign language should be cognitively demanding, and it can promote higher-order thinking skills such as hypothesizing or analysis. As Snow (1998) points out, the publication *New Ways in Content-Based Instruction* (Brinton and Master 1997) is organized around types of activities that involve "information management; critical thinking, hands-on activities; data gathering; and text analysis and construction" rather than around the traditional four skills, or even separate disciplines. This view is reflected in foreign language standards at the state level as well. For example, both the Wisconsin and Nebraska state standards suggest that both information and skills will be connected across disciplines.

Integrating Language Learning and Subject Content

As noted earlier, most foreign language teachers will view content from a language-driven perspective. That is, most language teachers will have language learning as a primary objective, and content from other disciplines will be at the service of language course objectives. When looking across the curriculum, language teachers may find it helpful to use the language curriculum as a criterion for making connections: How can the information and skills from this or that subject matter enable my students to become more proficient in the target language and/or gain greater insight into the target culture? There are probably as many right answers to that question as there are classes of teachers and their students. In the section that follows, some examples of connections with other disciplines are provided as a point of departure for thinking about curriculum integration. These are intended as examples of the realm of the possible, rather than an exhaustive list of the probable.

Connecting with Mathematics and Science. Mathematics provides many opportunities for connections. At the earliest levels of language proficiency students can practice numbers in cognitively demanding tasks. Many of the major conceptual tools of mathematics can be applied to almost any topic, and as such can fit well with the topics of the language classroom. For example, estimation and measurement can be used to predict and then calculate the size (height or weight) of classroom objects or the equivalent weights of fruits (How many grapes weigh the same as this orange?), or to calculate the ratio of the circumference of one's head to one's height. Number use and number patterns work well with both younger and older learners. While young students can engage in simple arithmetic operations, older students can use numbers to complete challenging number patterns (e.g., 3-7-15-31-?). Both young and older students can use numbers to predict and then measure the size of objects in inches or centimeters. The concept of percentages and the tool of graphing can be applied to the group work and class surveys that are common in communicative classrooms. Students can report the results of their surveys in percentages (e.g., 38% of our group and 67% of our class thinks the world will be a safer place in the year 2010). Survey results can also be graphed in various forms, both common and less common, such as bar and line graphs, pie graphs, or even box-and-whiskers or stem-and-leaf graphs.

Teachers can focus on specific language elements through connections with mathematics. Pair and group tasks can lead to reports that use the first-person plural forms of verbs and adjectives (e.g., we found . . . , our banana weighed . . . , 75% of us like to . . .) or to the third-person plural of the past tense (e.g., 18% of students went to the movies last weekend). In recent years, heavy emphasis on pair work has meant that many students get more practice in using the singular verb forms than in the plural forms. Reporting survey results or interpreting graphs and survey data can provide increased practice for needed forms.

Connections with science will depend on the grade level and topic. Some science topics work well for language learners, such as the migration of butterflies and weather/meteorology. Many students have a deep interest in the environment. Not only can students acquire language to describe the natural environment, they can also identify ways in which the environment can be protected, even in first-year classes at the secondary level. Natural phenomena (earthquakes, monsoons, tornadoes) can be linked to the language for identifying and describing geographic and topographic features. Grammatical skills and expression of language functions can be expanded through discussion of scientific phenomena. Students can describe (orally or in writing) the steps in an experiment (past tense) and the reasons for the results (describing cause-and-effect relationships) or hypothesize using if/then constructions.

Connecting with Social Studies. In the primary grades, social studies provides language practice and context for learning high-frequency vocabulary. In social studies, students learn about families, aspects of their community (where to buy things, modes of transportation, community services), and basic map skills. As students progress through the grades, study of national and world regions can provide a good link to foreign language. Study of the African continent allows students to achieve language objectives related to weather, numbers, or naming languages as they explore climatic characteristics of various regions; they can compare relative distances between cities in Africa, observe the percent of the population that lives in rural vs. urban areas, or identify the official languages of many African countries in the early part of the twentieth century as compared with its close. Study of U.S. or world history can allow students to further their language skills as they make comparisons between ways of life then and now (transportation in colonial times and today, changes in what is men's work/women's work or men's clothing/women's clothing).

Social studies is a particularly useful connection to the cultural objectives of the language curriculum. Many of the understandings students acquire in social studies can be applied to the study of the target culture. Many elementary and middle school teachers find it natural to relate aspects of life in a country studied in social studies with that of the target culture. Students of all ages can enhance their higher-order thinking by completing Venn diagrams (see Figure 4) that show similarities and differences between the target culture and one that is the focus of a social studies class. (Venn diagrams are used in many subjects of the school curriculum and provide a concrete springboard for compare/contrast tasks.) And because foreign language instruction and social studies share a common emphasis on developing multicultural perspectives, the culture standards delineated in Goal 2 can be addressed through links with social studies.

Specific language skills can be enhanced through connections with social studies. History texts allow students to observe the authentic use of the past tense(s) and can illuminate how choice of a specific past tense can affect

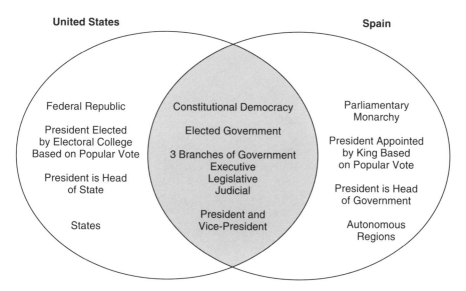

Figure 4
Political Systems

intended meanings. Students can be asked to describe historical events, as they are given cards with events indicated and verbs omitted or provided in infinitive form (Jamestown/to found/1607: *Jamestown was founded in 1607*). Students can make history time lines that show when specific events occurred, and also indicate the historical backdrop for those events (As World War II continued, more women joined the labor force). Both higher-order thinking and language skills can be promoted as students ponder the what if's of history: What if France had not sold the Louisiana Territory in 1803? What if Europe becomes a united single political entity? What if the Boxer Rebellion had succeeded?

Because many aspects of history and contemporary issues are multifaceted, social studies topics discussed in the language classroom provide opportunities to stretch and refine student skills in important language functions such as stating and defending a position. Carefully structured tasks in which students work toward the ability to express and counter viewpoints can result in modified debates in the language classroom even at the lower range of intermediate proficiency.

More-proficient students obviously can work with more-abstract content. For example, Stoller and Grabe (1997) describe a demography unit for university-level students. The unit includes discussion of population trends in both developing and developed countries, and the relationship between population trends and the environment. Students also explore the impact of population on air, water, and natural resources. Other examples may be found in the professional literature on content-based instruction for postsecondary students: Leaver and Stryker (1989) report on area studies taught in the foreign language at the Foreign Service Institute; numerous examples of models of language/content integration at the postsecondary level are found in Krueger and Ryan (1993) and Snow and Brinton (1997).

Connecting with the Arts. Many foreign language teachers are already making strong and useful connections with art and music. These connections can not only address the culture standards, but promote attainment of Goal 1 (Communication) as well. Possible connections between the arts and language learning will be familiar to teachers.

Some works of art can be viewed as "stories artists tell." In particular, portraits can be viewed as visual biographies. Teachers may ask students to describe what they see in purely objective terms (I see a little boy. He is wearing . . .). From there, students may be invited to interpret the portrait and to develop a story about the person. Teachers may provide additional information about the painting, its origins in time and place, and the subject, to weave together culture, history, and geography. Students may choose to revise their biographies based on this new information.

Works of art that depict events or groups of people can be used as a springboard for oral and written group tasks. Students can write skits to portray their response to a question such as: Imagine you were one of the people in this picture. What were you doing 10 minutes before the moment in this picture occurred? One hour afterward? Individual students may be asked to write in response to the question: Imagine you were one of the people in this picture. What were you thinking at the very moment the event in this painting occurred? If you could be any of the people you see pictured here, which one would you want to be and why?

Students can use landscapes or portrayals of events as a springboard for creating descriptions of settings for fictional narratives. Examination of texture and color can be used by students to generate oral or written descriptions of feelings evoked or to create analogies with senses (red tastes like . . . rough sounds like . . .).

Both music and art provide many avenues for developing language proficiency. Students may learn or write rhymes, chants, and poems, then tap out the beat; they can create movement, actions, or dance to accompany songs, rhymes, chants, and poems; or they can use different art media to illustrate songs, rhymes, chants, and poems. Teachers may use song lyrics to highlight vocabulary and grammar in context or ask students to write additional verses, new lyrics, or a summary of the lyrics in their own words. Elementary-grade teachers can research jump rope rhymes from U.S. culture and children's rhymes from other cultures. Students can act them out or set them to music. More-proficient students can give oral or written explanations of the game that goes with the rhyme. Students can play games from other countries, and then develop Venn diagrams that show how these games are similar to or different from games played here. Students can then explain orally and/or in writing the similarities and differences.

Not All Connections Are Equal

There are ways in which the disciplines can be exploited for language growth and ways in which each discipline has unique terminology or discourse features that may limit the ways connections are made (Met 1998; Met, forthcoming). Connections with English reading/language arts help improve both first- and foreign-language literacy through acquisition and application of learning strategies and processes. Reading skills can be enhanced in social studies, but may be limited in the area of mathematics and sciences because reading expository text in these areas requires a very different set of strategies from those used for narrative text or even expository text in the social sciences and humanities (Reehm and Long 1996). Similarly, the range of high-frequency vocabulary useful beyond the school setting that can be developed in the social sciences and humanities may be greater than in certain aspects of mathematics and science, where highly specific terminology may be restricted to these disciplines (e.g., *variables, pupa, anemometer*).

Standard 3.2: Acquire Information

Under Standard 3.2, students use the foreign language to acquire information and insights uniquely accessed through the language. Unlike Standard 3.1 (connections with other disciplines), the fields students may explore may not necessarily be tied to what they are learning in other subjects. An important feature of Standard 3.2 is the extensive flexibility inherent in the instructional experiences that may address this standard. The student may be a significant decision maker in determining what kinds of information to pursue, when, and how. And not all students have to make the same connections or acquire the same information: these may be driven as much by student choice as teacher decisions. In many cases, the information acquired will likely be applied beyond what occurs in formal schooling (Sandrock, personal communication). In this standard, a broader definition of content—that is, "anything of interest to the learner" (Genesee 1994)—may prevail, so that content may be academic content if that is what the student chooses, or it may reflect personal interests beyond academics. However, in keeping with the earlier definition proposed for content, the information students acquire and the fields in which it is pursued must be engaging to learners (which it is likely to be if chosen by the learners themselves) and represent some degree of cognitive demand.

In acquiring information that reflects students' personal academic or nonacademic interests, it is likely that students will make connections beyond the foreign language teacher's expertise, and new strategies for guiding and assessing student work may be required. Yet, even when teachers themselves are not knowledgeable in the arenas in which students actively acquire information, the classroom can provide students with the linguistic tools and strategies to access resources independently beyond the classroom walls.

Not only is there flexibility in the information students acquire and how they acquire it, but such flexibility allows for variation in the language outcomes that result from independent student work. Clearly, different students with different pursuits will come away with knowledge in differing lexical domains, grammar skills, or sophistication in expressing given language functions. And not all students may benefit equally in terms of the modes of communication or the traditional four skill areas. For many students, information may be acquired solely through the interpretive mode: some may only read and others may use only video to access information. And, within the interpretive mode, not all students will read the same kinds of material: some may read magazine articles and others access the electronic media. Some students may develop greater interpersonal communication skills than interpretive ones if they pursue personal interests through community outreach activities such as volunteer work or conducting telephone surveys on behalf of political candidates.

Standard 3.2: Connections to Goals and Standards

If the rationale for Goal 3: *Connections* reflects the goals of communicative language instruction, i.e., preparing students to function in the settings and topics they are most likely to encounter, then Standard 3.2 is a powerful mechanism for enabling students to do so. This standard clearly addresses the individual communicative needs of learners, and therefore also ties nicely to the standards in Goal 5: *Communities* (5.1: *Students use the language both within and beyond the school setting;* 5.2: *Students show evidence of becoming lifelong learners by using the language for personal enjoyment and enrichment*).

Perhaps one of the more appealing aspects of Standard 3.2 is inherent in the notion of perspectives. As the wording of the standard indicates, *"Students . . . recognize the distinctive viewpoints that are only available through the foreign language and its cultures."* As such, this standard can provide an effective channel for also attaining Goal 2: *Cultures*. As students use their language to recognize the distinctive viewpoints of the target culture, they acquire insights into the cultural perspectives that relate to a culture's products and practices. And just as students may pursue personal interests that lie beyond the expertise of the teacher, so too may students discover aspects of cultural perspectives unknown to the teacher. While many teachers are knowledgeable of cultural products and practices, the perspectives that drive them many not be as well known. Indeed, cultural perspectives have received insufficient attention in language teaching or in language teacher preparation in recent decades, so it is not surprising that less is known about them. Engaging students in discovering cultural perspectives as they acquire information and recognize viewpoints uniquely accessible through the language will strengthen attainment of both Goals 2 and 3. Cultural knowledge is important in reading academic texts. Students will need background knowledge to make appropriate inferences regarding the meaning of texts. Therefore, the tools teachers provide students as they prepare to pursue individual interests also promote Goal 2.

Students can also move toward attainment of Goal 4: *Comparisons* as they learn about the distinctive viewpoints of the target culture. Students deeply interested in sports might choose to read the sports section of a target language newspaper. They can observe which sports receive the most attention, and compare that to the sports section of the local paper. Other students might be interested in teen magazines or in polls and surveys conducted in the target culture. These provide unique access to the thinking of people in a given target culture locale. For example, high school students were given an article reporting the results of responses to the survey question, "What would you do with a million pesetas?" Students were able to compare the priorities of the Spaniards who responded to those in their local community. Teen magazines, which are often replete with such surveys, give students interesting ways to access the distinct viewpoints of their peers elsewhere.

Learning from Experience

As the language teaching profession increasingly aligns classroom instruction and learning experiences to the National Standards, new questions and challenges are bound to arise. Some will surprise us; others we may already have begun to anticipate. A few of the many questions that we will want to explore are briefly suggested below.

- How can language programs, particularly those in K–12 settings, continue to address articulation issues in order to work toward a seamless progression of knowledge and skills and yet still be responsive to learner interests? As already noted, most likely there will be variations in aspects of the language proficiency students acquire in addressing Standard 3.2. We will need to find ways to move away from some traditional foreign language curricula with their lockstep expectations for student achievement from level to level. That is, we will need to find ways to focus more on student proficiency than on achievement of specific language items, and recognize that proficiency may be demonstrated in different ways and using differing contents.
- How can students be assessed equitably in tasks and activities related to the Connections goal? To what degree should content knowledge be part of the assessment? Since one cannot communicate effectively without something to communicate about, surely topic knowledge will interact

with communicative proficiency. What criteria should teachers use to assess students and what relative weights should be given to those criteria? And how can teachers facilitate student learning in areas outside their own expertise and still effectively assess students?

• What models can be developed that allow teachers to work collaboratively with colleagues from other disciplines, given the constraints of schools (time available, number of students shared)? How can current collaborative models be expanded, and if necessary modified, to meet the needs of teachers in a range of grade levels and school organizational patterns? How can collaboration between content and language teachers be extended to shared approaches to student assessment?

• Given the many priorities for teacher professional development, how can teachers gain both confidence and increased competence in integrating content from other disciplines into their instructional program? Teachers will need to learn more about other disciplines so that rich and deep connections can be made. They will also find that teaching the content of other disciplines to learners with nonnative proficiency is facilitated by appropriate instructional strategies (Cloud 1998; Lorenz and Met 1988; Met 1994; Met 1989; Majhanovich and Fish 1988; Short 1997; Snow 1997; Snow 1987; Stole 1997). Snow (1998) suggests that integrating language and content learning expands teachers' instructional repertoire to include strategies for making content accessible. These strategies, in turn, facilitate language acquisition by making input comprehensible.

• What evidence can be marshaled to support the Connections goal? As is the case with many aspects of foreign language teaching in the United States, data derived from quantitative and qualitative research are needed to support the theoretical basis for integrating language and content instruction and for using language to acquire information. Genesee (1998) has suggested that there are compelling arguments to support the idea that content-based approaches to language teaching enhance student learning, but supporting research evidence is scarce to date.

Conclusion

National Standards for foreign language learning build on sound theory and practice both within and beyond the foreign language field. This chapter has examined how the Connections goal, in particular, is consonant with current theories about learning. Connecting across disciplines is not a goal unique to the language profession. Indeed, national standards in other disciplines, such as those in mathematics, include a similar goal. Interdisciplinary instruction and integrated curriculum have been the hallmarks of educational reform in schools across America. Notably absent from the discussions, unfortunately, have been foreign language educators, primarily because of the mistaken but common view that foreign languages are not part of the core curriculum. By making valid, rich, and multiple connections, language educators can increase their visibility and participation in the daily life of schools.

Beyond the theoretical bases for making connections, there are sound practical reasons as well. The Connections goal suggests an important role for using the foreign language to acquire information and gain access to the unique viewpoints of the language and culture. Within the field of language education, this aspect of the Connections goal provides important support for the other goals of the national standards for foreign language learning. Students gain communication skills, they gain insight into cultural perspectives, they can compare the viewpoints they encounter with their own, and they use language for personal enrichment both within and beyond the school setting. Thus, while aspects of the Connections goal may represent some new directions for language teaching, the two standards in this goal play an important role in the broader context of all five goals.

Foreign language study is an important and worthwhile endeavor for all America's students, regardless of age, ability, or geographic location. Languages should be worth learning as an academic pursuit in their own right as well as for their usefulness beyond academia. By working toward attainment of both standards in the Connections goal, language learners can address both of these worthy purposes. That is, the Connections goal promotes the intellectual development of learners. And because students use language to acquire information, particularly in areas of personal interest (whether vocational, avocational, or academic), making connections helps give the lie to the age-old plaint of language learners: *But I'm never going to use it!*

REFERENCES

Allen, W., Keith Anderson, and Leon Narvaez. 1992. "Foreign Languages Across the Curriculum: The Applied Foreign Language Component." *Foreign Language Annals* 25: 11–19.

Beane, James A. 1992. "Turning the Floor Over: Reflections on A Middle School Curriculum." *Middle School Journal* 23:34–40.

Brinton, Donna M., and Peter Master. 1997. *New Ways in Content-Based Instruction*. Alexandria, VA.: TESOL.

———, Marguerite Ann Snow, and Marjorie B. Wesche. 1989. *Content-Based Second Language Instruction*. Boston: Heinle and Heinle.

Brooks, Jacqueline, and Martin G. Brooks. 1993. *In Search of Understanding: The Case for Constructivist Classrooms*. Alexandria, VA: Association for Supervision and Curriculum Development.

Caine, R. N., and Geoffrey Caine. 1991. *Making Connections.* Alexandria, VA: Association for Supervision and Curriculum Development.

Cantoni-Harvey. Gina. 1987. *Content-Area Language Instruction.* Reading, MA: Addison Wesley.

Carson, Joan G., Josephine A. Taylor, and Laureen Fredella. 1997. "The Role of Content in Task-Based EAP Instruction," in Marguerite Ann Snow and Donna M. Brinton, eds., *The Content-Based Classroom.* New York: Longman.

Center for Applied Linguistics. 1997. *Directory of Total and Partial Immersion Programs in U.S. Schools.* Washington, DC: Center for Applied Linguistics.

Chamot, Anna Uhl, and Lisa Kupper. 1989. "Learning Strategies in Foreign Language Instruction." *Foreign Language Annals* 22: 13–28.

Cloud, Nancy. 1998. "Teacher Competencies in Content-Based Instruction," in Myriam Met, ed., *Critical Issues in Early Second Language Learning.* Glenview, IL.: Scott Foresman–Addison Wesley.

Crandall, Jodi, and G. Richard Tucker. 1990. "Content-Based Instruction in Second and Foreign Languages," in Amado Padilla, Halford H. Fairchild, and Concepcion Valadez, eds., *Foreign Language Education: Issues and Strategies.* Newbury Park, CA.: SAGE.

Cummins, James. 1981. "The Role of Primary Language Development in Promoting Educational Success for Language Minority Students, " in *Schooling and Language Minority Students: A Theoretical Framework.* Sacramento: California Department of Education.

Curtain, H. A., and Carol Ann Pesola. 1994. *Languages and Children: Making the Match.* New York: Longman.

Genesee, Fred. 1994. *Integrating Language and Content: Lessons from Immersion.* Santa Cruz, CA: National Center for Research on Cultural Diversity and Second Language Learning.

———. 1998. "Content-Based Language Instruction," in Myriam Met, ed., *Critical Issues in Early Second Language Learning.* Glenview, IL.: Scott Foresman–Addison Wesley.

Grabe, William, and Fredricka Stoller. 1997. "Content-Based Instruction: Research Foundations," in Marguerite Ann Snow and Donna M. Brinton, eds., *The Content-Based Classroom.* New York: Longman.

Hawkins, Mary Louise, and M. Dolores Graham. 1994. *Curriculum Architecture.* Columbus, OH: National Middle School Association.

Jacobs, Heidi. 1989. *Interdisciplinary Curriculum: Design and Implementation.* Alexandria, VA: Association for Supervision and Curriculum Development.

Jensen, Erik. 1998. *Teaching with the Brain in Mind.* Alexandria, VA: Association for Supervision and Curriculum Development.

Jurasek, Richard. 1988. "Integrating Foreign Languages into the College Curriculum." *Modern Language Journal* 72:52–58.

Krueger, Merle, and Frank Ryan. 1993. *Language and Content: Discipline- and Content-Based Approaches to Language Study.* Lexington, MA: D.C. Heath.

Leaver, Betty Lou, and Stephen B. Stryker. 1989. "Content-Based Instruction for Foreign Language Classrooms." *Foreign Language Annals,* 2:269–75.

Lorenz, Eileen B., and Myriam Met. 1988. *What It Means to Be an Immersion Teacher.* Rockville, MD: Office of Instruction and Program Development, Montgomery County Public Schools.

Messick, Rosemary G., and Karen Reynolds. 1992. *Middle Level Curriculum in Action.* New York: Longman.

Met, Myriam. 1989. "Walking on Water and Other Characteristics of Effective Elementary School Teachers." *Foreign Language Annals* 22:175–83.

———. 1994. "Teaching Content Through a Second Language," in Fred Genesee, ed., *Educating Second Language Children.* Cambridge: Cambridge University Press.

———. 1995. "Foreign Language Instruction in Middle Schools: A New View for the Coming Century," in Rick Donato and Robert M. Terry, eds., *Foreign Language Learning: The Journey of a Lifetime.* Lincolnwood, IL: National Textbook Company.

————. 1998. "Curriculum Decision-Making in Content-Based Second Language Teaching," in Fred Genesee and Jasone Cenoz, eds., *Beyond Bilingualism: Multilingualism and Multilingual Education.* Clevedon, Eng.: Multilingual Matters.

————. Forthcoming. "Enhancing Second Language Development Through Content-Teaching." *Infancia y Aprendizaje* (Spain).

Met, Myriam, H. Anderson, E. Brega, and N. Rhodes. 1983. "Elementary School Foreign Language: Key Link in the Chain of Learning," in Robert G. Mead, ed., *Foreign Languages: Key Links in the Chain of Learning.* Middlebury, VT.: Northeast Conference on the Teaching of Foreign Languages.

O'Malley, J. Michael, and Anna Uhl Chamot. 1990. *Learning Strategies in Second Language Acquisition.* New York: Cambridge University Press.

Oxford, Rebecca. 1990. *Language Learning Strategies: What Every Teacher Should Know.* New York: Newbury House/Harper and Row.

Palmer, Joan. 1991, "Planning Wheels Turn Curriculum Around." *Educational Leadership.* 49:2, 57–60.

Reehm, Sue P., and Shirley A. Long. 1996. "Reading in the Mathematics Classroom." *Middle School Journal* 27 (5):35–41.

Ryan, Frank. 1994. "Languages Across the Curriculum: More Than a Good Idea," in H. Stephen Straight, ed., *Language Across the Curriculum. Translation Perspectives VII.* Binghamton, NY: Center for Research in Translation, State University of New York at Binghamton.

Sandrock, Paul. 1998. Personal communication.

Short, Deborah J. 1997. "Reading and 'Riting and . . . Social Studies: Research on Integrated Language and Content in Secondary Classrooms," in Marguerite Ann Snow and Donna M. Brinton, eds., *The Content-Based Classroom.* New York: Longman.

Sizer, Theodore. 1992. *Horace's School.* Boston: Houghton Mifflin.

Snow, Marguerite Ann. 1987. *Immersion Teacher Handbook.* Los Angeles, CA: Center for Language Education and Research, University of California.

————. 1997. "Teaching Academic Literacy Skills: Discipline Faculty Take Responsibility," in Marguerite Ann Snow and Donna M. Brinton, eds., *The Content-Based Classroom.* New York: Longman.

————. 1998. "Trends and Issues in Content-Based Instruction," in William Grabe, C. Ferguson, R. B. Kaplan, G. R. Tucker, and H. G. Widdowson, eds., *Annual Review of Applied Linguistics.* New York: Cambridge University Press.

Snow, Marguerite Anne, and Donna M. Brinton. 1997. *The Content-Based Classroom.* New York: Longman.

Stole, Carole. 1997. "Pedagogical Responses from Content Faculty: Teaching Content and Language in History," in Marguerite Ann Snow and Donna M. Brinton, eds., *The Content-Based Classroom.* New York: Longman.

Stoller, Fredricka L., and William Grabe. 1997. "A Six-T's Approach to Content-Based Instruction," in Marguerite Ann Snow and Donna M. Brinton, eds., *The Content-Based Classroom.* New York: Longman.

Straight, H. Stephen. 1994. *Language Across the Curriculum. Translation Perspectives VII.* Binghamton, NY: Center for Research in Translation, State University of New York at Binghamton.

Vars, Gordon F. 1987. *Interdisciplinary Teaching in the Middle Grades: Why and How.* Columbus, OH: National Middle School Association.

5

Comparisons: Towards the Development of Intercultural Competence[1]

Alvino E. Fantini

School for International Training
Brattleboro, Vermont

I. Comparisons and the Five C's: An Overview

You can't discuss the ocean with a well frog—
he's limited by the space he lives in.
You can't discuss ice with a summer insect—
he's bound to a single season.
You can't discuss the Way with a cramped scholar—
he's shackled by his doctrines.

—Chuang Tzu, 4th Century B.C.

The inclusion of *Comparisons* as one of five goal areas of the National Standards for Foreign Language Learning represents a truly significant development in the field of language education. The purpose of this goal area, while simply stated—"(to) develop insight into the nature of language and culture" (*Standards for Foreign Language Learning* 1996:53)—can lead to potentially powerful and exciting implications. Moreover, this goal is explicit acknowledgment that study of a second or foreign language and its culture

Alvino E. Fantini (Ph.D., University of Texas) is director of Bilingual-Multicultural Education and a faculty member of the MAT Program at the School for International Training in Brattleboro, Vermont. Fantini gained distinction for his sociolinguistic research on dual languages acquisition. His key professional concern focuses on the nexus between language, culture, and worldview. Besides conducting U.S. Peace Corps training for 16 countries, he guided materials development in more than 30 languages and completed a series of intercultural orientation guides. Fantini is also an international consultant and a recent president of the Society for Intercultural Education, Training and Research (SIETAR). His most recent work is *New Ways in Teaching Culture* (TESOL: 1997).

contributes in an important way to the education and development of every learner. In elaborating the rationale behind the Comparisons goal area, the standards document further states that "students benefit from language learning by discovering different patterns among language systems and cultures. Through the study of a new language system and the way such a system expresses meanings in culturally appropriate ways, students gain insights into the nature of language, linguistic and grammatical concepts, and the communicative functions of language in society, as well as the complexity of the interaction between language and culture" (*SFLL* 1996:53).

In addition, the Comparisons goal area includes two standards: Standard 4.1 states: "Students demonstrate understanding of the nature of language through comparisons of the language studied and their own" (*SFLL* 1996:9). This standard focuses on the effect that learning a new language has on the learner's ability to develop hypotheses about how language works and the role that language plays in one's life. The implications are many, but one can infer that learners go beneath the surface structure to explore how language expression carries meaning, how meaning is construed in language, and how different languages construe meaning differently. Standard 4.2 adds: "Students recognize that cultures use different patterns of interaction and can apply this knowledge to their own" (*SFLL* 1996:9). This standard suggests that throughout the language learning process, students explore both similarities and differences inherent in the perspectives, practices, and products of the native and second cultures. Again, learners go beyond the surface to investigate how language affects and reflects culture, how language and culture are interrelated, and how together both language and culture influence one's view of the world.

While the Comparisons goal and its standards provide an exciting vision for language learning, the notion that proficiency in another language and competence in its culture provide powerful insights into one's own is hardly new. Not only has this idea served as a basic tenet in the field of intercultural education, but it has appeared throughout the history of education and is echoed in other disciplines like philosophy, psychology, anthropology, and linguistics. This is also captured in the lines above, written so many centuries ago by the Chinese philosopher Chung Tsu.

Highlighting learning of the second language-culture (LC2) is, of course, extremely important, but a Cultures goal alone would be incomplete without also explicitly and systematically engaging in Comparisons. Moving beyond study of the LC2 to comparative work (i.e., intercultural exploration) greatly expands traditional foreign language (FL) concerns and promises important and significant rewards. A recently published case study piloting the standards, with a special focus on Comparisons, documents the learning of Arabic by African American students. This report provides an early glimpse of some of the benefits of comparative work among learners in an inner-city classroom (Moore and English 1997:173–205). Testimonies of countless other individuals who have undergone an intercultural experience provide further support for the Comparisons goal.

Comparisons[2] is, of course, inextricably linked to the Cultures goal. Yet it also deepens the study of cultures by investigating the LC2 and one's native language-culture (LC1) in addition to the underlying causes and consequences of their cultural differences. Comparisons ensure the deepening of the learner's self-awareness, an often untapped potential arising from the provocativeness of intercultural comparisons, to which language contributes a major part. This may explain why it is so common to hear individuals who have spent time in a foreign culture say, "You know I learned so much about the host language and its speakers, but guess what: I learned even more about myself." Many in the intercultural studies field believe that self-awareness is undoubtedly the most important benefit of cross-cultural contact. This awareness is enhanced by including Comparisons as a bona fide aspect of the FL experience.

The idea that FL teachers might include Comparisons along with the other four goal areas—Communication, Communities, Connections, and Cultures (*SFLL* 1996:9)—ensures learner exposure to *all* of the multiple benefits of second- or foreign-language culture learning. Considered holistically, these may be characterized as *intercultural competence*, an ability that enables individuals to operate effectively and appropriately in more than one language-culture, and an ability that is increasingly valued and needed in today's world and in the years ahead. This chapter, then, explores the Comparisons goal area—the theoretical and conceptual aspects that underlie it, the rationale for considering the development of intercultural competence as an overriding goal, and the implications and applications of intercultural explorations in the language classroom.

Beyond Culture: The Intercultural Dimension

Whereas target-culture exploration is often part of FL teaching—albeit sporadically and inconsistently—comparative work is seldom included in FL classroom activities. Nonetheless, Comparisons has been central to the work of intercultural educators and trainers who, early on, recognized that learning about another culture enhances learning about one's own. Experiencing a different culture—and the more esoteric or bizarre (from the eyes of the beholder), the better—surfaces provocative questions, not only about the new experience at hand but also about what one has always taken for granted— one's own language-culture. While exploring the new LC, the learner is able to look back on his or her own from a new vantage point. This is true whether the experience occurs across an ocean or within one's own neighborhood— it can be equally true in the FL classroom.

Exploring Comparisons initiates varying degrees and levels of interpersonal and intercultural learning. While a classroom can never fully substitute for direct experience in a field situation, creative, thoughtful, and systematic attention to comparisons work can still produce significant growth. The degrees and levels of growth may be represented as a continuum of interrelated possibilities, since development in one area enhances development in others:

(LC1) Intrapersonal/Interpersonal $\longleftrightarrow$ Intercultural/Intracultural (LC2)
[– variables +]

For example, as an individual interacts with others (even those of a similar LC background), perspectives are gained on how he or she is being perceived. In this sense, *inter*personal learning contributes to *intra*personal learning (on the left side of the continuum). Similarly, interaction with those from a different LC background provides opportunities to reflect on one's own LC1 and contributes to *inter*cultural learning (on the right side of the arrow). And, as one gains experiences with many individuals from the LC2, one begins to recognize differences among its members as well, leading to an understanding of diversity within cultures that breaks down erroneous or overgeneralized stereotypes (the *intra*cultural dimension). This process of inspection (of that which is different) and introspection (of oneself and of one's own language-culture) is the essence of the Comparisons goal area— learning about self and others.

Clearly, the degree, amount, and complexity of social variables increase or decrease as one moves along the continuum from either left to right or right to left (signified by - *variables* +). Movement toward the left suggests interactions only with those of the same LC1 (where divergent variables, like language and cultural patterns, decrease and their impact on interactions is low) versus contact with those from a different LC (where variables increase, especially language and cultural patterns, and their impact on interactions is therefore high). Interaction among interlocutors of different LCs is severely constrained by lack of a common language and culture and tends to be far more labored, with less chance of success. Comparisons elucidate the variables present at various points along the continuum and highlight the factors that aid intercultural communication.

To sum up, as one interacts with others (even those of the same LC), one learns about oneself (the inter- and intrapersonal levels), just as when one interacts with those of a different LC, one learns both about the LC2 and more about one's own LC (the intercultural dimension). In-depth exploration of the LC2 can also lead to insights about diversity within the LC2 (the intracultural) and possibly about diversity within one's own culture as well (also intracultural). Viewed this way, language educators can play an important role in helping their learners' development at all points along the continuum. This type of growth enables effective and appropriate interaction not only with diversity in the world at large but also with diversity within one's own neighborhood. For those students who may never have an opportunity to travel abroad, the latter may be even more important.

Language Education and the Intercultural Field

Although Comparisons, i.e., intercultural exploration, represents a new venture for many teachers, Comparisons has been at the very core of the intercultural field. While this field is quite new in contrast to FL education, it has developed rapidly during the past quarter of a century. Unlike FL education, however, its roots are found outside formal educational settings—in government (e.g., in the U.S. Peace Corps and Foreign Service), educational exchange (through programs conducted by pioneer organizations like The Experiment in International Living, the American Field Service, and Youth for Understanding), and more recently, in international business and multinational corporations. In all of these areas, individuals are engaged in the experience of living, working, or studying in a foreign culture. Their needs are immediate and intercultural success is central to their purpose. Organizations that prepare individuals for such cross-cultural situations labor continually to develop and refine models and procedures to ensure the effective functioning of their participants.

Much of the work done by interculturalists is disseminated through journals sponsored by kindred organizations like SIETAR International (the Society for Intercultural Education, Training and Research). As the premier professional society concerned with intercultural matters, SIETAR has helped develop the field into what it is today, and it currently coordinates more than thirty-five affiliate chapters around the world. With Cultures and Comparisons now explicit goals of FL education, language teachers can learn much about these areas from their interculturalist colleagues, just as interculturalists can learn much about language preparation for cross-cultural situations from FL teachers.

Surprisingly, too few interculturalists have language and linguistics as part of their formation; it is even more surprising to find interculturalists and some TESOL educators (Teachers of English to Speakers of Other Languages) without proficiency in a second tongue. Without a second-language experience, they are deprived of the insights and benefits that derive from grappling with communication on someone else's terms. Despite any understanding *about* other cultures, the monolingual professional is limited to intellectualized endeavors when *concepts* about other LCs are not also accompanied by *direct experience*. Lacking alternative forms of communication, they are constrained to perceive, conceptualize, formulate, and express thoughts from a single vantage point. Multiple perspectives are difficult in such cases. And despite their ability to discuss intercultural concepts in their own tongue, their understanding remains vicarious, a situation that Fishman (1976) characterized as "monocular vision . . . leading to narrow smugness and a smug narrowness."

In this sense, language educators are in a more favorable position. They already possess varying degrees of language proficiency and cultural competence. And because language is more tangible and easier to document than culture, they are better able to analyze and understand their data. For this reason, much of what we have gleaned about languages from a linguistic perspective has helped to inform our understanding of culture. This should not come as a surprise, since language reflects and affects culture. The utility of this linguistic insight to intercultural efforts is well supported in works by Edward Hall and expressed in his succinct proposition that "culture is communication" (1973:97), which we might invert to also say that "communication is culture."

Further analysis of this statement deepens its significance even more. It is said, for example, that the anthropoid became *homo sapiens* only through language acquisition. Language enables human qualities by helping us to learn from symbolic and vicarious, in addition to direct, experiences. It helps us to organize and formulate thoughts, as well as to convey them in turn to someone else. Without language, none of this is possible. Stated another way, language is the construct that enables culture development through interaction and communication with other people.

Studies of wolf children and other feral children, and those of older individuals raised in isolation, dramatically attest to the constraints that lack of a language exerts on their development (e.g., Brown 1958; Curtiss 1977; Lane

1976; Rymer 1993; Schaller 1991). But for individuals undergoing *normal* development, language affects and reflects culture just as culture affects and reflects what is encoded in language. Although language and culture are not a perfect mirror of each other, a dynamic relationship exists between them. Whorf and Piaget observed this intertwining, although each emphasized a different aspect. (Piaget in Pulaski 1971; Steinfatt 1989; Whorf 1956). No matter which is stressed, it is clear that language and culture belong together. Foreign language teachers proficient in other languages, while enjoying the advantage of direct experience with alternative communication systems, may now wish to draw further from intercultural research. This is especially true if exploration of Comparisons is to be effective.

II. From Communicative Competence to Intercultural Competence

> We shall not cease from exploration and the end of all our
> exploring will be to arrive where we started and know the
> place for the first time.
>
> —T. S. Eliot

Rethinking Communicative Competence

Whereas speech signals are typically a major part of most communication systems, other forms are also employed: written symbols, signed language, gestures, and so forth. No matter which are used, communicative exchanges combine multiple forms as part of one's total *communicative competence.*

Introduction of the notion of communicative competence in the language field a number of years ago signaled an important conceptual shift that broadened our understanding of language. For many, it served as a reminder that teaching language involves more than the linguistic component alone, even though grammar work continued to be a major focus of classroom teaching for many years. And communicative competence was also reflected in various newer approaches to foreign language teaching. For interculturalists, the notion of communicative competence led to research that included culture-specific ethnographic studies. Much of this work was based on Hymes's framework (1972) and other efforts to extend his sociolinguistic framework to intercultural interaction (Collier 1989). Their endeavors, however, remained focused mostly on the communicative rules of interaction rather than on language itself. A holistic model combining both was clearly needed, especially for preparing learners to operate in a second communication system.

The Foreign Language Standards do just that—they expand our focus beyond linguistic dimensions of language and address other areas that are equally sanctioned, highlighted, and encouraged. Communicative competence is an apt term for this whole because it addresses multiple aspects of the communication process. The conjoining and inseparability of language and culture is further ensured through a second and related term that may be useful to introduce at this point: *linguaculture* (also *languaculture*). This term has begun to appear increasingly in the literature in recent years and refers to both conceptual and operational dimensions (Kramsch 1989; Agar 1994; Fantini 1995:149).

Various components of communicative competence are included in an expanded view of foreign language subject matter. Omaggio, for example, reviewed several constructs based on Canale and Swain, as well as theorists like Campbell and Wales, Hymes, and Munby, and identified four areas: (1) grammatical competence, (2) sociolinguistic competence, (3) discourse competence, and (4) strategic competence (1986:7). No matter how represented, it is clear that language *learning* and language *use* involve multiple facets. In my own construct, depicted in Figure 1, four components are also

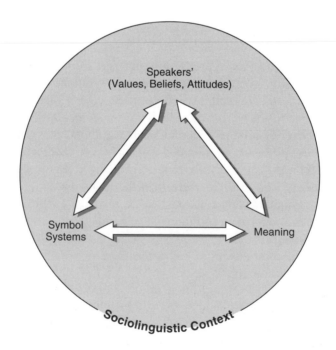

Figure 1
Communicative Competence: Components and Interconnections

posited, although slightly reconfigured (three of which directly correspond to the *practices, products, perspectives* scheme used in the Standards document). To elaborate further, three of the components are: the speakers of the language and their attendant values, beliefs, attitudes, etc. (or practices); the meaning or semantic component (or perspectives); and the symbolic component, whether written and/or spoken symbols, gestures, etc. (or products). The third component also includes

- a linguistic dimension (the sounds, signs and/or graphemes, forms and grammar of language, which is commonly the major focus of language teachers);
- a paralinguistic dimension (tone, pitch, volume, speed, and affective aspects); and
- an extralinguistic dimension (nonverbal aspects such as gestures, movements, grimaces).

These components are interrelated and mutually affect each other (signified by the two-directional arrows). They are also modified in accordance with their use in a particular social context (signified by the circle). When context is considered, the fourth component, sociolinguistic context, becomes apparent. This fourth component consists of a repertoire of communicative choices, each appropriate (i.e., normal or *unmarked*) for a given situation and, conversely, inappropriate (or *marked*) when improperly employed. All four components are acquired in overlapping stages from one's earliest years as part of native communicative competence. This understanding underscores what one also needs in order to be competent in a second or third system, since every linguaculture in the world possesses these areas, although the details within each will obviously differ. For further discussion of communicative competence, see Chapter 2.

Exploring Intercultural Competence

Earlier it was suggested that there may be an even larger goal that subsumes all five goal areas. This megagoal may be characterized as the development of intercultural communicative competence (ICC) or, more simply stated, intercultural competence (IC). This holistic view is widely shared to varying degrees by colleagues in disciplines other than foreign languages. Many professionals in ESOL, bilingual education, intercultural education, multicultural education, ethnic heritage and ethnic revival education, and international and global education, for example, share the desire to help learners develop the awareness, attitudes, skills, and knowledge (captured in the acronym A+ASK, explained below) which can prepare them for successful participation in another cultural group.

The addition of the term *intercultural* to *communicative competence* recognizes that communicative competence in a *second* language is needed to take one beyond one's native competence. It also recognizes the impact that a second, third, or fourth communicative competence produces on one's LC1 (or among several in the case of the multilingual-multicultural person). One does not *add* LC2 competence without also experiencing its effects on the existing paradigm. Quite the contrary, the LC1 becomes increasingly susceptible to introspection and change as one interacts and reflects about the LC2 and LC1 and the dynamic between them. Moreover, because second competence creates new options, the development of ICC leads to unanticipated consequences. The more deeply one enters the LC2, the more challenging and complex the interactions between the LC1 and LC2. The Comparisons goal explores these phenomena and their effects on the learner. In this sense, then, the development of intercultural competence leads beyond monolingualism-monoculturalism to varying degrees of adaptation (or rejection), adjustment, assimiliation, and/or to bilingual-bicultural functioning. These outcomes represent different scenarios within the cross-cultural process and depend entirely on the choices each learner makes.

Constructs of Intercultural Competence

An understanding of communicative competence, then, is critical to our interest in intercultural communicative competence—truly the province of the Comparisons goal area. The addition of the *intercultural* component acknowledges the dynamic interaction between one's native (and limited) CC1 and the target CC2, which occurs when they are in contact. (See Figure 2.)

Although a notion of intercultural competence is widely held, as with CC, various characterizations exist with regard to its definition and its components (Dinges and Baldwin in Landis 1996). An analysis of articles by two researchers that examine ICC reveals three common dimensions:

- the ability to establish and maintain relationships,
- the ability to communicate with minimal loss or distortion, and
- the ability to attain compliance toward some mutual goal (Martin 1989; Wiseman and Koester 1993).

Curiously, all three seem as much a part of interpersonal competence as they are of intercultural competence. Once again, what differs perhaps is the

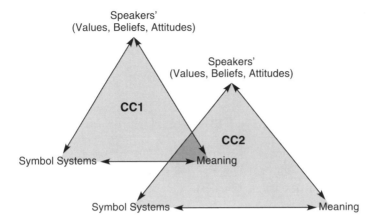

Figure 2
Communicative Competence in Two Different Language-Cultures

degree and complexity of variables that mediate interactions among the individuals involved. Clearly, the second dimension—*the ability to communicate with minimal loss or distortion*—speaks more directly to language teachers. Yet all are relevant to foreign language education. Learners will need to be able to establish relationships and to accomplish tasks with members of the target culture in addition to being able to communicate.

Success in an intercultural context clearly calls for some degree of IC competence in both language and culture. Although communication could conceivably also transpire in one's own tongue, IC competence assumes communication (at least at certain times and circumstances) will also take place in the target language. In today's world, reliance on our own ethnic or native competence alone is not enough; we must also be able to deal with people from other languages and cultures *on their own terms and in their own language.*

Having identified various dimensions of IC competence, many researchers have gone on to explore behavioral attributes that are most related to intercultural success. The traits most commonly cited include: respect, patience, a sense of humor, tolerance for ambiguity, flexibility, empathy, nonjudgmentalness, openness, curiosity, and motivation, among others (e.g., Kealey 1990:5; Kohls 1979:72). These traits are often found in cross-cultural inventories (e.g., Kelley and Meyers 1992) that guide the objectives on which training plans are designed. One wonders, of course, whether or not such traits can be developed in individuals who do not already exhibit them. Nonetheless, intercultural efforts attempt to help learners clarify those traits they already possess, to understand their significance to intercultural adaptability, and to develop abilities for intercultural success. These dimensions of IC competence, their behavioral manifestations, and the relevant abilities all suggest new areas of work for the foreign language teacher intrigued with the Comparisons goal.

III. Other Aspects of Comparisons

> In the beginning was the Word. And the Word was made flesh.
> It was so in the beginning and it is so today. The language, the
> Word, carries within it the history, the culture, the traditions, the
> very life of a people, the flesh. Language is people. We cannot
> even conceive of a people without a language, or a language
> without people. The two are one and the same. To know one is
> to know the other.
>
> —Sabine Ulibarri

Language educators and interculturalists, then, together have a role to play in developing intercultural competence. With few exceptions, however, interculturalists often overlook (or leave to language teachers) the task of developing language proficiency (Ting-Toomey & Korzenny 1989), just as language teachers often overlook (or leave to interculturalists) the task of developing intercultural abilities. Ironically, this occurs despite our acknowledgment of the inseparability of language and culture. Although this notion is widely held, few understand explicitly the interconnections implied in the notion of linguaculture. This is what we will examine next.

Language and Worldview: Components and Interconnections

> A different language is a different vision of life.
>
> —Fellini

It has already been stated various times that language both reflects and affects one's worldview. Language provides a sort of road map as to how one perceives, interprets, thinks about, and expresses one's views of the world. But what do we mean when we use the term *worldview* (or *Weltanschauung* in German, *vision du monde* in French, *cosmovisión* in Spanish, *visão global do mundo* in Portuguese)? What are its components, how are they interconnected, and how do language and culture mediate (inter)cultural processes?

Language (i.e., communicative competence, the expanded notion of our subject matter) reflects and reinforces the particular view we hold of the world. In linguistic terms, the influence of language on culture and world-view is called *language determinism* and *relativity;* that is, the language we acquire influences the way we construct our model of the world (determinism). And if this is so, other languages convey differing visions of that same world (relativity). Hall alludes to this phenomenon when he states: "Man is the model-making organism par excellence . . . Grammars and writing systems are models of language," while also cautioning that "all models are incomplete. By definition, they are abstractions and leave things out" (1976:10–11). Another writer, Kurt Vonnegut, addresses these notions even more directly:

> I've often thought there ought to be a manual to hand little kids, telling them what kind of planet they're on . . . called *Welcome to Earth* . . . . And one thing I would really like to tell them about is cultural relativity. . . . A first grader should understand that his culture isn't a rational invention; that there are thousands of other cultures and they all work pretty well; that all cultures function on faith rather than truth; that there are lots of alternatives to our own society . . . Cultural relativity is . . . defensible (and) attractive. It's also a source of hope (1974:276).

This long-debated theory of language determinism and relativity, known as the Sapir-Whorf hypothesis, raises intriguing issues related to cross-cultural effectiveness. It clarifies why each person comprehends and expresses from a particular vantage point, complicating interactions among those operating from different competency systems (Steinfatt 1989; Whorf 1956). And it reminds us of the difficulty of setting aside our own cultural lenses.

How effectively and appropriately, then, can an individual behave in an intercultural context with—or without—proficiency in the language of the target culture? These words suggest two viewpoints on this issue. Whereas effectiveness is a judgment based on one's own perspective, appropriateness depends on judgments based on the host's perspective. And although communication across cultures may occur in one's own language (an expectation often held by many English speakers), it is qualitatively different to communicate in one's native language rather than in the host language—whether it be Spanish, French, German, Swahili, or another tongue. Whatever the case, L2 proficiency is critical to effective *and* appropriate functioning in cross-cultural situations and to the development of other views of the world. Exposure to a third or fourth language, needless to say, is even better because it helps to reconfigure polarizations in worldviews, which often occur even in the minds of bilingual-bicultural individuals.

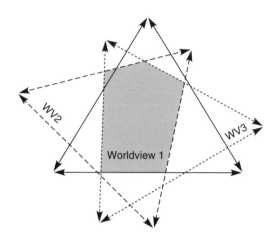

Figure 3
Three Different Worldview Configurations

The illustration in Figure 3 depicts the components of each linguaculture, how they form a cohesive worldview, and how worldviews differ from each other.

While each worldview consists of the same interrelated components, the details of the components themselves vary from LC to LC, resulting in differing realizations for each speaker. This explains why developing an LC2 involves more than mastery of language as tool (the surface features). It also requires grasping how the components are reconfigured. For this reason, LC2 acquisition transforms and expands one's view of the world. And although each view differs (in particular aspects), it is possible that they all share some aspects (the shaded areas where triangles overlap). In other words, despite the marvelous diversity and creativity reflected in the world's linguacultures, they may share a common core of *universals,* a notion that researchers have only recently begun to investigate seriously.

Unfortunately, success with one's native LC does not guarantee success with an LC2. In fact, the LC1 may be one's biggest impediment to fully acquiring a second. Establishment of the first paradigm commonly inhibits adults from developing a second, at least not without serious questioning, deep scrutiny, and reflection, unlike young bilinguals who have already established *dual* paradigms in their earliest years (Fantini 1985). For older individuals, developing intercultural competence comes with a cost—with challenges, surprises, and reservations. And anyone who has undergone an intercultural experience knows that we make choices at every turn, and that the choices we make bear consequences—for ourselves and for those with whom we interact (Adler 1976).

Language-Culture as Fundamental Paradigm

Language is perhaps our most fundamental human and humanizing paradigm. Because language mediates everything we do, it is fundamental to our humanness. But exactly how does it do this? Another scheme, known as the Input-Output Framework (Figure 4), tries to depict how language exteriorizes one's perceptions of the world as it in turn frames one's internalized view.

To elaborate further, we (Interlocutors 1 and 2) find ourselves always in a given context (external world). And in each situation, each person (in accordance with his or her language, culture, and experiences) selectively attends to (i.e., perceives) certain aspects of that context. Perceptions (apprehended through the various senses) are formulated into concepts or thoughts (essentially a mental process). However, to communicate thoughts to someone else requires reformulating them into tangible manifestations (provided by one's available language system). Thoughts are *reinterpreted* and grouped by semantic features (still at an abstract level) to be shaped as signs or words (i.e., they are given morphological form, albeit still at an abstract level) and then ordered sequentially (since language is conveyed linearly, i.e., one word placed after another in a sequence dictated by the available syntactic system),

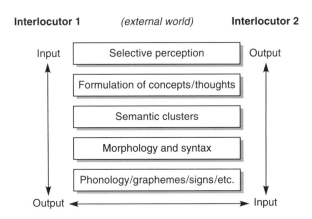

Figure 4
An Input-Output Framework

then couched within existing language symbols (sounds, script, gestures, and so forth), and finally expressed physically. Mental aspects of this process (up to the moment of physical manifestation) are called competence, while the physical expression is called *performance* (corresponding to deep and surface structures in Chomsky's generative-transformational scheme) (Chomsky 1965).

Whereas we gather input through perception, our output is expressed through tangible symbols. Input and output are connected within each speaker through mental processes mediated at both deep and surface levels by the person's language system. Language symbols provide the *substance* that allows thought to be exteriorized and communicated to others. Where interlocutors share the same LC, output from the first speaker provides comprehensible input for the second. Hence, they alternately reverse the process during dialog, at times moving from perception to thought to expression (from input to output); and at others, receiving someone else's symbolic output as their input. In this case, the process is reversed (within the interlocutor) to create a facsimile of the other's mental representations (therein providing a vicarious way of experiencing and knowing). This process of converting perception to thought and thought to language, however, requires fragmenting holistic *experience* in accordance with the existing *word categories* in one's own tongue, since the words of languages are discrete units, conveyed only one at a time.

In this way, language serves as a basic classificatory system, segmenting and fragmenting our notions of the world into available word categories while also grouping and combining categories of words in other ways. That is, all words provide more general or more narrow specifications, based on clusters of semantic features that constitute their meaning. Moreover, words cohere in hierarchies, from more general to more specific, sharing many of the same semantic features with others yet always retaining at least one feature that distinguishes them from all others. Finally, word hierarchies also mesh into hetararchies (i.e., a hierarchy of hierarchies). For example, if we consider the group of words we call nouns, we can see how nouns fit within a larger hetararchy (moving upward) just as we can also identify a hierarchy of words within the category of nouns (moving downward) (Anglin 1970, 1995). (See Figure 5.)

In this example, *chair* and *horse* share the semantic features that both are nouns and both are tangible, but differ because the second has the additional feature *animal*. Likewise, *chair, horse,* and *man* share the features of noun, and tangible, whereas the last has the additional feature *human*. Each new word is distinct from the other nouns because, while it shares features

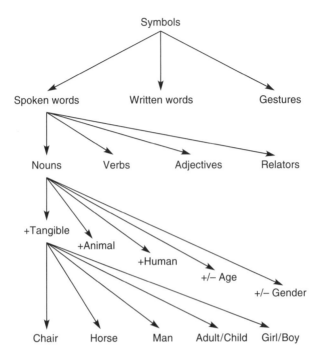

Figure 5
A Word Hierarchy

with them, it always has at least one further specification. In fact, for each word to be distinguishable from all other words, it must always have at least one distinctive feature. Whereas all languages cluster semantic features in hierarchical ways, which features of *reality* they encode, how features are clustered into word categories, and how categories are organized hierarchically vary by language system. Acquiring our native tongue, then, means acquiring the classificatory scheme intrinsic to that tongue. We learn both to generalize (moving up the hierarchy) *and* to specify (moving down the hierarchy) about the things of the world as we encode concepts into the words of our language. In turn, the words of our language lead us to preexisting and widely held cultural concepts.

In brief, each linguaculture provides its own historically and culturally rooted hetararchy. If not a fact of the world, it is indeed a fact of language and culture. Hall acknowledges this when he says, "[T]here is no necessary connection between these symbolizations and what occurred. Talking is a highly selective process . . . highlighting some things at the expense of some other things" (Hall 1973:97–98). We recognize, then, that language-thought connections are arbitrary conventions or, put another way, conventionalized arbitrariness. Yet once a connection is established, the relationship remains rather fixed (although it may also shift over time) and is usually unquestioned by the speakers of that language.

These connections between experience, thought, and expression are how language reflects and affects culture and how together, language and culture influence worldview. Because this process begins so early in life, it is understandable why we might take our LC1 for granted, unaware that our first paradigm provides not merely a *neutral* communication system but a pervasive medium that influences every aspect of our lives. A second LC experience is provocative precisely because it exposes us to an alternative: another system and one that would otherwise be impossible to imagine from our current perspective. It stimulates questions that may never occur to us to ask about our native language, culture, and worldview. These are the very questions that are at the heart of Comparisons work.

Language—A Two-Edged Sword

Six blind men on their way to visit the Rajah encountered an elephant. Not being able to see it, they each felt the elephant with their hands to determine what sort of creature it was. . . .

—Popular Folktale

Language is often likened to a two-edged sword: while it communicates, it can also excommunicate. It includes those who share the system, but it also excludes those who do not. Language also has the power to liberate and constrain. Our ability to symbolize, for example, allows us to move freely, albeit conceptually, through time and space. We can recall and speak of things past, just as we can project our ruminations into the future merely by uttering words. Yet there is no way to retrieve the past nor ensure the future; we can only symbolize about them while we remain always in the present moment and place. However, our faith in words is so great that we can viscerally experience the *reality* of something we never witnessed directly at all.

Although language conveys thoughts and experiences, it sometimes also constrains and contradicts them. Through language we learn, for example, that things are not always what they seem (the introduction to the well-known folktale above serves as an excellent reminder of this). In fact, much of what we learn and know we really do not *know* at all, at least not directly. Our knowledge is tremendously augmented, however, through language use. Much of schoolwork illustrates how much learning is accomplished through language without involving concomitant experience. Language permits contemplating the impossible and exploring the unfathomable. We talk about concepts as difficult and as abstract as *death,* for example, which we can never know directly, at least not in life. It is difficult to imagine life without our ability to symbolize, just as it is difficult to imagine how we might think or know differently if we spoke a language other than—or in addition to—our native tongue. Comparisons between and across linguacultures help us to understand that this is so.

Beyond the Native Paradigm

> An unreflected life is hardly a life worth living.
>
> —Socrates

Much of the discussion about Comparisons to this point may appear outside of usual concerns of language teachers. Taken seriously, it requires rethinking the purposes and benefits of LC2 development by directing attention to the learner's understanding of both the LC1 and LC2. However, this understanding also has to do with alternative ways of seeing and knowing—options not easily accessible to a monolingual-monocultural person. Alternative thinking (also known as zigzag thinking and creativity) has been promoted by many educators, scholars, and scientists. It is reflected in the maxim "looking out is looking in," often heard among interculturalists. And it is captured in a well-known quote from Albert Einstein, who stated that "no problem can be solved from the same consciousness that created it. We must learn to see the world anew" (Einstein in Fantini 1995:141). "Seeing the world anew" (i.e., going beyond one's own linguaculture) and becoming a more creative, divergent thinker are important outcomes of work with the Comparisons goal.

When the larger goal of ICC development and its attendant A+ASK dimensions are considered, the necessity of comparative work becomes even clearer. The Comparisons goal develops the learner's knowledge, skills, and attitude (toward self and others), but most of all, it is concerned with awareness. This last area deserves further elaboration, since educators already work with knowledge and, to some extent, skills. Many are also familiar with a taxonomy developed a number of years ago that expanded educational objectives even further by adding the third area of affect (or attitude) to knowledge (or cognition) and skills (or behaviors) (Bloom 1969). Awareness increasingly seems to be another essential component and one that is especially relevant to ICC development. For this reason, interculturalists already commonly address awareness and affect along with knowledge and skills.

Figure 6
The A+ASK Paradigm

Language teachers now also need to consider how awareness and attitude are important dimensions of foreign language work.

Awareness appears to be of a different order than the other three areas of our expanded taxonomy and, for this reason, it is placed at the center of the A+ASK acronym (see Figure 6). Awareness emanates from learning in the other areas but it also enhances development in the other areas. For many in the intercultural field, awareness (of self and otherness) is a keystone on which effective and appropriate interactions depend. Writers from various disciplines have been intrigued with awareness and have explored its role further. Stevens (1971), Curle (1972), and Gattegno (1976), among others, cite awareness as the most powerful dimension of the A+ASK quartet. And the Portuguese expression *concientização* (signifying *critical consciousness* or *awareness*) has become an international word through the works of Paulo Freire (1970, 1973, 1998).

Awareness is in and of the *self* (and it is always about the self in relation to someone or something else). Hence, awareness is always *self*-awareness and to say *self*-awareness is redundant. Awareness involves exploring, experimenting, and experiencing (the subtitle of Stevens's book) (1971). It is reflective and introspective, and in turn, it can be optionally expressed or manifested both to the self and to others. Awareness is difficult to reverse; that is, once one becomes aware, it is difficult to return to unawareness (although one may try to deceive oneself, the self usually knows this). Awareness leads to deeper cognition, skills, and attitudes just as it is also enhanced by their development. It is pivotal to cross-cultural entry and acceptance by members of other cultures on their terms (and for this reason, it has a role in most cross-cultural orientation models). Freire adds several other observations (1970, 1973, 1998):

- *concientização* is awareness of selfhood;
- *concientização* is a critical look at the self in a social situation;
- it can produce a transformation of the self and of one's relation to others;
- it can lead to dealing critically and creatively with reality (and fantasy); and
- it is the most important task of education.

Awareness development figures into work with the Comparisons goal too. Educators need to ask: What role should awareness have in the educational process? How can I work on awareness development? And even more challenging—How can I monitor and assess its development? These issues will be taken up below; for the moment, however, it should be obvious that Comparisons requires reexamining the educational content and processes of both curricula and lesson plans.

IV. Insights from the Intercultural Field

> You cannot teach a person anything. You can only help him to find it for himself.
>
> —Galileo Galilei

Systematic and ongoing comparing and contrasting is at the heart of Comparisons exploration. In the process, the learner uncovers cross-cultural similarities and differences. However, contrasts can be either minimized or maximized in the mind of the learner. For example, novices in an intercultural situation may downplay differences ("People are basically the same everywhere") or exaggerate them ("These people are really strange"). Cross-cultural models from the intercultural field help in all of these areas and are discussed below. For the moment, however, let us examine various insights extant in the intercultural field that can serve as further backdrop for our thinking about the Comparisons goal in instruction.

Some Relevant Notions

Comparisons are always rooted in the perspective of the onlooker and this, in and of itself, presents special problems. While interculturalists value non-judgmentalness, the fact is that we always attempt to make sense (and therefore make judgments) of every situation we encounter. However, we must be aware of this bias, since it is nearly impossible to set it aside. We need to recognize that we always see things through our own cultural lenses, which skew our assessment in every situation. For this reason, it is probably more accurate to speak of *suspending* judgment rather than making no judgment at all. Interculturalists highlight this phenomenon by distinguishing between *etic* and *emic* perspectives, i.e., interpreting another culture from the outside as a foreigner (the etic) versus how members of other cultures explain themselves (the emic). In most cases, etic and emic perspectives do not match, but insiders are not always necessarily more accurate in portraying their own culture either. We have already discussed the fact that natives are often quite unaware of their own linguaculture. Awareness on the part of both insiders and outsiders, then, aids mutual understanding and for this reason is essential to positive intercultural interactions.

It is also important to note that LCs are not monoliths but tend to display varying degrees of uniformity or diversity within themselves. Small societies—island cultures and the like, for example—often exhibit higher degrees of uniformity and have lesser tolerance of variation or noncomformity. Such cultures are said to be *high-context* cultures. This means that values, beliefs, behaviors, etc., are so widely shared among its members that they are implicit and therefore there is little need to discuss them explicitly. In contrast, *low-context* cultures display more diversity among groups and individuals and the differences among them are greater. In these cases, it is often necessary to explain oneself, one's motivations, and one's behaviors because they can be more easily misunderstood. Teachers dealing with LCs spread over wide geographical areas may find these to be lower-context situations. French and Spanish teachers conducting lessons aimed at the Comparisons goal, for example, will need to explore similarities and differences not only across LCs but also within the target LC.

Finally, Comparisons exploration focuses on *culture-specific* differences (those between two specific LCs) just as it may also investigate *culture-general* issues (those that apply to intercultural processes regardless of the LCs involved). While exploration of the target LC is common, the possibility of great diversity in low-context situations raises questions about what cultural aspects to teach without overgeneralizing. Bullfights in Hispanic cultures, for example, elicit differing reactions from Hispanics, depending on their background and location. While some are staunch *aficionados,* others dislike or even strongly protest the practice. In some countries, bullfights are common and popular (Spain, Mexico, Colombia), in others they occur occasionally (Venezuela, Bolivia), and in others they rarely occur at all (Guatemala, Nicaragua). Thoughtful culture-specific exploration avoids overgeneralizing and portraying the wider culture monolithically when, in fact, it is not.

Conversely, Comparisons also inspects culture-general phenomena, that is, those issues and processes that occur independently of the specific LC in question. Interculturalists often take a culture-general approach when preparing individuals for several cultures at the same time. Language educators can do the same with low context situations. In both cases, important learnings are made possible by extrapolating issues and processes from culture-general contexts and by focusing on culture-specific tasks.

Maps and Types of Culture

Numerous culture models can help with Comparisons goal work. An example of one such model is Hall's *Map of Culture,* found in his earliest work, *The Silent Language* (1959:173–174). This map is essentially a grid formed by various categories across the top and down one side, representing ninety-nine culture areas. These areas help in systematizing contrastive work across LCs. Although useful, the grid may be overly complex for most teachers for whom contrastive work is only part of their plan.

A more simplified version is found in another map of culture, known by its acronym NAPI-KEPRA+H, which stands for categories found in its left-hand and top columns (Fantini 1984). This framework presents elements found in any cultural context down the left-hand column (e.g., natural environment, artifacts, people, and information or communication), and cultural groupings or processes across the top (kinship, economic, political, religious, and other associations) . The resultant grid (Figure 7) provides an abbreviated culture map that is much easier to use for comparative purposes.

	Kinship	Economics	Politics	Religion	Associations
Natural Environment					
Artifacts					
People					
Information/ Communication					
Historicity (i.e., +/− time dimension/past and/or future)					

Figure 7
The NAPI-KEPRA+H Framework

Historicity (represented by the H of KEPRA+H), adds a temporal dimension that enriches the task. Students may explore any one of the grid boxes at other points in time—how it was in the past (e.g., last month, last year, 50–100 years ago) or how it might be in the future (e.g., next month, next year, 50–100 years from now), prompting learners to investigate past and future as well as current cultural contrasts.

Whereas many activities are designed to explore specific cultural aspects, this framework helps to systematically track culture components and their interconnectedness. Stated another way, the grid ensures a holistic view of the target culture at any given moment in time (synchrony) as well as over time (diachrony). It suggests areas where learners may engage with native speakers and it encourages both passive roles (e.g., merely observing for low-level language students) and active roles (by participating where possible for intermediate- to advanced-level language students). It also provides an ongoing way of visiting and revisiting the target culture, deepening understanding and involvement at each stage. Finally, it draws on the students' current knowledge, involves them in further research using local resources as available (when used in the learner's own culture), or going out into communities (when conducted in the host culture) (see procedures in Fantini 1997:52–56).

A third way of researching cross-cultural contrasts is suggested in the Nichols Framework (1990), shown in Figure 8. This model is in the form of a grid and posits universal themes for a systematic comparison of the cultural orientation of various groups.

In this grid, axiology refers to the principle on which a culture rotates; epistemology to its origins, nature, and methods of knowledge; logic to approaches to correct reasoning and valid thought processes; and process to methods of exploring and finding knowledge. Down the left side, Nichols tentatively categorizes various ethnic groups in accordance with their presumed worldview orientation. It should be easy to see how this grid can be utilized in conducting intercultural comparisons.

A final model is a Sociocultural Grid based on a sociological framework. This grid identifies three culture components: A+S+M. That is: Artifacts (things people make), Sociofacts (how, where, when, and why people come together), and Mentifacts (what people think or believe) (Fantini and Fantini 1997:57–61). These components are directly akin to the three P's cited in the Standards document representing Products (Artifacts), Practices (Sociofacts), and Perspectives (Mentifacts) (SLL 1996:43). However called, it is important to note how the components interconnect. No matter which component one begins with, the other two can always be related. For example, if we take an item like *sandwich* (or cross, vacuum cleaner, rice bowl, baguette,

Ethnic Groups/ Worldview	Axiology	Epistemology	Logic	Process
European Euro-American	*Man-Object* The highest value lies in the object or in the acquisition of the object.	*Cognitive* One knows through counting and measuring.	*Dichotomous* Either/Or	*Technology* All sets are repeatable and reproducible.
African Afro-American Native American Hispanics Arabs	*Man-Man* The higest value lies in the interpersonal relationships between men.	*Affective* One knows through symbolic imagery and rhythm.	*Diunital* The union of opposites.	*Niuology* All sets are interrelated through human and spiritual networks.
Asian Asian-American Native-American Polynesian	*Man-Group* The highest value lies in the cohesiveness of the group.	*Conative* One knows through striving toward the transcendent.	*Nyaya* The objective world is conceived independent of thought and mind.	*Cosmology* All sets are independently interrelated in the harmony of the universe.

Figure 8
The Nichols Framework

etc.)—essentially an artifact (or product)—we can consider first of all what a sandwich is (e.g., lunch, snack, bread and cold cuts, etc.). We can then explore what (or who), when, and how people use the sociofact (or practice), in this case a sandwich (e.g., working people, students, for picnics, bite size for cocktails, cut into little triangles for small children, etc.). And finally, we can investigate what the notion of sandwich represents or means (e.g., portable, inexpensive, quick, common fare)—the mentifact (or perspective). Similarly, if we choose the item *wedding* (a sociofact), we can discuss the things (artifacts) related to this social occasion in our own culture (or in the target culture)—such as cake, rings, wedding dress, etc.—and then explore the significance or meaning behind each (the mentifacts). After exploring connections among artifacts, sociofacts, and mentifacts, students can go on to compare and contrast these across cultures. Note can be made where connections among components do *not* also correspond across cultures plus special language related to each area. In short, the ASM (or PPP) framework enriches exploration by ensuring that cultural items are not dealt with inadequately in isolation, while also surfacing language expressions related to each area and to the whole.

V. Developing ICC: Models, Content, and Processes

The adoption of new areas from the standards will require teachers to think about how to address them in a curriculum plan. Happily, in the case of the Comparisons goal, teachers can draw on existing models and methods and on content and processes already extant. A recently published survey of intercultural communication courses at colleges and universities in eleven countries provides a wealth of information about relevant content and processes for Comparisons work (Fantini 1997b). Although the survey addresses seven areas, only Parts 5 through 9 are pertinent here: (5) Curriculum design; (6) Content areas; (7) Course implementation and delivery; (8) Materials and resources; and (9) Assessment. Much of the information that follows is taken from this survey.

Cultural Entry Models

Numerous cultural entry models are cited in Part 5 of the survey, dealing with curriculum design. Each model is based on a particular orientation, e.g. chronological progression, developmental sequences, stages, and phases typically experienced by intercultural sojourners, etc. Yet all are concerned with cross-cultural contact, entry, choices and options, and the consequences of sojourner choices in terms of host reactions. Most models outline various stages typically undergone during intercultural exposure. How far one progresses through these stages and how much one adapts is a matter of personal choice. Individual choices range from rejection of the target culture (usually countered by similar reactions on the part of hosts) to surface and sometimes deep adjustment. Sojourners who learn to operate in a rather native-like fashion may be perceived (or accepted) as a member of the host society. Those who adjust contextually to two (or more) cultures in such a fashion tend to be fairly bilingual-bicultural (or multilingual-multicultural), i.e., individuals comfortable within, and accepted by, members of each context. Those who adjust to the point of also losing their original identity (or sometimes rejecting their native culture) present cases of assimilation (sometimes voluntarily taken on by the sojourners and sometimes forced upon them by others).

Most cultural models will be a boon to foreign language teachers engaged in the Comparisons quest. As each stage of a model is considered, discussions of similarities and differences, contrasts and comparisons, are stimulated. Models help raise poignant issues of awareness, attitude, skills, and knowledge needed for further entry into the target culture. Learners who reach a plateau in their cross-cultural development can focus their discussion on choices they make, given the contrasts, what helps or hinders further progress, and possible strategies for further achievement. (Journals are extremely helpful in tracking their entry.) Such discussions invariably promote deeper inspection of the values and beliefs that learners most cherish.

Three cultural entry models will provide some examples. The first, with a psychological orientation, posits various "Stages in Developing an Intercultural Perspective" (Hoopes in Pusch 1979). These stages proceed from ethnocentrism to awareness, then understanding, acceptance/respect, appreciation/valuing, selective adoption (of aspects of the target culture), and finally (depending on the choices made), assimilation, adaptation, or biculturalism/multiculturalism. Movement from one stage to the next requires expansion of the learner's intercultural perspective as well as development of the A+ASK as needed. As the teacher engages learners at each stage, he or she will uncover a wealth of activities to help explore the target culture, the learner's perspective, and the competencies needed at each level.

A second model, based on intercultural processes, identifies "Seven Concepts in Cross-Cultural Interaction" (Gochenour and Janeway 1993:1). This model assumes that the person involved in a cross-cultural situation is central to the success of the interaction and that the *process* of an individual's interaction with people in an unfamiliar culture depends on his or her awareness of that process. Seven elements about the learner form the framework (pp. 3–5):

1. establish contact and essential communication;
2. establish bona fides (i.e., one's role) and be accepted (i.e., be allowed to exist);
3. observe what is going on and sort out meanings;
4. establish a (new) role within the role definitions of the host society;
5. develop conscious knowledge of oneself—as a center, as a cultural being, and as one taking responsibility;
6. conscious development of needed attributes and skills—mental, emotional, and physical;
7. conscious establishment of self-sustaining and meaningful relationships within the host culture.

Taken together, these concepts provide the basis for an entire training or education design with relevant activities appropriate for work at each stage.

A third model, based on a developmental perspective, is an adaptation of the Hoopes framework already cited. Bennett (1993) posits six stages along a continuum, progressing from ethnocentrism to ethnorelativity. The first three are ethnocentric stages, while the last three are ethnorelative stages, signaling an important shift midway when one moves beyond ethnocentrism. The ethnocentric stages are: (1) denial (isolation and separation); (2) defense (denigration, superiority, reversal); and (3) minimization (physical universalism and transcendent universalism). The ethnorelative stages are: (4) acceptance (respect for behavioral difference and respect for value difference); (5) adaptation (empathy and pluralism); and finally (6) integration (contextual evaluation and constructive marginality) (Bennett 1993:29). This model can be especially productive within foreign language education because it suggests both a sequence and activities appropriate for each stage. Moreover, taken together, the stages progress toward the development of intercultural sensitivity and competence; and in all cases, comparative work is imperative.

Content

Teachers can pursue Comparisons work in both the areas of language and culture at all proficiency levels. But what are some content areas that are appropriate for contrastive exploration? Clearly, the Comparisons goal begins with and builds on Cultures goal exploration, but it also goes far beyond. In the language area, one might immediately think of contrastive linguistic approaches, although this was not the motivation for a Comparisons goal. Beyond traditional linguistic contrasting (at phonological, morphological, and grammatical levels), however, one could certainly also compare paralinguistic and nonverbal behaviors, as well as explore contrasts in meaning and other aspects of communicative competence. Both these areas would add important and interesting dimensions.

Many intercultural activities address precisely these concerns; some are quite simple, while others are more complex. For example, the *Toe to Toe* exercise is quite simple in its exploration of proxemic preferences (an aspect of nonverbal behavior) and how we feel when space and distance factors are altered (Fantini 1984:35). Students are asked to stand and find a conversation partner. After a few moments of conversing, they are asked to stand facing each other with their toes touching. Discussion later focuses on whether they engaged in this awkward situation, whether they compensated by modifying other behaviors (leaning backward, moving one's face to one side, etc.), and how they felt and why. Other nonverbal aspects to explore are haptics (touching patterns), kinesics (body movements and gestures), olfactics (smell), oculesics (eye contact patterns), and chronemics (the timing and patterns of interacting in speech). Chronemics is especially fruitful, since many cultures value little or no overlap in turn taking during a conversation (i.e., mono-chronic cultures such as the Japanese, Anglo English speakers, etc.) while others practice significant overlap (i.e., polychronic cultures typical of Latins, Mediterraneans, Arabs, etc.). Being able to engage appropriately in conversation, whether mono- or polychronic, is an important part of inter-cultural competence. Inappropriate turn taking may often irritate the speakers, affect the interaction in a negative way, and reduce the chances of developing a significant relationship.

Whatever areas are involved, however, work in the A+ASK dimensions continues throughout (that is, once aware, we go on to explore how and why we feel the way we do about some particular aspect, develop our ability to perform whether or not we choose to incorporate a particular behavior, and expand our knowledge of a particular item). An example of this is the learning of appropriate ways to greet in a Francophone or Hispanic milieu, considering the social context and attendant factors. At the cognitive level, we may *know* how to greet (e.g., two to four kisses on the cheeks among female French speakers, depending on regional variations, a handshake fol-lowed by an *abrazo,* or embrace, plus a closing handshake among Mexican Spanish speakers, etc.). *Knowledge* of when, how, and with whom to greet in this manner needs to be accompanied by *practice* so that the act feels natural and automatic; however, we must also examine how we *feel* about per-forming this act and *why.* Together, these three aspects enhance intercultural *awareness* about contrasts in greetings between both cultures.

Processes

Besides content, one also needs to consider processes that are most effective for conducting Comparisons work. Processes, of course, have to do with course delivery and implementation. One part of the ICC Survey deals with course implementation and delivery and will again be instructive (Fantini 1997b). It is common to find that inductive, participatory, and experiential approaches are widely popular among interculturalists, since these all help learners to discover their own insights and clarify their own perspectives. Of these, experiential activities are most unique to intercultural work. One model in particular deserves comment.

The Experiential Learning Cycle (see Figure 9), popularized by Kolb (1984:21) a number of years ago, is based on Kurt Lewin's concept of feed-back processes. This model posits a four-stage cycle as a continuous learning process, with both active and passive, and concrete and abstract dimensions.

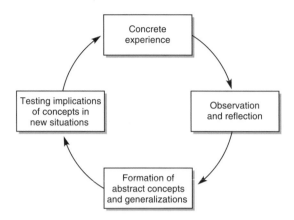

Figure 9
The Experiential Learning Cycle

In this model, concrete experience is followed by observation and reflection, which in turn leads to the formation of abstract concepts and generalizations. These then lead to the formulation of hypotheses to be tested in future action, which in turn leads to new experiences. Kolb offers several observations about the model (20–38):

- the learning cycle is continuous and recurring;
- the direction that learning takes is governed by one's felt needs and goals, since we seek experiences related to our goals;
- learning is erratic and inefficient when objectives are not clear;
- learning styles are highly individual in both direction and process (i.e., some individuals value certain stages more than others).

This model has proven quite effective for intercultural work because it ensures clarity of goals, provides a process, identifies various stages within each cycle, and guarantees student involvement.

A Syllabus–Lesson Plan Model

A helpful device for guiding the design of both a course syllabus and individual lesson plans is the Process Approach (PA) (Fantini and Dant 1993). This model ensures inclusion of culture-intercultural dimensions during language study by positing seven stages:

1. Presentation of new material
2. Practice of new material within a limited and controlled context

3. Explanation or elucidation of the grammar rules behind the material, where necessary or useful (more appropriate for adolescent and older learners than for young children)

4. Transposition and use of new material (cumulatively with other materials previously learned) into freer contexts and more-spontaneous conversation

5. Sociolinguistic exploration of the effect of social context on language use, emphasizing the appropriateness of specific language styles (as opposed to grammaticality)

6. Culture exploration for determining appropriate interactional strategies and behaviors, while also learning about values, beliefs, customs, etc., of the target culture

7. Intercultural exploration, i.e., comparing and contrasting the target culture with the student's native culture

Most teachers are quite familiar with Stages 1–4 (often preceded by a warmup); Stages 5–7 are perhaps less common. Their inclusion, however, ensures that language work is complemented by explicit attention to sociolinguistic, cultural, and intercultural aspects. Since language texts usually focus on language structure and, more recently, on communication (Stages 1–4), the teacher is left to develop Stage 5–7 activities, if they are presented at all. The PA framework lays out an explicit process that clarifies objectives and appropriate activities at each stage. It aids in selecting, sequencing, and evaluating learning/teaching activities. These can be chosen because of their match with the learning objectives for each stage rather than drawn at random from a bag of tricks. The framework also reminds the teacher to include Stage 5–7 activities on the assumption that he or she already has a repertoire of Stage 1–4 activities. The chart in Figure 10 provides some illustrative activities appropriate at each of the seven stages (81).

Following are a few additional suggestions for using this framework. For example, the process is cyclical, and stages should be built in cyclically throughout the syllabus and lesson plans. Not all the stages need to be covered in a single lesson; rather, several lesson units may be required before starting the cycle anew. Also, the stages need not be followed linearly as sequenced in the framework. Although one could begin with Stage 1 and continue sequentially through 7, one could also start at another point. For example, one might start with Stage 6 (or 5 or 7), providing a cultural event as the starting point for the language lesson that follows and flows from it. In this way, language work is framed within a cultural context. Moreover, teachers will also discover that certain activities may overlap several stages all at once, while others focus on only a single stage. Finally, the teacher with

---

Presentation of New Material
A full or abbreviated dialog
A two-line exchange (question/answer)
Manipulation of cuisenaire rods (à la Silent Way)
Others _____

Practice in Context
Pattern practice (all types of drills)
Controlled narrative and questions
Structured conversation or other activity
Others _____

Grammar Exploration
Grammatical explanation of rules
Students figure out rules (à la Counseling Language Learning)
Use of grammar reference books
Others _____

Transposition (or Use)
Unstructured or free conversation
Manipulation of visual aids, objects, and so on
Free narratives
Games
Others _____

Sociolinguistic Exploration
Research on aspects of language use
Simulations and role-play (with varying social factors such as age, sex, role, etc.)
Practice with interactional strategies (e.g., greeting, commands, interrupting, etc.)
Others _____

Target Culture Exploration
Cultural operations (e.g., making a sandwich, a taco, etc.)
Panel and/or group discussion of cultural themes (e.g., family unit, time concepts,
    respect systems, humor, personal hygiene, etc.)
Video segments of events in the target culture
Others _____

Intercultural Exploration
Comparing and contrasting TC and students' own culture(s)
Exploring cultural contact and entry choices and consequences
Exploring causes for culture bumps, shock, or stress
Others _____

Figure 10

A Process Approach Framework: A Syllabus–Lesson Plan Schema

deductive preferences may choose to present Stage 3 before Stages 2 and 4 (in other words, grammar work before practice and use). The inductively inclined teacher, on the other hand, may prefer to present Stage 2 before Stage 3 (i.e., presentation and practice followed by the rules). What remains important, however, is that language and culture exploration is integral to the plan, complemented by work toward the Comparisons goal.

IC Activities for the FL Classroom

The activities respondents list in the ICC survey is incredibly varied (Fantini 1997:139–40). They include discussion, lecture, readings, exercises, small-group tasks, case studies, simulations/skits, observational tasks, exploration tasks, collaborative learning activities, panels, role-plays, field research, debate, interviews, videos, small-group discussion of journals and home-work, interaction with an intercultural pal, summary translation, participation in public lectures, slides, and library research. Outside-of-class activities cited include interaction/interviews with persons of another culture (e.g., interviewing native speakers, foreign student partners, community activities), fieldwork (e.g., drop-offs, site visits, ethnographies, field trips), writing tasks (e.g., papers, critical incidents, journals, reflective essays), media and theater tasks (viewing films, reading newspapers, presenting skits), projects (collaborative tasks, oral reports, exploratory tasks), and other (research, practicing skills, internships).

Most classroom teachers are familiar with many of these activities and can certainly add others to the list. Some activities are more appropriate for Cultures and Comparisons goals, however, than others. Following are illus-trations of several activities specific to Culture-Comparisons work. Although the first two are primarily Cultures activities, they are easily adaptable for Comparisons exploration as well; the rest are all intercultural exploration techniques (adapted from Fantini 1997a). Some activities will require some fluency in the target language; but even in these cases, most can be modified for use at lower proficiency levels or conducted in the learner's native language.

1. What's Going On Here? (Culture Contexts) (Fantini 1997a:122–23)

Overview

This activity utilizes the power of video to bring a cultural segment to the classroom, allowing students to test their understanding with and without language by tuning in to contextual information and trying to make sense of what they see. Only later is the sound track added. A segment may be taken, for example, from a sitcom of the target culture (e.g., *The Bill Cosby Show* in U.S. culture).

Objectives

1. To experience an event in the target culture
2. To figure out what's going on contextually with and without the use of language
3. To learn language relevent to the context depicted

General

Levels—All

Preparation time—15 minutes

Class time—20 to 30 minutes

Material needed—5 minutes of an appropriate video segment

Procedure

1. Record a 5-minute video segment of an appropriate television sitcom or movie. Choose a sequence that depicts a brief comprehensible event that does not require knowing the entire story.
2. Play the segment first without the sound track (volume turned off) and ask students to figure out: (a) Who are the people involved? (b) How are they related to each other? (c) Where are they? (d) What are they doing? (e) What are they saying? (f) What is the story line?
3. When the segment is over, ask students to discuss their answers to the questions, attempting to recreate the story line together.
4. Ask what clues (e.g., nonverbal, contextual) helped them to figure out the story.
5. Play the segment again, this time with the sound track (volume turned on), and ask the students to reconsider their original interpretation.
6. Discuss revisions they may have made in the story and what these were based on (e.g., was it the way something was said, or did their understanding of words or expressions in the target language influence the revision?).

Additional Comments

1. This activity can be used for exploring contextual and nonverbal dimensions of one's native language and culture as well as with

language learners at all levels of proficiency in the target language. In the latter case, beginners with little or no comprehension can rely on contextual cues and affective aspects of language, while more advanced students can try to match their initial inferences with what they understood when the volume was turned up.

2. Intermediate- to advanced-level students can also be asked to explore cultural and contextual aspects in greater depth because they will understand more of the spoken dialogue.

3. This activity can be followed with intercultural exploration by discussing how context and nonverbal dimensions contribute to communication, i.e., what misinterpretations were made and why, and in the case of language learners, how our native language and culture influence how we make sense of any given situation (i.e., how our *cultural lenses* work).

2. Everyday Tasks (Operations) (Fantini 1997a:124–25)

Overview

This activity falls into a category of tasks known as *operations,* that is, ordinary activities found in everyday life that reflect cultural information. This particular example, designed for an ESOL situation, offers an amusing yet real way of witnessing a common experience of many U.S. children. The activity involves preparing a peanut butter and jelly sandwich while learning relevant vocabulary and practicing language at the same time. Using this example as a model, identify appropriate operations in the target culture.

Objectives

• To experience an everyday task common to the target culture
• To develop vocabulary and expressions appropriate to the task
• To practice language in context

General

Levels—All

Preparation time—10 minutes

Class time—20 to 30 minutes

Materials needed—Jar of peanut butter, jar of grape jelly, loaf of white bread, dish, knife, napkin, table

Procedure

1. After placing students in a semicircle so that all can see, prepare a peanut butter and jelly sandwich in front of the class.

2. Before beginning the task, describe some of its cultural context (e.g., many U.S. children like to take these sandwiches to school for lunch or for a snack; they often enjoy this with milk; etc.).

3. While preparing the sandwich, describe its preparation in considerable detail at each step in the process (e.g., first you take two slices of soft white bread, choose the preferred type of peanut butter, spread the peanut butter on the bread, spread the grape jelly over the peanut butter, cut off the crust, and then cut the sandwich into small triangles, etc.).

4. After talking through the steps while making the sandwich, ask students to do a variety of things; for example, restate the steps (in the present tense), restate the procedure (in the past tense), direct you or another student to do the activity once again (using the imperative).

5. Have students discuss their reactions to this cultural event and why (offer sandwich wedges to those who wish to taste this snack); then have them comment on favorite snacks in their own culture(s) (e.g., who prepares them, who eats them and who does not, whether the snack is a personal like or is common in their culture).

6. Repeat the operation, having students provide instructions. Follow them literally and precisely and often funny things will result, dramatizing the need for linguistic accuracy and precision. You may then repeat the activity a third time, having students direct another student and interrupting periodically to ask: What did he (she) just do? What is she (he) going to do next? In this way you can elicit verb forms in the past or future.

Additional Comments

1. This activity can emphasize language use and/or culture exploration, depending on the course needs. It can also lead to intercultural exploration by stressing comparative and contrastive aspects of common everyday tasks.

2. Think of other operations or everyday tasks performed in the target culture around which you can develop further lessons.

3. Have students think of everyday tasks common to their own culture or the target culture and come to class prepared to demonstrate and explain them to other students.

3. Exploring Cross-Cultural Miscommunication (Bosher in Fantini 1997a:169–73)

Overview

This activity requires students to write a description of a situation they have experienced with a native of the host culture that resulted in cross-cultural miscommunication. In order to familiarize students with what is expected, present examples of some typical situations beforehand.

Objectives

- To demonstrate awareness of cultural assumptions in everyday situations that can lead to cross-cultural miscommunication
- To develop vocabulary to describe cultural situations and the miscommunications that can result

General

Level—Intermediate +

Preparation time—35 minutes

Class time—Two class sessions, several days apart. 50 minutes, first day; 20 minutes, second day

Resources needed—Pencil, paper, students who have traveled abroad, teacher who is experienced in the host culture

Procedure

1. Select several cultural episodes (critical incidents) that would be interesting to or relevant for your students (e.g., episodes that involve social interaction with members of the host culture, educational situations, etc.).
2. Photocopy descriptions of the episodes separate from the possible interpretations and separate from the explanations. Or, alternatively, make overhead transparencies for a class reading of the episodes.
3. Read through the description of the episode with students. Explain any vocabulary words with which students may be unfamiliar. Ask students if they have experienced such a situation with members of the host culture and how they felt about it.
4. After students have discussed the content of the episode, hand out copies or project the transparencies of the possible interpretations of the incident. Ask students which interpretation they would choose and why, based on their cultural assumptions.

5. Offer your opinion about the most appropriate interpretation of the situation based on the cultural assumptions of the host culture.

6. When discussion of the possible interpretations has run its course, provide copies of the overhead with the explanations of the possible interpretations. Have students discuss differences between what is considered appropriate behavior in their native culture and in the host culture, using the cultural episode as an example.

7. Repeat this procedure once or twice, depending on student interest and time available.

8. Divide students into small groups. Ask them to write a description of a situation that one or more of them experienced with members of the host culture that resulted in a cross-cultural misunderstanding.

9. Have students complete the description of the cultural episode, and provide several possible interpretations of the incident for homework. Although students do not have to explain their interpretations, they should be ready to discuss the most appropriate interpretation of the incident, based on assumptions of the host culture. Encourage students to seek out representatives of the host culture for assistance in correctly interpreting the situation from their perspective.

10. When students have finished writing cultural episodes, arrange students from two groups into a circle, with students from each group facing each other. Have the groups exchange their cultural episodes, and read the episode of the other group, as well as the possible interpretations. Students should discuss their interpretations of each situation and the differences between the assumptions of their own culture and the host culture.

Additional Information

As a follow-up activity, encourage students to develop strategies for interpreting and responding appropriately in cross-cultural situations to reduce the potential for miscommunication. For example, students could talk with the other person about what has gone wrong when there has been a misunderstanding.

4. Comparing Cultural Events (Fitzgerald in Fantini 1997a:174–75)

Overview

Students sometimes lack the confidence to engage in conversation or practice their language skills with native speakers of the target language. One reason for this is a fear of not knowing how to act. This activity enables students to discuss behavioral differences appropriate for a given situation.

Objectives

- To demonstrate awareness of different cultural practices in different cultures
- To learn appropriate behavior for a given situation
- To practice informal letter writing skills

General

Levels—Any

Preparation time—5 minutes

Class time—1 hour

Material needed—5- to 10-minute film clip

Procedure

1. Select a short film clip that shows a cultural event in the target culture, such as a dinner party, a birthday party, holiday celebrations.
2. Give students the chart in Figure 11 and ask them to complete the first column while watching the clip.
3. After viewing, ask students in groups to discuss what takes place in their own culture. Have them complete the last column of the chart.
4. Ask students to imagine they are living in the target culture environment, and having attended the event shown in the film clip, they decide to write a letter to a friend telling him or her about the event.

Additional Information

1. The activity leads nicely into project work. Ask the students, in groups, to find additional materials about the cultural event (e.g., pictures, photographs, articles, clothes).
2. If you have available space in the classroom the students can design a "cultural wall" to display their work and materials.
3. A cultural library is an effective way of storing students' work. Ensure that it is accessible to other students and teachers in the school who may be interested in finding out about different cultural habits.
4. To demonstrate their understanding of the different cultural approaches to an event, students could perform a short role-play.

Appendix

Name of Event:

Name of Event:

_____

Student's Country: _____   Host Culture: _____

Where is the event taking place?

_____

Who or what is involved?

_____

Column 1	Column 2

What is happening?

_____   _____
_____   _____
_____   _____
_____   _____
_____   _____

Figure 11
Sample Chart

5. Culture Shocks (Lange and Park in Fantini 1997a:176–77)

Overview

A Steven Spielberg movie, *Indiana Jones and the Temple of Doom,* showed an exotic table setting covered with sumptuous food, which the Western guests were anticipating with delight, only to discover, when they lifted the lid, a pile of steaming hot monkey brains. Similarly, this activity generates shocking or surprising cross-cultural incidents and also helps students learn how to express their reactions through language.

Objectives

- To understand cultural differences, especially those with a potential for provoking shocking reactions
- To practice the language associated with reactions such as shock, surprise, delight, etc.

General

Level—Advanced
Preparation time—5 minutes
Class time—1 hour
Materials needed—None

Procedure

1. Give several examples of how you were surprised at the way certain things were done in the target culture—events that made you more aware of your own cultural values; e.g., astonishment at people slurping noodles, your alarm (quite often accompanied by screams) at seeing a whole fish (with its eyes staring up at you) on a plate, or if you were given a gift of a silkworm to eat (a luxury for the giver but horrifying to the receiver), how you might react and why.

2. Practice language that will help students to express their reactions and how to explain politely the reason for their reaction.

3. Ask each student to think of a situation where she or he experienced or observed someone undergoing an unusual emotional experience arising from cultural differences and to write the situation down on a piece of paper. (Make sure students maintain a neutral stance in their description.)

4. Then, in rotating pairs, they interview a number of people and take notes, asking them what their reaction would be in that situation and why.

5. After students summarize their findings on real and possible reactions related to actual or imaginary experiences in the host culture, conclude the activity by comparing and contrasting what are considered rude/tactful/polite reactions and the different effects they have on people of the target culture.

6. Turn off the Stereo(type) (Nakata in Fantini 1997a:206–207)

Overview

Asking learners to identify stereotypes they hold about members of the target culture and about themselves helps bring these into awareness. Discussion and comparison of widely held stereotypes help point out vast discrepancies and, in the process, help reduce students' stereotypical impressions while they are learning more about each other.

Objectives

- To explore assumptions students hold about various cultures
- To explore the validity of these assumptions
- To reduce overgeneralized stereotypical impressions that are commonly held

General

Levels—Any

Preparation time—10 minutes

Class time—1 hour

Materials needed—None

Procedure

1. Provide students with a copy of the sheet in Figure 12 and ask them to fill it in.
2. Then have them form small groups and compare their responses.
3. Have them use the sheet to develop a questionnaire for people from the culture being stereotyped to ask whether they believe the stereotype is valid or not.

Americans

are always _____.

are never _____.

are sometimes _____.

like _____.

don't like _____.

French

are always _____.

are never _____.

are sometimes _____.

like _____.

don't like _____.

Mexicans

are always _____.

are never _____.

are sometimes _____.

like _____.

don't like _____.

I / We

am/are always _____.

am/are never _____.

am/are sometimes _____.

like _____.

don't like _____.

Figure 12
Identifying Stereotypes

4. Have the groups report their findings to the class.

5. Hold a discussion on the use and validity of stereotypes.

Additional Information

Interviewing people from various cultures about positive and negative aspects of English-speaking people, of themselves, and of each other, could be one follow-up activity to continue the exploration of stereotypical impressions. Substitute other groups in the form as appropriate to your situation.

In addition to these examples, a wealth of other activities are available in intercultural publications.

Assessment

Foreign language educators who incorporate new standards goal areas into their work will also face new assessment challenges, especially in the Comparisons goal area. To aid in thinking about assessment, the Standards document provides "Sample Progress Indicators" for each of the standards and at various grade levels (*SFLL* 1996:54–57). However, evaluating progress toward the development of intercultural competence and the A+ASK dimensions presents additional challenges. Whereas teachers know how to assess knowledge and skills, awareness and attitude have seldom been part of assessment; they are also less subject to quantification and documentation. Yet, if all four dimensions are important to Comparisons goal work, all will require some form of monitoring and evaluation.

Fortunately, approaches to assessment have changed in recent years. In the language field, these changes occurred in part because proficiency assessment provides better indicators of language performance than the more traditional letter or number grades used to evaluate academic achievement. This trend has been coupled with a move toward global assessments that include the learner in the evaluative process. Portfolio assessment is a good example of such an approach that continues to gain in acceptance, and examples of portfolio approaches are also cited in the Standards document (*SFLL* 1996:90–91). Together, proficiency and portfolio approaches provide a good base for assessing Comparisons outcomes as well. However, two other widely used instruments may also help assess intercultural competence.

The first is a Cross-Cultural Adaptability Inventory (CCAI) (Kelley and Meyers 1992). Although this instrument would not normally be used by a language teacher as published, what it measures and how it does this is pertinent. The CCAI responds to several concerns related to the development of intercultural competence. These are to (1) understand the factors or qualities that enhance cross-cultural effectiveness; (2) assess those factors or qualities in which one is strong and those needing improvement; (3) decide whether to seek an experience in a culturally diverse context (i.e., whether to live, study, or work in a different culture); (4) prepare to enter another culture through training; and (5) improve interactional skills with people from other cultures.

The inventory cites both personal characteristics and learnable behaviors and is designed to assist in determining the extent to which learners exhibit those characteristics most correlated with effectiveness with people from another culture. Four areas are identified: emotional resilience, flexibility/openness, perceptual acuity, and personal autonomy. High scores in these four areas indicate greater chances of cross-cultural adaptation and success. A correlated Action-Planning Guide provides ideas for increasing one's cross-cultural adaptability in each area. The process and content of the inventory, together with the guide, can aid the foreign language teacher and learners (through self-assessment) in identifying and working on factors associated with cross-cultural success.

The second instrument is a tool developed for use by both learner and teacher to help in assessing intercultural competence development. It is known as the YOGA Form (*YOGA* stands for Your Objectives, Guidelines, and Assessment) (Fantini 1995) and includes the four areas of A+ASK (plus language proficiency) at four developmental levels—from intercultural sojourner (short-term experiences of about four to six weeks, typical of high school vacation trips or summer exchanges); academic semester abroad programs and internships (of a longer duration of about four to eight months); a professional level (appropriate for staff working in an intercultural or multicultural context); and specialists (trainers and educators who conduct intercultural orientation). Figure 13 shows an excerpt from the sojourner level, which is to be used both for self-evaluation and assessment by another party ("0" is nil and "5" is high development).

When the ACTFL Proficiency Scale is utilized to assess language proficiency in conjunction with this form, it provides a fifth indicator of intercultural competence development.

Awareness *I demonstrate awareness of*

- differences in language and culture.   0 1 2 3 4 5
- my negative reactions to these differences
  (fear, laughter, disgust, superiority, etc.).   0 1 2 3 4 5
- how the context affects/alters my interaction with others.   0 1 2 3 4 5
- how I am viewed by members of the host culture.   0 1 2 3 4 5

Attitude *I demonstrate that I am ready and willing to*

- interact with members of the host culture (I don't avoid them;
  I don't always seek the company only of my compatriots, etc.).   0 1 2 3 4 5
- learn from my hosts, their language and their culture.   0 1 2 3 4 5
- try to communicate in the host language.   0 1 2 3 4 5
- behave in ways judged "appropriate" by my hosts.   0 1 2 3 4 5
- deal with the emotions and frustrations caused by my
  participation in the host culture in addition to the pleasures
  which it offers.   0 1 2 3 4 5

Skills

- I demonstrate flexibility when interacting with persons
  from the host culture.   0 1 2 3 4 5
- I use models appropriate to the host culture.   0 1 2 3 4 5
- I avoid offending my hosts with my behavior, dress, etc.   0 1 2 3 4 5
- I am able to contrast the host culture with my own.   0 1 2 3 4 5
- I use strategies which aid my adaptation and reduce
  cultural stress.   0 1 2 3 4 5
- I develop strategies for learning the host language
  and about the host culture.   0 1 2 3 4 5

Knowledge

- I can cite a basic definition of culture and identify
  its components.   0 1 2 3 4 5
- I can contrast aspects of the host linguaculture with my own.   0 1 2 3 4 5
- I know the essential norms and taboos (greetings, dress,
  behaviors, etc.) of the host culture.   0 1 2 3 4 5
- I recognize signs of culture stress and I know strategies
  for overcoming them.   0 1 2 3 4 5
- I know some techniques for maximizing my learning
  of the host language and culture.   0 1 2 3 4 5

Figure 13

YOGA Assessment Form (Sojourner Level)

VI. Looking Ahead

> Who the hell do you think you are to say the world is so and
> so . . . just because you think the world is so and so? Who gave
> you the authority? . . . The world is a strange place . . . full of mystery
> and awe.
>
> —Carlos Castaneda

The Comparisons goal, and the Cultures goal are extremely important areas of foreign language education whose time for systemic development has come. Fortunately, writers of the Standards document were visionary in their conception and incorporated Comparisons as an explicit goal of foreign language learning. As a result, the standards provide strong support for working toward developing intercultural competence in our learners. Moreover, they signal the possibility of increased cooperation between language educators and interculturalists in order to accomplish this. As they explore this goal, foreign language educators will benefit greatly by drawing on work already done by interculturalists, just as interculturalists will certainly benefit from closer involvement with FL educators.

Comparisons exploration adds important new dimensions to the learning traditionally promoted within the study of a foreign or second language. For that exploration to proceed at all, however, requires the ongoing work of culture exploration—*culture* both with a big *C* and a little *c* (i.e., the culture of the arts, literature, music, etc., as well as the everyday culture of the speakers of the target tongue). Comparisons work is based on the systematic comparing and contrasting of the learner's linguaculture and the one under study, seeking out both differences and similarities and possibly discovering in the process universal dimensions as well that flow from our shared humanity. It is clear that in addition to scrutiny of the target culture, Comparisons ensures that learners also develop awareness of their own culture, otherwise taken for granted because we seldom have cause to question and inspect what we have always been assumed to be the *way of the world*. In this sense, Comparisons exploration will surely add much to the general education of every learner as well.

Pursuit of the Comparisons goal helps the learner break out of the limited paradigm of monolingualism and monoculturalism, and in the process, out of an ethnocentric view of the world. It moves the learner further down the path toward bilingualism and biculturalism as he or she acquires new ways of perceiving, thinking, knowing, and doing. It provides the learner not only with more knowledge but different knowledge—the learner will not only know more, but know differently as he or she learns to understand through new ways of making sense and meaning of the world.

Challenges

> If you find a path with no obstacles, it probably doesn't lead anywhere.
>
> —Anonymous

Foreign language educators will need to meet several challenges if Comparisons goal work is to be effective. Most practicing FL teachers today were educated before Comparisons (and other goal areas) were either widely understood or addressed. As the expanded goals become more widely adopted and implemented, teacher education programs presumably will begin to address them more systematically as part of teacher preparation. In the meantime, however, practicing teachers will need to find ways to further their development in these areas through collegial collaborations as well as through professional workshops and institutes. Together, we are breaking new ground.

A related concern is that most approaches of the past quarter of a century, while expanding methodological options, provide little guidance in several new goal areas. Each approach—audiolingual, silent way, counseling language-learning, total physical response, and others—contributed fresh perspectives to the teaching-learning process, but like all paradigms, ignored others. While utilizing to advantage what each has to offer, we must also recognize that no one approach is suited for all purposes or all learners.

Although such approaches can at times create a satisfying learning experience, they are capable of generating their own *methodological* culture. Methodological cultures seldom bear any semblance to the ways of interacting and communicating appropriate to the target culture. No matter how successfully one manipulates cuisenaire rods when teaching Italian (*à la* silent way, for example), although the learner may develop self-reliance in figuring out grammatical structures, it reveals little about interactive behaviors appropriate among Italians. Indeed, most approaches are unconcerned with the vision of language learning reflected in the five goals, and especially Comparisons. It will be the task of foreign language educators to rethink curriculum planning and implementation if Comparisons work is to succeed.

In carrying out Cultures and Comparisons work, teachers will also need to assess their current level of competence. A Teacher YOGA Form provides such an instrument, addressing six commonly acknowledged competency areas (Fantini in Freeman 1993:43–45):

- Interpersonal Relations
- Cultural/Intercultural
- Language/Linguistics
- Language Acquisition and Learning

- Language Teaching (including curriculum design and lesson planning, implementation, and assessment)
- Professionalism

For our present purpose, however, we are concerned with Cultural/Intercultural Competencies, presented in Figure 14. The key used is as follows (with +/– to indicate intermediate points):

0 = NA (Not applicable)

1 = Need for growth/development

2 = Acceptable

3 = Competent

The form may be used in three ways:

- To clarify objectives for interns (in a preservice case) or for practicing teachers (in an inservice case)
- To provide guidelines for periodic monitoring over time (e.g., during an internship), or for a longer duration (in the case of the practicing teacher)
- To establish common assessment procedures for use at various moments by both intern/teacher and observer/mentor/supervisor

In other words, it provides formative, summative, and normative indicators by focusing on where the teacher is at the moment, how the teacher is getting along, and how the teacher fares within each competency area.

Finally, as Lindquist and Rosen (1997:1) point out in a discussion relating foreign language standards to their own experience with mathematics standards, "[D]eveloping the standards is only the beginning—the excitement and hard work are yet to come." In that same volume, Phillips stresses the importance of collaboration among professionals to develop effective classroom practices, to reform curriculum, and "the need for experimentation, reflection, and reform," which will in turn inform the Standards. "Gone forever are the days of narrowly defined outcomes and prescriptive approaches derived from a neat but inadequate theory of learning" (Phillips 1997:xiii).

Inclusion of sociocultural dimension in the lesson:

— is aware of and attentive to sociolinguistic variables $\quad$ 0/–1+/–2+/–3+

— uses appropriate target language/social interactional activities $\quad$ 0/–1+/–2+/–3+

— addresses target language culture in different content
and context areas: readings, discussions, topics, etc. $\quad$ 0/–1+/–2+/–3+

Presence of cultural dimension in classroom dynamics:

— is sensitive to/respects student cultural differences $\quad$ 0/–1+/–2+/–3+

— uses the cultural diversity of students to advantage $\quad$ 0/–1+/–2+/–3+

— fosters students' interest in and understanding
of the target culture $\quad$ 0/–1+/–2+/–3+

— creates opportunities for students to experience the target
culture (not just the "methodological" culture) $\quad$ 0/–1+/–2+/–3+

— fosters students' respect for cultural diversity $\quad$ 0/–1+/–2+/–3+

Inclusion of intercultural dimension

— compares and contrasts target and native cultures $\quad$ 0/–1+/–2+/–3+

— explores intercultural processes (stages, options,
consequences) $\quad$ 0/–1+/–2+/–3+

— responds to intercultural conflicts if they arise $\quad$ 0/–1+/–2+/–3+

— explores impact of language on intercultural entry $\quad$ 0/–1+/–2+/–3+

**Aware of, sensitive and responsive to, intercultural
challenges of the teaching situation:**

— in the classroom $\quad$ 0/–1+/–2+/–3+

— in the institution $\quad$ 0/–1+/–2+/–3+

— in the community $\quad$ 0/–1+/–2+/–3+

— and in the target culture (if applicable) $\quad$ 0/–1+/–2+/–3+

Others: _____ $\quad$ 0/–1+/–2+/–3+

_____ $\quad$ 0/–1+/–2+/–3+

Figure 14
YOGA Teacher Assessment Form—Part II. Culture/Intercultural Teacher Competencies

The Potential—Transcending

Developing intercultural communicative competence for ourselves and for others is a shared challenge—for language educators and interculturalists alike—but its attainment promises significant rewards. Intercultural competence offers the possibility of transcending the limitations of one's singular worldview. "If you want to know about water, don't ask a goldfish," is a quote frequently heard among interculturalists. Those who have never experienced another culture nor labored to communicate through a second language, like the goldfish, are often unaware of the very milieu in which they have always existed. Contact with other worldviews through an expanded vision of language study can result in a shift of perspective, along with a concomitant appreciation for the diversity and richness of human beings. This paradigm shift is the kind that one writer portrayed as a historic revolution, one that occurs within the head and the mind, as personal transformation, and *change from the inside out* (Ferguson 1980:17–20).

As language educators, we may indeed have a significant role in that revolution. A concern with cross-cultural effectiveness and appropriateness—coupled with second- or foreign-language development—will, it is hoped, lead beyond tolerance and understanding to a genuine appreciation of others. For this to happen, however, we need to develop the awareness, attitudes, skills, and knowledge that will make us better participants on a local and global level, able to understand and to empathize with others in new ways. Exposure to more than one language, culture, and worldview, in a positive context, offers such a promise. The goal of Comparisons, when thoughtfully considered and consistently implemented in the foreign language curriculum, can help move us closer to that promise.

NOTES

1. The author is indebted to Dr. Patrick R. Moran, a colleague and faculty member, for his comments and suggestions in preparing this chapter, and to Shirley Capron, Research Librarian at the School for International Training, who provided valuable research assistance.
2. Note: In this article, the term "Comparisons," when capitalized, refers to the Comparisons goal area of the National Standards.

REFERENCES

Adler, Peter S. 1976. "Beyond Culture Identity," in Larry A. Samovar & Richard E. Porter, eds., *Intercultural Communication.* 2nd ed. Belmont, CA: Wadsworth.

Agar, Michael. 1994. "The Intercultural Frame." *The International Journal of Intercultural Relations* 18:2. New York: Pergamon.

Anglin, Jeremy M. 1995. "Classifying the World through Language." *The International Journal of Intercultural Relations* 19:161–81. New York: Pergamon.

————. 1970. *The Growth of Word Meaning.* Cambridge, MA: MIT Press.

Bennett, Milton J. 1993. "Towards Ethnorelativism: A Developmental Model of Intercultural Sensitivity," pp. 21–71 in Michael Paige, ed., *Education for the Intercultural Experience.* Yarmouth, ME: Intercultural Press.

Bloom, Benjamin S. 1969. *Taxonomy of Educational Objectives: The Classification of Educational Goals.* United Kingdom: Longman Group.

Bosher, Susan. 1997. "Exploring Cross-Cultural Miscommunication," in Alvino E. Fantini, ed., *New Ways in Teaching Culture.* Alexandria, VA: TESOL.

Brown, Roger. 1958. *Words and Things.* New York: The Free Press.

Carbaugh, D., ed. 1990. *Cultural Communication and Intercultural Contact.* Hillsdale, NY: Lawrence Erlbaum.

Castaneda, Carlos. 1972. *Journey to Ixtlan: The Lessons of Don Juan.* New York: Simon & Schuster.

Chomsky, Noam. 1965. *Aspects of the Theory of Syntax.* Cambridge, MA: MIT Press.

Collier, M. J. 1989. "Cultural and Intercultural Communication Competence." *The International Journal of Intercultural Relations* 13:287–302.

Crawford-Lange, Linda M., and Dale L. Lange. 1984. "Doing the Unthinkable in the Second Language Classroom: A Process for the Integration of Language and Culture," pp. 139–77 in Theodore V. Higgs, ed., *Teaching for Proficiency: The Organizing Principle.* The American Council on the Teaching of Foreign Languages Foreign Language Education Series. Lincolnwood, IL: National Textbook.

Curle, Adam. 1972. *Mystics and Militants.* London: Tavistock Publications.

Curtiss, Susan. 1977. *Genie: A Psycholinguistic Study of a Modern-day "Wild Child."* New York: Academic Press.

Dinges, Norman G., and Kathleen D. Baldwin. 1996. "Intercultural Competence: A Research Perspective," pp. 106–23 in Dan Landis and Rabi S. Bhagat, eds., *Handbook of Intercultural Training,* 2nd ed. Thousand Oaks, CA: Sage Publications.

Fantini, Alvino E, ed. 1997a. *New Ways in Teaching Culture.* Alexandria, VA: TESOL.

————. 1997b. "A Survey of Intercultural Communication Courses," *International Journal of Intercultural Relations* 21:125–48. New York: Pergamon Press.

————, ed. 1995. Special Issue on Language, Culture and World View. *International Journal of Intercultural Relations* 19:2. New York: Pergamon Press.

————. 1995. The YOGA Form on Assessing Intercultural Competence. Brattleboro, VT: School for International Training. Unpublished.

————. 1993. "Teacher Assessment," pp. 43–55 in Donald Freeman and Steve Cornwell, eds., *New Ways in Teacher Education.* Alexandria, VA: TESOL.

————. 1985. *Language Acquisition of a Bilingual Child.* Clevedon, Avon, England: Multilingual Matters; also 1982. *La acquisición del lenguaje en un niño bilingüe.* Barcelona: Editorial Herder.

————, ed. 1984. *Cross-Cultural Orientation: A Guide for Leaders and Educators.* Brattleboro, VT: The SIT Bookstore.

————, ed. 1984. "Exploring the Community," in *Getting the Whole Picture.* Part III, pp. 22–53. Brattleboro, VT: The SIT Bookstore.

———— and William P. Dant. 1993. "Language and Intercultural Orientation: A Process Approach," pp. 79–96 in Theodore Gochenour, ed., *Beyond Experience,* 2nd ed. Yarmouth, ME: Intercultural Press.

Fantini, Beatriz C., and Alvino E. Fantini. 1997. "Artifacts, Sociofacts, Mentifacts: A Sociocultural Framework," pp. 57–61 in Alvino E. Fantini, ed., *New Ways in Teaching Culture.* Alexandria, VA: TESOL.

Ferguson, Marilyn. 1980. *The Aquarian Conspiracy.* Los Angeles: J. P. Tarcher.

Fishman, Joshua. 1976. Bilingual Education: An International Sociological Perspective. Recorded keynote address. San Antonio: Fifth International Bilingual Education Conference.

Fitzgerald, Susan. 1997. "Comparing Cultural Events," pp. 174–175 in Alvino E. Fantini, ed., *New Ways in Teaching Culture.* Alexandria, VA: TESOL.

Freire, Paulo. 1998. *Teachers as Cultural Workers: Letters to Those Who Dare Teach.* Boulder, CO: Westview Press.

———. 1973. *Education for Critical Consciousness.* New York: Continuum.

———. 1970. *Pedagogy of the Oppressed.* New York: Continuum.

Gattegno, Caleb. 1976. *Educational Solutions Newsletter: On Knowledge.* V:5, New York: Schools for the Future.

Gochenour, Theodore. 1993. *Beyond Experience: The Experiential Approach to Cross-cultural Education.* Yarmouth, ME: Intercultural Press.

——— and Anne Janeway. 1993. "Seven Concepts in Cross-cultural Interaction: A Training Design," pp. 1–9 in Theodore Gochenour, ed., *Beyond Experience: The Experiential Approach to Cross-cultural Education.* Yarmouth, ME: Intercultural Press.

Gudykunst, William B., and T. Nishida. 1989. "Theoretical Perspectives for Studying Intercultural Communication," pp. 17–46 in M. K. Asante & W. S. Gudykunst, eds., *Handbook of International and Intercultural Communication.* Newbury Park, CA: Sage.

Hall, Edward T. 1959. *The Silent Language.* Greenwich, CT: Fawcett Publications.

———. 1976. *Beyond Culture.* New York: Doubleday.

Hoopes, David. 1979. "Intercultural Communication Concepts and the Psychology of Intercultural Experience," in Margaret Pusch, ed., *Multicultural Education: A Cross-cultural Training Approach.* Yarmouth, ME: Intercultural Press.

Hymes, Dell. 1972. "Models of the Interaction of Language and Social Life," pp. 1–72 in J. Gumperz & D. Hymes, eds. *Directions in Sociolinguistics: The Ethnography of Communication.* New York: Holt, Rinehart & Winston.

Kealey, Daniel J. 1990. *Cross-cultural Effectiveness: A Study of Canadian Technical Advisors Overseas.* Hull, Quebec: Canadian International Development Agency.

Kelley, Colleen, and Judith Meyers. 1992. *The Cross-cultural Adaptability Inventory.* Yarmouth, ME: Intercultural Press.

Kohls, L. Robert. 1979. *Survival Kit for Overseas Living.* Chicago: Intercultural Network/SYSTRAN Publications.

Kolb, David A. 1984. *Experiential Learning: Experience as the Source of Learning and Development.* Englewood Cliffs, NJ: Prentice Hall.

Kramsch, Claire. 1989. "New Directions in the Teaching of Language and Culture." Occasional Papers. Baltimore, MD: Johns Hopkins University. Unpublished.

Lane, Harlan. 1976. *The Wild Boy of Aveyron.* Cambridge, MA: Harvard University Press.

Lange, Elizabeth, and Jong-oe Park. 1997. "Culture Shocks," in Alvino E. Fantini, ed., *New Ways in Teaching Culture.* Alexandria, VA: TESOL.

Lindquist, Mary Montgomery, and Linda P. Rosen. 1997. "Professional Collaboration: A Perspective from the Mathematics Standards," in June K. Phillips, ed., *Collaborations: Meeting New Goals, New Realities.* Lincolnwood, IL: National Textbook Co.

Martin, Judith N., ed. 1989. "Special Issue: Intercultural Communication Competence," in *International Journal of Intercultural Relations* 13:3. New York: Pergamon Press.

Moore, Zena, and Mark Anthony English. 1997. "Linguistic and Cultural Comparisons: Middle School African American Students Learning Arabic," in June K. Phillips, ed., *Collaborations: Meeting New Goals, New Realities.* Lincolnwood, IL: National Textbook Co.

Nakata, Yoshiyuki. 1997. "Turn Off the Stereo(type)," pp. 206–207 in Alvino E. Fantini, ed., *New Ways in Teaching Culture.* Alexandria, VA: TESOL.

National Standards in Foreign Language Education Project. 1996. *Standards for Foreign Language Learning. Preparing for the 21st Century.* Lawrence, KS: Allen Press.

Nichols, Edwin J. 1990. *The Philosophical Aspects of Cultural Difference.* SIETAR Summer Institute. Washington, DC: Georgetown University. Unpublished handout.

Omaggio, Alice. 1986. *Teaching Language in Context.* Boston, MA: Heinle & Heinle.

Phillips, June K., ed. 1997. *Collaborations: Meeting New Goals, New Realities.* Lincolnwood, IL: National Textbook Co.

Pulaski Spencer, M. A. 1971. *Understanding Piaget.* New York: Harper & Row.

Pusch, Margaret, ed. 1979. *Multicultural Education: A Cross-cultural Training Approach.* Yarmouth, ME: Intercultural Press.

Pyke, R. 1966. *Language in Relation to a United Theory of the Structure of Human Behavior.* The Hague: Mouton.

Rymer, R. 1993. *Genie: An Abused Child's Flight from Silence.* New York: HarperCollins.

Schaller, Susan. 1991. *A Man without Words.* New York: Summit Books.

Steinfatt, T. M. 1989. "Linguistic Relativity: Toward a Broader View," pp. 35–78 in S. Ting-Toomey and F. Korzenny, editors. *Language, Communication and Culture: Current Directions.* Newbury Park, CA: Sage.

Stevens, John O. 1971. *Awareness: Exploring, Experimenting and Experiencing.* Moab, Utah: Real People Press.

Ting-Toomey, S., and F. Korzenny, eds. 1989. *Language, Communication and Culture: Current Directions.* Newbury Park, CA: Sage.

Vonnegut, Jr., Kurt. 1974. *Wampeters, Foma and Granfallons.* New York: Delacorte.

Whorf, Benjamin L. 1956. *Language, Thought and Reality.* Cambridge, MA: The MIT Press.

Wiseman, R. L., and J. Koester, eds. 1993. *Intercultural Communication Competence.* Newbury Park, CA: Sage.

Appendix

A Selected Bibliography of Intercultural Resources

Althen, Gary, ed. 1994. *Learning Across Cultures.* NAFSA: Association of International Educators.

Brislin, Richard, and Tomoko Yoshida. 1994. *Intercultural Communication Training: An Introduction.* Thousand Oaks, CA: Sage Publications.

———, eds. 1994. *Improving Intercultural Interactions: Modules for Cross-cultural Training Programs.* Thousand Oaks, CA: Sage Publications.

Fantini, Alvino E., ed. 1997. *New Ways in Teaching Culture.* Alexandria, VA: TESOL.

———, ed. 1984. *Cross-cultural Orientation: A Guide for Leaders and Educators.* Brattleboro, VT: The SIT Bookstore.

———, ed. 1984. *Getting the Whole Picture: A Student's Field Guide to Language Acquisition and Culture Exploration.* Brattleboro, VT: The SIT Bookstore.

———, ed. 1984. *Beyond the Language Classroom: Identifying and Using Resources for the Development of Communicative Competence.* Brattleboro, VT: The SIT Bookstore.

Fowler, Sandra M., and Monica G. Mumford, eds. 1995. *Intercultural Sourcebook: Cross-cultural Training Methods.* Vol I. Yarmouth, ME: Intercultural Press.

Gaston, Jan. 1984. *Cultural Awareness Teaching Techniques.* Brattleboro, VT: ProLingua Associates.

Gochenour, Theodore, ed. 1993. *Beyond Experience: The Experiential Approach to Cross-cultural Education.* Yarmouth, ME: Intercultural Press.

Kohls, L. Robert. 1979. *Survival Kit for Overseas Living.* Chicago, IL: Intercultural Network/SYSTRAN Publications.

——— and John M. Knight. 1994. *Developing Intercultural Awareness: A Cross-cultural Training Handbook.* Yarmouth, ME: Intercultural Press.

Landis, Dan, and Rabi S. Bhagat, eds. 1996. *Handbook of Intercultural Training.* 2nd ed. Thousand Oaks, CA: Sage Publications.

Lustig, Myron W., and Jolene Koester. 1993. *Intercultural Competence: Interpersonal Communication Across Cultures.* New York: HarperCollins College Publishers.

Pusch, Margaret, ed. 1979. *Multicultural Education: A Cross-cultural Training Approach.* Yarmouth, ME: Intercultural Press.

Ricard, Virginia B. 1993. *Developing Intercultural Communication Skills.* Malabar, FL: Kreiger Publishing Company.

Seelye, H. Ned. 1996. *Experiential Activities for Intercultural Learning.* Vol I. Yarmouth, ME: Intercultural Press.

Storti, Craig. 1997. *Culture Matters: The Peace Corps Cross-Cultural Workbook.* Washington, DC: Peace Corps Information Collection and Exchange.

Summerfield, Ellen. 1997. *Survival Kit for Multicultural Living.* Yarmouth, ME: Intercultural Press.

Tomalin, Barry, and Susan Stempleski. 1993. *Cultural Awareness.* New York: Oxford University Press.

Vogel Zanger, Virginia. 1993. *Face to Face: Communication, Culture, and Collaboration.* Boston, MA: Heinle & Heinle.

Weeks, William, Paul B. Pedersen, and Richard W. Brislin. 1979. *A Manual of Structured Experiences for Cross-cultural Learning.* Yarmouth, ME: Intercultural Press.

Wiseman, R. L., and J. Koester, eds. 1993. *Intercultural Communication Competence.* Newbury Park, CA: Sage.

6

Meeting the Needs of All Learners: Case Studies in Computer-Based Foreign Language Reading

Mary Ann Lyman-Hager
San Diego State University

Joanne Burnett
University of Southern Mississippi

Introduction

Within the framework of the standards, it is stated that in order to attain the Five Cs of foreign language study, "students require a foreign language program that provides rich curricular experiences" (National Standards in Foreign Language Education Project 1996:28). The computerized reading of an excerpt from *Une vie de boy* (Oyono 1956) offers one such possibility for

Mary Ann Lyman-Hager (Ph.D., University of Idaho), professor of French in the Department of French and Italian and director of the National Foreign Language Center at San Diego State University, teaches courses in second language acquisition theory and the appropriate uses of multimedia and technology in foreign language instruction. Her research interests include theory-based applications of distance education and multimedia technologies in language learning, and research in second language reading. Her articles have appeared in *Foreign Language Annals, The Modern Language Journal,* the *CALICO Journal, Le Journal du Multimédia, The French Review,* the *IALL Journal,* and others. She has co-authored a book on using the Internet in teaching basic French (*Surf's Up*) and has authored a multimedia CD-ROM for teaching French texts and literature at several levels, *A l'Aventure.*

Joanne Burnett (Ph.D., Pennsylvania State University) is an assistant professor of French and second language acquisition at the University of Southern Mississippi. She is a frequent conference presenter on issues related to technology and the language classroom and is co-author of an interactive reading of *Le Rossignol* on the CD-ROM program *A l'Aventure.* She teaches all levels of French language and civilization and courses on methodology and language acquisition in the Master of Arts in the Teaching of Languages program at USM.

enriching the study of French. It particularly focuses on meeting Standard 1.2 on interpretive communication:

> The Interpretive Mode is focused on the appropriate cultural interpretation of meanings that occur in written and spoken forms where there is no recourse to the active negotiation of meaning with the writer or the speaker. Such instances of "one-way" reading or listening include the cultural interpretation of texts, movies, radio and television broadcasts and speeches. Interpreting the cultural meaning of texts, oral or written, must be distinguished from the notion of reading and listening "comprehension," where the term could refer to understanding a text with an American mind set. Put another way, interpretation differs from comprehension in that the former implies the ability to "read (or listen) between the lines" (*SFLL* 1996:32–33).

The computerized reading of a Francophone African text additionally allows students to work on aspects of the Cultures Standard 2.2, which calls for students to focus on what are termed the "tangible products of the culture studied," such as a literary excerpt, as well as Comparisons Standard 4.2, which asks students to expand their understanding of culture by comparing the culture studied to their own. As part of the weave of curricular elements (*SFLL* 1996:29), technology in the form of a computerized reading may be an appropriate medium for blending several standards goals at once.

The *Une vie de boy* computer program[1] —which provides cultural, grammatical, and lexical glosses in English and French for the first 1,754 words of the Cameroonian novel—allows the student to attain information about language structure, reading strategies, and cultural information critical to understanding the context of this culture. These three areas all correspond to elements in the curricular weave in the standards document. (A printout of two computer screens from the program is found in Appendix A.) The program's eight-page introductory section additionally presents an explicit, systematic discussion of potentially beneficial strategies to be used by the users, sets the context for the Oyono text, and outlines the use of the various types of glosses available in the computer program.

The first chapter of *Une vie de boy* (Oyono 1956) additionally affords the learner a "complete" story, which has aesthetic and pedagogical merits over fragmented excerpts usually found in beginning readers. (The events of the first chapter actually take place before the main events of the novel and can be used as an introduction to a reading of the whole novel.)[2] Additionally, the program may meet the needs of a variety of learners in view of the on-line helps and the self-paced manner in which it may be approached. It may also offer a starting point for entry into the literate skills necessary for students to become lifelong learners of a target language, an ultimate goal of the standards initiative.

Although it is clear that computer technology can mediate a variety of learning circumstances, without continued research and attention to how the technology is exploited by all learners—the successful student as well as those who experience less success—both in language and in computer use, technological innovations may not provide the enriching curricular experiences hoped for.

This chapter summarizes the findings of an earlier research study carried out at the Pennsylvania State University (Lyman-Hager, Davis, Burnett, and Chennault 1993) in which successful vocabulary retention was attained for third-semester French students using the program, and presents a detailed analysis of three problematic cases drawn from the same pool of students who completed the computerized reading. Recall protocols, vocabulary tests, pre-class student questionnaires, and software evaluation protocols were combined with the tracking data (which recorded every keystroke made by the student) to help determine how students made use of informational glosses and how they interpreted the text as a result. As the individual analyses will reveal, all three students struggled with the text to the extent that this particular program's capabilities were not sufficient in and of themselves to bring about basic comprehension of the text for two of the students or assist in high levels of vocabulary retention for all three. Meeting the needs of all learners within standards guidelines may mean that alternative learning approaches will have to be developed for the various standards, with the realization that some standards will be affected in different ways for different learners. Analyzing readers' problems of miscomprehension and misinterpretation as well as difficulties with lexical acquisition is a first step. A greater challenge lies in designing both technological and curricular programs to better meet the needs of individual readers such as these.

Background to the Study

Reading is central to the goal areas of Cultures, Connections, Comparisons, and Communication and is therefore considered as important an area to school success as is first language reading to general academic learning. Foreign language reading in particular is an area thought to be well suited to technological applications (Blake 1992). What do we know about the nature of reading in this new medium? Although Grabe (1996) asserts that we have learned a great deal about reading in the past years (citing significant research in the areas of cognitive and educational psychology), this research may be limited to reading in print-based media and in first languages.

Intermediate-Level Foreign Language Reading

Students have expressed great difficulty in reading foreign language texts, particularly when so many vocabulary words are unknown. This is not surprising. In the past decade, oral communicative competence has received much greater attention in foreign language education than have literary skills. In response to this, many faculty currently favor a four-skills (plus culture) curricular approach in lower levels of French language instruction, stressing the building of transferable skills and strategies among all four skills (listening, speaking, reading, and writing) and the interaction of linguistic and cultural phenomena. (It is anticipated that as faculty gain familiarity with the standards they might find that the framework of communicative modes—interpersonal, interpretive, and presentational—facilitates greater interaction than the former notion of skills and culture.) Moreover, there is considerable pressure on the undergraduate foreign language curriculum to include voices from diverse cultures. Likewise, educators are called upon to produce graduates who exhibit cultural sensitivity and who also have excellent oral and written communication skills. It is clear that we need to examine new methods for out-of-class individualized study with an eye to improving the balance of the four skills and cultural awareness in the curriculum. The enhancement of literacy skills, and reading in particular, appears to be at the heart of the dilemma. Students' understanding of the underlying cultures (especially of those that are unfamiliar) is closely interrelated to their reading proficiency, as culture plays a critical role in reading (Feldman 1990; Hewitt 1990; Swaffar, Arens, and Byrnes 1991).

The third semester at the university, in particular, marks the beginning of the emergence of solid intermediate-level skills for most learners. Learners at this stage transfer many of the previously learned rules of L2 grammar, their newly acquired L2 vocabulary, and their prior knowledge of the L2 culture to new situations (as described in the ACTFL Provisional Proficiency Guidelines 1989). Learners are also developing reading skills and interpretative strategies to deal with authentic documents of various lengths and cultural "weights" (i.e., difficulties and/or densities), such as reading an advertisement for an apartment rental or a short literary excerpt about life in a French subsidized housing project, texts included in the third-semester textbook *Allons Voir Les Français et Les Francophones!* used at Penn State, the site of this study. Likewise, at this stage the learner is forming lasting impressions of French and Francophone culture, and the notion of inclusion of typically underrepresented linguistic, cultural, or ethnic groups.

Computer-Assisted Reading in a Foreign Language

Several computerized foreign language reading programs exist currently on the market.[3] However, for the creators of the computerized version of *Une vie de boy,* none of these provided the opportunity to

1. follow a specific theoretical model of reading comprehension;
2. record students' behaviors while they are reading on-line;
3. create a shell for use in other languages and with other types of glosses, such as multimedia, digitized video and audio glosses; and
4. offer the intermediate-level learner a rather unique African perspective on Francophone culture.

Insofar as reading strategies may be operationalized in the form of computer glosses, the program's tracker could show how the students availed themselves of these glosses. Where students exhibited an unusual or quite divergent understanding of the text[4] the researcher and/or teacher could return to the computer tracking records for that student and literally "track the learner's path" through the text in order to determine how the student might have used the available information more to her advantage.

Little research exists to measure the real costs of integrating computers into the curriculum and the short- and long-term influence of computer use on learning. However, we now have enough computers in educational settings to determine how, under what conditions, and to what degree computers can affect student learning (Bozeman and House 1988). Indeed, we needed to build into the program clear-cut measures of effectiveness in order to insure continued institutional support of our approach. Two pilot studies accompanied the development of the final product. The first, conducted in the spring of 1991 after the design of the screen and glossing capabilities, determined which words and concepts students needed to know to understand the text. The second revealed which of the computer's hypertexual glosses students would select and how these glosses might affect individual readers' comprehension and interpretation.

Spring 1991: Using Student Input to Determine Glossing Content

The process of creating a glossing program or providing dictionary definitions and cultural information, references, and grammar notes was as important as the product in the interactive reading project. This process, described more thoroughly in Davis, Lyman-Hager, and Hayden (1992), involved gathering user input from French 3 students and teaching assistants about the selection of actual words to be glossed in the program. They randomly assigned sections of French 3 students to one of three treatments:

1. reading through the text quickly and circling unknown words;
2. reading the text and then immediately afterward writing recall protocols[5] in English; and
3. reading the text quickly, then writing definitions in English for preselected, underlined words.[6]

Researchers then compared this student-derived data with a ranking of "difficult words and concepts" by teaching assistants who had familiarity with the reading and knowledge of their students' performance in reading authentic texts in French.[7]

This first 1991 study occurred prior to the construction of the program and was very important in determining unknown vocabulary and students' global comprehension of the text. Nineteen sections of third-semester French language classes in the spring of 1991, plus eight teaching assistants, were used in this study. Results of the three treatments were combined to form a "master list" of words to be glossed. Students' responses to the text determined the actual content of the program. Problematic words that were identified by all three means of assessment were selected for inclusion in the computer program. The software development team entered the words to be glossed in an Excel spreadsheet, allowing for a single word to be glossed up to seven different ways.[8] The main program was written in Toolbook,[9] which allows for the creation of "hotwords" that could be linked to the Excel spreadsheet glossing entries in the seven categories. Native speakers, cultural informants, outside evaluators, and teaching assistants verified the accuracy of the content of the glosses. The program was ready for large-scale implementation with third-semester French students in the fall of 1992.

The Fall 1992 Study

The software authors had felt that it was critical to determine which types of glosses readers seemed to prefer for this particular text. They also wanted to know whether or not the computer treatment (more particularly, the coding capabilities of the computer, which allow instantaneous look-ups) offered significant long-term benefits to intermediate-level readers in French. These benefits would be measured by scores on a vocabulary-in-context quiz given the week after the treatment to both computer and noncomputer sections—and in learners' evaluations of both types of reading (print and nonprint). The vocabulary study was published in Lyman-Hager et al. (1993), and data from that study are listed in Appendix B. In addition, cases from the computerized reading group would be examined to see what strategies users actually used to assist in their comprehension and interpretation of the excerpt. Would this type of computerized "hypertextual" reading offer significant advantages to intermediate French language students—in terms of student usage of the entire variety of glosses found in the computer-mediated form of text, learning gains in vocabulary acquisition,[10] and improved strategy use? How do students who use the computer program process text differently from one another?

The study incorporated all fifteen sections of French 3 at the Pennsylvania State University in the fall of 1992. Graduate assistants charged with teaching sections of French 3 distributed an Informed Consent Form during the first week of class, along with a preclass questionnaire. The purpose of the questionnaire was to determine incoming students' various reasons for studying French, as well as their prior instruction or knowledge of the French language and of other languages. Midway through the semester, as a part of the regular course work in the language laboratory, researchers randomly assigned sections of students to either the computer or the noncomputer reading group.

The two types of readings were available in the University Learning Center multimedia laboratory for a three-day period. Thus, all students read the Oyono text in either computerized or print form in the Learning Center. Those students using the computer program received their glossing helps "on-line," while students in the noncomputer treatment group had access to pages of glosses and illustrations drawn directly from the computer program. Both treatments could opt to have the story "read" aloud by authentic speakers of French from Francophone Africa, either on audiotape or, in the case of the computer group, in on-line, digitized audio format. For difficult-to-define concepts, both treatments had access to the same pictures, although the print ones were in black and white rather than in color. Thus, the actual content of each treatment was virtually identical. The interaction of the student with the glosses in the computerized reading, however, is very different, and this is the concept we were trying to access with the computer versus noncomputer research design. The pages of text in the "default" form of the computer (before any words are selected to be glossed) are free of any potential distracting explanations. It is the individual student who selects help when needed.

There were no time limits set for either treatment, and all students were given instruction sheets and were monitored by student lab attendants, who signed the students' questionnaires to indicate that standardized procedures had been followed. Time spent on the computer program was recorded by the tracker under the students' ID numbers, as were the number of keystrokes, requests for word definitions in English and in French, cultural information, relations among characters, and requests to hear accompanying audio. The amount of time students spent looking at introductory material, and precise information about how they interacted with the program, were available through an examination of the tracking data.

Immediately after each treatment, students filled out an evaluation form and a recall protocol form, where they were asked to write, in English, their recollection of significant events in the story. At the beginning of the following week, students discussed the story in class following a uniform question-and-answer sheet, then immediately took an in-class vocabulary quiz composed of words that the teaching assistants had agreed were the most critical to the story. (Consensus on the twenty "critical" words included on the vocabulary quiz had been obtained earlier by having each of the eight teaching assistants independently read the passage and circle words they felt that students would absolutely need to understand to be able to make sense of the text.) The words were presented in the context of the original text on one page, with a matching column format on the second page.[11]

Instruments of this evaluation include tracker data from the computer program, questionnaire data, and software/reading program evaluations given to each student. The procedures of the study involved

1. examining recall protocols in detail to determine student retention of the story following computer and noncomputer treatments;

2. analyzing results of preclass questionnaires (on the axes of motivation and prior experience in the language) of noncomputer and computer groups; and

3. scoring the vocabulary quiz and running statistical tests on the computer and noncomputer groups to see if treatment had an effect on performance in this area.

Thus, the first study helped answer whether computer-assisted reading can make a difference in learners' vocabulary acquisition, one of the first important problems foreign language readers encounter. Use of the program as a substitution for a similar reading in the curriculum was repeated once per semester over a subsequent three-semester period (Spring, Summer, and Fall of 1993) to determine what strategies or aids learners choose in response to the task of reading unfamiliar material, a task encouraged in the national standards. Tracking data from this period has offered evidence that students using the computerized version of *Une vie de boy* retained more of the story's key words.[12] Additionally, students preferred the computerized version of the reading to the print version. (Appendix C summarizes the results of the courseware/reading evaluation.) The tendency of these students to prefer the quick English definition to other types of glosses, even when the efficacy of these other glosses was explained, was also strongly documented by tracking records. (See also Davis and Lyman-Hager 1997 for similar results.)

For the present study, three students from the 1992 study who did not fit the pattern of greater success on vocabulary measures and who presented rather unusual recall protocols, which summarized what they viewed as the main points of the story, were chosen from the larger pool of students. In order to have a more complete understanding of the difficulties encountered in reading comprehension, data were taken from a variety of sources:

1. preclass questionnaires;

2. tracking data of the computer program;

3. questionnaires taken just after the computer treatment;

4. recall protocols taken just after the post-treatment questionnaire;[13] and

5. vocabulary retention quizzes taken a week later.

Three Case Studies

No single study can deal with all the variations that teachers will need to consider when trying to integrate the standards into their language curriculum. This study tackles only one element: *interpretive communication via computerized print material.* Although the following individual cases were randomly assigned by section to the computerized treatment, their selection for analysis here was nonrandom. These students are described in detail in order to illustrate the power of combining data from multiple sources to shed light on individual learners' responses to text in a foreign language and on the highly individualized manner in which they process it. Additionally the study clarifies the role computer technology plays within the context of the standards for three relatively unsuccessful readers of a piece of literature that is set in a culture unfamiliar to most U.S. students.

Their initial selection was based on the striking differences in their approaches to the recall protocol task, and on the fact that all are from English-speaking families and of the same gender (female), thus eliminating possible gender explanations for the interpretations expressed on the protocol. Additionally, all three students scored below the mean for the computer group on the vocabulary retention quiz, indicating that they may be processing information differently from others (of both genders) in the computer group and that a closer analysis of their individual reading strategies might yield insights into how to strengthen their vocabulary recall skills. (The names of these students, obviously, have been changed to protect their anonymity.) Familiarity with the story is necessary to understand the students' recall protocols, so the Oyono text is reprinted in Appendix D.

Student Profile for Sara

Sara is 23 and in her third semester of college French, her ninth semester of college. She started in Spanish in her sixth semester of college but discontinued it after a semester. She is in French to satisfy the language requirement only. She reports that she usually uses the computer for word processing assignments.

Sara appeared to value the presentation, the learner interaction, and the content about equally, giving either a 4 or 5 for all items. Interestingly, she placed stars on the items with which she strongly agreed, i.e., those questions asking whether the content of the reading was easier to digest in this format, whether this method of instruction made her want to learn more about what happened next in the story, and whether using this method seemed superior to traditional methods. However, she gave a rating of 2 to the question asking if an audio recording of the text would aid her understanding of it. In fact, examining her tracking data, we found that she only used the audio once, for the pronunciation of the word *invita*.

Sara's Vocabulary Quiz

She received a 9/20, which is more than one standard deviation from the computer group's mean score of 14.1 on the vocabulary quiz. She missed the words *rosin, tordre, fouet, plaies, bagarre, fendre,* and *esquiver,* despite having looked them up and despite having looked up *fendre* and *esquiver* twice. However, she correctly defined both *case* and *gourmandise,* having looked up *case* twice, once in French and once in English, and *gourmandise* four times in English. On the last page of the reading, not only did she look up *leur gourmandise,* but she also looked up *ta gourmandise.* This makes one wonder whether it was the possessive pronouns she did not understand or the word *gourmandise* of which she needed to be reminded. Nevertheless, the English translation of *gourmandise* as "glutton" appears in the first sentence of her recall protocol. So we can assume that this word was understood after the reading was completed.

Sara's Recall Protocol Analysis

CASE #1

Recall Protocol 10:00 a.m., Nov. 2, 1992

Joseph was beaten up by his father who thought he was a glutton & for some reason his father wanted to beat up the girl's parents. Joseph goes to live with the priest who treats him well & lives happily with him & his mother still loves him. He visits his sick uncle who is eating porcupine. His mother is famous for how she prepares it & Joseph's father keeps threatening he will make Joseph sleep w/ his mother. This would embarrass Joseph so he chooses to live with the priest.

Sara

She spent about 53 minutes viewing the program. She spent little time with the introductory material and instead began reading the text right away. In the beginning she relied on the strategy of looking up words in French, for a total of 22 words. Then she decided to read through the pages of the story, perhaps to see how much lay ahead of her, since she spent less than four seconds on each page. She returned to page 3, looked up 10 more French definitions before changing strategies and relying on English definitions exclusively for a total of 128 words. She looked up English definitions much more often than the norm for the computer group. After looking up 33 French definitions, she did not return to the strategy of looking up words in the target language, except for one time for the word *alignait,* which she looked up both in French and English. Additionally, she requested information about relations among characters—*maître, ce maudit Blanc, du vieux Tinati*—and culture—*le révérend père Gilbert, le boy.* The only grammar lookup was for the *passé simple* of the verb *devenir: devins.* There is evidence that Sara reread portions of the text. On the second page of the story, She looked up *mangeurs d' hommes* in one paragraph and then looked up seven more words from the following paragraph before looking up *mangeurs d' hommes* again from the preceding paragraph. More evidence of her use of rereading as a strategy happened later. During the part of the story where there is argument about Toundi's mother saving some porcupine for him to eat, Sara looked up *gardé* then *marmite,* followed by *son bégaiement, gardé,* and *marmite* again. She looked up *marmite* once more on the following page of the story and subsequently correctly identified the word on the vocabulary quiz.

Out of a total of thirteen written pausal units,[14] Sara had nine that can be considered directly related to the story. Sara's miscomprehension may stem in part from the fact that she does not know why there was fighting among the villagers, making no reference to the sugar cubes the priest has thrown to them. She believed that Tinati is a girl ("the girl's parents") despite Toundi's having referred to him (in the text itself) as *mon compagnon* and having said *il m'avait tordu le bras*. Looking up the category RELATIONSHIP and discovering the relation of Tinati to Toundi would have perhaps cleared up this miscomprehension. Sara's sense of chronology is also somewhat confused in that she had the visit to the uncle after Toundi had gone to live with the priest. She reasoned that Toundi decided to live with the priest because his father threatened him about sleeping with his mother.

She appeared to be processing in a "bottom-up" manner, which may account for her lack of temporal coherence. She also seemed to follow her own strategies for reading, which differed from those outlined for her in both the handout of instructions given to her by the lab attendants and the introduction to the program. Sara needs to confirm meanings and strengthen her mental representation of the story. More cultural helps about the nature of insults and use of such language in Cameroonian culture could perhaps be helpful for students, like Sara, to avoid incorrect elaborations such as those found in her recall protocol.

Sharon's Student Profile

Sharon studied French in junior high (7th and 8th grades) and Spanish for four years in high school. She returned to the study of French in college, where she had one semester prior to this one. She also took Russian for one semester. She is taking the course to fulfill the language requirement for graduation. She indicated that she is 21 years old and has used a word processor for most writing assignments at the university.

Sharon appeared satisfied with the content, presentation, and learner interaction of the program, rating all categories as 4s. However, she had no opinion about whether French definitions would help her understanding of the text. But she gave a rating of 5 to the statements, "I think more cultural information would have helped my understanding of the text," and "I found the English definitions critical to my understanding of the text." One complaint, however, was that she wished "the female attendant at Sparks Bldg. would have known how to work the computers"—then she "would not have had to wait 40 minutes"—before being able to use the program. She had no opinion about whether "this method of instruction made her want to learn more about what happened next in the story," yet she gave a rating of 4 (indicating strong agreement) to the program evaluation's statement: "This method for the content seems superior to traditional methods of learning."

Sharon's Vocabulary Quiz

She correctly defined only 8 words out of 20 on the vocabulary quiz, which is also more than one standard deviation below the average for the computer group. She missed the words *case, veiller, rotin, marmite, gourmandise,* and *esquiver,* even though she had looked them up. She had looked up *gourmand* twice and *gourmandise* once and various forms of *esquiver* three times, but this was to no avail. (In fact, all three students missed *esquiver* on the quiz.) She looked up *croûtes de gales* only once, however, and the correct translation of "scabies" is written in her recall protocol. She also correctly defined *prêtre,* and the tracker shows that she looked it up twice. There seemed to be no correlation between the number of times a word was looked up and it being correctly defined on the vocabulary quiz. We could speculate that *croûtes de gales* (a rare skin condition) might have been perceptually salient for Sharon.

Sharon's Recall Protocol Analysis

CASE #2

Recall Protocol   10:25 a.m., Oct. 30, 1992

La Vie de Boy concerned the life of Taoundi—his desires to do things that his father disagreed with and his endurance to his fathers physical abuse. We are introduced to Toundi and immediately involved in the violence that occurs between his family. When wishing to do something his father does not approve of, his father gets angry and states that because Toundi is his <property>, he should do just as he (his father) says. He seeks refuge at his uncles house (who has scabies?) and something happens at dinner time that makes Toundi's mother cry. For the first time, Toundi wishes to kill his father. Later, Toundi converts to Catholicism and this infuriates and disappoints Toundi's father—who then refuses him to live in the family hut. Toundi's mother is saddened but blesses Toundi and tells him to bathe in the river if he ever becomes sick. Toundi then lives a happy life w/ Father Gilbert.

Sharon

Even though she had to wait at the center to use the program, she spent a total of 71 minutes on the program, which is significantly longer than other students studied. She also spent time reading the introductory material to the text (3 minutes 23 seconds). In contrast to Sara, her lookups were almost exclusively in English, 141 total, with the exception of *la vitesse* and *esquivai*, which she looked up in French. The only grammar explanation was for the subjunctive of the verb *finir: finisse*. She had nine cultural lookups: *Fia, le trou de mon anus, moitié, plonger, le boy, une culotte kaki, tous les gamins,* and *une goutte de mon liquide.*

Although her vocabulary quiz was not the best of the computer treatment subjects', curiously, her recall protocol is one of the best ones. Out of a total of twenty pausal units, seventeen are directly from the story. The only distortion in her recall is her statement that Toundi seeks refuge at his uncle's house, which does not happen in the story. Evidence of story elaboration in her recall is seen when she writes that Toundi's conversion to Catholicism infuriates his father. Still, she spends the longest time of the three profiled students on the program, and this may be one reason why her recall is good. Her essay shows that she is capable of temporal organization and understanding the major themes of the story. What is less clear is how to reinforce vocabulary retention for both Sara and Sharon. Michelle, the subject of the following case study, unlike the other two women, had a higher vocabulary quiz score and seems to be better at recognizing cognates and words that are similar to English, but fails to comprehend the major story line.

Michelle's Student Profile

Michelle studied French for the first time in college and is 20 years old. This is her third semester of college French. In high school she studied Spanish for four years. Unlike the other two women in this study, she writes that she is motivated to study French because she is interested in specific aspects of the culture, particularly civilization, history, and the language. She does not use the computer for word processing, so this may be her first experience with computers.

On the evaluation of the computer program, she demonstrated great satisfaction with the instructional quality of the program in general, giving ratings of 5s. She ranked the tools as equally helpful, giving 4s. The presentation of the material and the learner interaction were highly rated as 5s. Her attitude about the experience was also quite positive. However, she had no opinion as to whether the content of the program was appropriate for her level of learning or whether the content of the program was appropriate for students of French at this level.

Michelle's Vocabulary Quiz

Her score of 12 was below the mean for the computer group, but better than the other two subjects' scores, and within one standard deviation of the average score. On the vocabulary quiz, she missed the words *singer, croûtes de gales,* and *gourmandise,* and yet had looked them up once. On the other hand, she correctly defined *bienfaiteur, sacristie, païens, crever, marmite,* and *prêtre,* and these were also looked up only once. One explanation for her retention or recognition of these words and not others may be that four of the previous words are cognates or very similar to the English: "benefactor," "sacristy," "pagans," and "priest."

Michelle's Recall Protocol Analysis

CASE #3

Recall Protocol   8:15 p.m., Oct. 29, 1992

I remember a lot about how Toundi's father was killed. I know it had some-thing to do with him fighting with others about lumps of sugar, but I didn't understand why. His abdomen was pierced and he died.

Even though his father has died, Toundi thinks he is to blame and talks to his father in his diary. I think he is also describing a fight with someone in his diary.

Then I caught something about a starving porcupine. References to mis-sionaries in their lives kept appearing. I may be off-balance about the meaning of all this. I'm not really sure.

Michelle

She spent 44 minutes with the program, which is less than average for the computer group. From looking at her individual profile on the tracker, we learned that she approached the task as instructed by the program, i.e., she read the introductory pages, then tried a few vocabulary lookups. She then listened to the entire story, for 9 minutes 33 seconds. (Few learners listened that long to the program, especially in proportion to the short amount of time she spent on the program.) She scrolled backwards through the story to get to the beginning and then began to read the story in earnest, looking up words. All of her definitional lookups were in English. She sought cultural references for *prêtre, Maka,* and the exclamation *aaaaaaaaaakiéééé.* Her grammar searches were for the *passé simple* of verbs *pleurer, paraître,* and *devenir.* After finishing the story, she apparently scrolled backwards through the story.

Out of a total of 12 pausal units, she only has two that make correct reference to the story. From analyzing the recall protocol, in light of the tracker, she seemed to be a top-down reader; that is to say, she attempted to get the general picture first. Her protocol showed some frustration and only a vague understanding of content, which was evident in statements such as "I may be off-balance about the meaning of all this. I'm not really sure." The details of individual words' meanings did not seem to concern her. She had a total absence of chronology in her narrative as well as many distortions. She believed Toundi's father died by being pierced in the abdomen after having himself fought over the sugar cubes. She also believed Toundi talked to his father via the diary. She then mentioned a starving porcupine at the end of the essay, yet she had looked up *porc-épic, moitié, fourmis,* and *l'un des pièges.* We can only assume that she confused half-eaten—*moitié devoré*—with the concept of starving.

She also seemed to have difficulty figuring out to which character personal pronouns and possessive adjectives are referring, and this lack of attention to detail causes her to confuse who is fighting over the sugar cubes and to whom Toundi is writing in his diary. More importantly, Michelle may have confused *mon père* (meaning father/priest) with Toundi's real father/*père,* and this confusion may have led to wrong schemata formation from the beginning of the reading, thus distorting the rest of the story and leading her down the wrong textual path, so to speak. There were also big jumps in her lookups, sometimes as many as 57 points between words. For example she looked up *privez-le,* which is word/expression # 470 in the program database, but her next lookup was not until word #527, *parut.* This jump took place during the infamous porcupine story. It seemed that she rushed through the program, not spending an adequate amount of time digesting the material. Even though she followed the instructions to get the overall picture of the story by reading it through first and listening to the audio, this was not a totally helpful strategy in her case, as it did not aid in her general comprehension. She looked up fewer words than the other two women and spent less time on the computer, but managed to receive a better score on the vocabulary test. While Sara and Sharon could potentially benefit from on-line help directly related to vocabulary-building strategies, Michelle may need comprehension checks programmed throughout the story or classroom discussion and individual attention from the instructor while reading. If we were to judge Sara's and Michelle's recall protocols with regard to the Interpretive standard, both would fall significantly short of the mark. Although Sharon, weak in vocabulary, performed at a higher level of reading comprehension, textual interpretation still remains somewhat low. The standards guidelines remind educators that

> Since the Interpretive Mode does not allow for active negotiation between the reader and the writer or the listener and the speaker, it requires a much more profound knowledge of the culture from the outset. The more one knows about the other language and culture, the greater the chances of creating the appropriate cultural interpretation of a written or spoken text. It must be noted, however, that cultural literacy and the ability to read or listen between the lines are developed over time and through exposure to the language and culture. (*SFLL* 1996:33)

Conclusions

While it is impossible to generalize from only three cases, it seems that for these learners, vocabulary recognition and retention based on performance in a text-specific vocabulary quiz were not related to reading comprehension or interpretation. Moreover, programmed on-line helps and instructions were either ignored or when used failed to help in the ways the software authors had envisioned.

Reading is a difficult enough task in one's native language, where social contexts and meanings provide support to the important schematic intonation upon which new information (input) is scaffolded (Vygotsky 1962; Hatch 1993). Reading in a foreign language becomes all the more difficult when learners do not have the essential background information to build upon (Bernhardt 1990; Hewitt 1990). A major area for investigation of second language acquisition processes, according to Blake, is vocabulary acquisition. Studies by Miller and Gildea (1987) have shown that having "instantaneous access to lexical information, as one does through an interactive computer system, aids vocabulary development immensely" (19). Our 1992 study confirms this, but individual cases drawn from the sample indicate that students process information very differently and can perhaps benefit from a more individualized approach to enhancing foreign language reading comprehension skills and related vocabulary retention.

Reading comprehension and interpretation of texts are promising areas for technology-enhanced research and merit special attention in light of the emphasis placed on both in the national standards. Computers offer the means to accomplish this type of research. For university and secondary teachers alike who desire to integrate the standards guidelines and technology into their foreign language curricula, data analysis using several instruments, such as illustrated above, might yield an initial profile of individual readers who seem to be initially "at risk" in their foreign language career. Early analysis and instructional intervention may aid these learners immeasurably. Interviewing the students shortly after they had finished the protocols would have also strengthened these individual case studies.

A number of additional research questions follow related to the study of individual learners:

- Will those learners who have access to tools that aid comprehension and that, at the same time, model a variety of good reading strategies become better readers of subsequent texts presented later on in the curriculum?

- Is there a relationship between certain types of learners and the types of lookups they choose?

- Will their lookups on the computer, because it is so easy to do, assist with or impede retention and comprehension?

- In view of the relatively easy procedure of clicking on a mouse for information, do computerized readings remove a sense of responsibility on the part of the students to work harder at understanding and interpreting the text?

- If they do not understand a word, or if they lack background knowledge of the culture, will this lack of understanding lead to an incorrect global interpretation of the story?

And finally we additionally need to know more about students' cognitive processes involved in reading foreign language texts—how individual students map certain concepts to preexisting and new knowledge. These questions and others offering insights as to how L2 readers might structure incoming knowledge are a part of continuing research efforts.

In the years that followed this research, the *Une vie de boy* program served as a prototype for other foreign language literary glossing endeavors at the university. From 1995 to 1997, twenty other authentic texts designed for a variety of levels and several different genres were annotated electronically and combined on a CD-ROM, entitled *A l'Aventure* (Lyman-Hager 1997). The recent appearance of and growing emphasis among educators on the national standards make this type of authentic, culturally dense reading all the more relevant to secondary and post-secondary language learners, in particular with relation to standards goals for Cultures and Comparisons. In particular, Francophone African readings such as *Une vie de boy* offer new perspectives on faraway cultures and allow for rich comparisons with practices from the students' hearth culture.

Clearly, new approaches and materials will be needed to equip the global electronic schoolhouse of the year 2000 as well as meet the needs of all of our learners. Technology will be able to play an important role in this restructured school, particularly in the area of "authentic performance assessment in foreign language education" (Nielson and Hoffman 1996:123). The opportunity exists to mediate the world of the learner and the text in new ways. The overarching goal for technology within the standards is for students to take advantage of new technological advances to strengthen linguistic skills, establish communication with pen pals and peers, and learn more about contemporary target cultures and communities. Great hope has been placed in the Internet and computers in general as providers of authentic materials and as mediators of unfamiliar cultural and linguistic materials. Research of the kind reported in this chapter is essential for educators and instructional designers alike to work toward fully realizing technology's potential and to create and update programs, both technological and curricular for the schoolhouse of the future and its students.

NOTES

1. The Bernhardt model of reading inspired the seven types of glosses used in the program designed for use in this research. The original Bernhardt categories are: Word Recognition, Phonemic/Graphemic Decoding, Syntactic Feature Recognition, Intratextual Perception, Prior Knowledge, and Metacognition. The glosses created in the Une Vie de Boy program are: Pronunciation, English Definition, French Definition, Grammar, Cultural Information, Relationship, and Picture.

2. This understanding can be exhibited by recall protocols, a procedure advocated by Bernhardt and Lee as a useful measure of understanding.

3. These programs include Blake's Recuerdos de Madrid, the various programs of the Transparent Language, Inc., and a program by Geoffrey Hope of the University of Iowa.

4. The introductory chapter selected for the computer program Une Vie De Boy (Oyono, pp. 15-23) relates the chain of events that initially led Toundi away from his village, his family, and his friends—and into the world of the French colonizers (first a Catholic priest, then the Commandant). The action in the novel's introductory chapter selected for glossing describes Toundi's relationship with his father and mother and his attraction to the lifestyle of the Catholic priest, which lead to a final blow-up with his father and alienation from his family.

5. This is not attributable to the fact that the material is simply on the computer but rather to the notion that more information can be glossed in a variety of ways in this format. The glosses, especially the French and English definitions and the pictures, may serve as a type of feedback mechanism when the student is fairly certain of the word's meaning but needs a quick confirmation.

6. According to Lee and Bernhardt, the recall protocol technique is an ideal method of testing reading comprehension insofar as the vocabulary is not suggested by the test itself but is, rather, supplied by the student writing her recollections of the story.

7. This list was further distilled to determine the twenty most important words, which formed the contents of the vocabulary-in-context quiz given later, in the second study using the program.

8. Excel (version 4.0 was used in this program initially) is by Microsoft Corporation.

9. Morris Weinstock and Lorinda Brader were the chief programmers of Unc Vie de Boy, while graphic artists and instructional designers from Penn State's Educational Technology Services group also contributed greatly to the program's creation.

10. These words are: bienfaiteur, case, veiller, lâcher, rotin, tordre, singer, sacristie, fendre, fouet, croûtes de gales, païens, plaies, marmite, gourmandise, prêtre, bagarre, esquiver, crever, and maudir.

11. It was not possible to determine what readers actually looked up and how they looked up the words from the print version because of the lack of an appropriate "tracking device." Furthermore, the number of actual glossing possibilities on paper was severely reduced, precisely because of the nature of the enhanced coding capabilities of the computer, where every "je" or "te" could be linked electronically to a type of concept map indicating the relationship of the word to the character in the story.

12. This was reported in Lyman-Hager et. al. as a part of the 1993 CALICO Symposium Proceedings. The presentation itself elaborated on the 1992 study and included the case studies included in this article.

13. A full description of the program, including sample screens, is found in Lyman-Hager, Mary Ann and James N. Davis, "The Case for Computerized Reading: Une Vie de Boy." The French Review. Vol. 69, No. 5, 775-790. April 1996.

14. An equal number of sections was chosen from which subjects were randomly selected. After that, 35 students were randomly selected from the non-computer treatment group and 37 from the computer treatment group. Parametric T-tests for independent samples were carried out for the dependent variable, the vocabulary quiz scores, of the two treatment groups. Non-parametric Mann-Whitney U tests were performed on the two treatment groups for measures (motivation, experience, sex, and other languages studied) obtained from the questionnaire filled out by all students during the first week of the semester. Results of these separate tests are listed in Tables 1 and 2 of Appendix D. The non-computer and computer groups were compared on measures of prior experience in the language, other languages, and motivation, and no significant differences between the groups were found.

15. The table in Appendix C summarizes the results of the courseware/reading evaluation.

16. The Recall Protocol consisted of a blank paper with the following instructions at the top: "After you have finished reading the passage several times (as per the instructions enclosed with your packet attached to the Une Vie de Boy program), please write down on this sheet of paper what you remember from the story. You may write however long you like, but do not look at the text again or speak with other students to refresh your memory while you are thinking and writing. Although this is not a test, it is a part of your French 3 program, so do your best.

REFERENCES

American Council on the Teaching of Foreign Languages. 1989. "ACTFL Provisional Program Guidelines for Foreign Language Teacher Education." *Foreign Language Annals* 21:71– 82.

Bernhardt, Elizabeth B. 1990. "A Model of L2 Text Construction: The Recall of Literary Texts by Learners of German," pp. 21–43 in Angela Labarca, ed., *Issues in L2: Theory as Practice/Practice as Theory.* Norwood, NJ: Ablex.

Blake, Robert J. 1992. "Second Language Reading on the Computer." *ADFL Bulletin,* 24,1:17– 22.

———.1991. *Recuerdos de Madrid/Memories of Madrid.* Lexington: D.C. Heath.

Bozeman, W., and J. House. 1988. "Microcomputers in Education: the Second Decade." *T.H.E. Journal* 15:82–86.

Bragger, Jeannette D., and Donald B. Rice. 1992. *Allons Voir: Les Français et Les Francophones!* Boston: Heinle & Heinle.

Davis, James N., Mary Ann Lyman-Hager, and Susan B. Hayden. 1992. "Assessing User Needs in Early Stages of Program Development: The Case of Foreign Language Reading." *CALICO Journal* 9:21–27.

Davis, James N., and Mary Ann Lyman-Hager. 1997. "Computers in L2 Reading: Student Performance, Student Attitudes." *Foreign Language Annals* 30:58–72.

Feldman, Doris S. 1990. "The Role of Universal Knowledge versus Culture Specific Knowledge for Comprehending Text," pp. 88–105 in Angela Labarca, ed., *Issues in L2: Theory as Practice/Practice as Theory.* Norwood, NJ: Ablex.

Grabe, William. 1996. "Developments in Reading Research and Their Implications for Computer-Adaptive Reading Assessment." Paper presented at San Diego State University, November.

Hatch, Evelyn. 1983. *Psycholinguistics: A Second Language Perspective.* Rowley, MA: Newbury House.

Hewitt, Nancy Maisto. 1990. "Reading, Cognitive Style, and Culture: A Look at Some Relationships in Second-Language Acquisition," pp. 62–87 in Angela Labarca, ed., *Issues in L2: Theory as Practice/Practice as Theory.* Norwood, NJ: Ablex.

Lee, James F. 1986. "On the Use of the Recall Task to Measure L2 Reading Comprehension." *Studies in Second Language Acquisition* 8:83–93.

Lyman-Hager, Mary Ann. 1997. *A l'Aventure:* CD-ROM. New York: John Wiley and Sons.

Lyman-Hager, Mary Ann, James N. Davis, Joanne Burnett, and Ronald Chennault. 1993. "Une vie de boy: Interactive Reading in French," in Frank L. Borchardt and Eleanor M. T. Johnson, eds., *Proceedings of the Computer Assisted Learning and Instruction Consortium 1993 Annual Symposium on Assessment.* March.

Miller, George A., and Patricia M. Gildea. 1987. "How Children Learn Words." *Scientific American* 257:94–99.

National Standards in Foreign Language Education Project. 1996. *Standards for Foreign Language Learning: Preparing for the 21st Century.* Lawrence, KS: Allen Press.

Nielson, Mel, and Elizabeth Hoffman. 1996. "Technology, Reform, and Foreign Language Standards: A Vision for Change." pp. 119–37 in Robert Lafayette, ed., *National Standards: A Catalyst for Reform.* Lincolnwood, IL: National Textbook Company.

Oyono, Ferdinand. 1956. *Une vie de boy.* Paris: Julliard.

Quinlan, Michael. 1989. *Transparent Language.* Hollis, NH.

Swaffar, Janet K., Katherine M. Arens, and Heidi Byrnes. 1991. *Reading for Meaning: An Integrated Approach to Language Learning.* Englewood Cliffs, NJ: Prentice Hall.

Vygotsky, Lev S. 1962. *Thought and Language.* Cambridge: The MIT Press.

Appendix A

Computer Screens

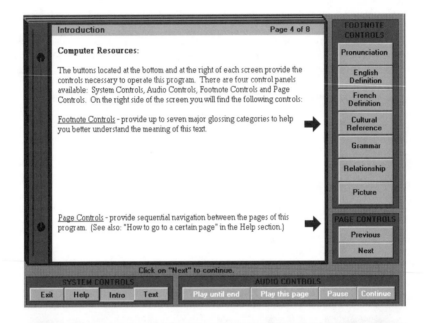

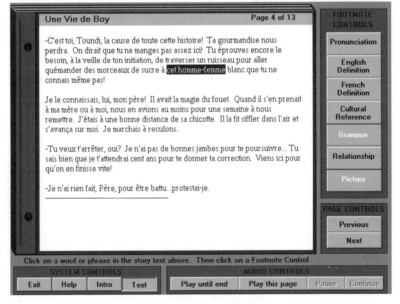

Appendix B

Tables

TABLE 1

T-Tests for Independent Samples of Treatments: Vocabulary Quiz Scores (20 items)

	N	Mean	Standard Deviation	Standard Error	Separate T Value	Variance 2-Tailed Prob
NC	35	11.69	4.575	.773		
C	37	14.14	3.457	.568		
					–2.55	013*

*Significant at the .05 level
NC = Noncomputer
C = Computer

TABLE 2

Mann-Whitney U—Wilcoxon Rank Sum W Test for Independent Samples of Treatments

Prior Experience or Instruction in the French Language by Treatment (Noncomputer /Computer)

Cases	Median	Mean	U	W	Z	2-Tailed P
35 NC 37 C						
	4.00	3.8125	605.5	1235.5	– 4851	.6276

Motivation to Learn or Perfect the French Language by Treatment (Noncomputer/Computer)

Cases	Median	Mean	U	W	Z	2-Tailed P
35 NC 37 C						
	3.0	2.5833	591.0	1221.0	– .6661	.5054

Other Languages Studied or Spoken by Treatment (Noncomputer /Computer)

Cases	Median	Mean	U	W	Z	2-Tailed P
35 NC 37 C						
	.000	.3889	625.5	1255.5	– .2935	.7691

Appendix C

Summary of Questionnaire Data for Computer and Noncomputer Groups

Question content: The wording variations on the questionnaire for the two groups (Computer **C** versus Noncomputer **NC**) are enclosed in square brackets. For the most part, the word "computer" or "presentation" is substituted by "reading" and "materials." A Likert scale range of 1–5 was used.

Content

1*   The content of the program [reading] is appropriate for my level of learning.
     Mean Values C = 3.43   NC = 2.91
     0.46

2   The content of the program [reading] was clearer to me after I used it.
     Mean Values C = 3.95   NC = 3.46
     0.49

3+   I understood the goals of the program [reading].
     Mean Values C = 4.00   NC = 2.86
     1.14

4   The content [of the reading] is presented clearly and logically.
     Mean Values C = 3.81   NC = 3.46
     0.35

5   The content [of the reading] is appropriate for students of French at this level.
     Mean Values C = 3.59   NC = 2.97
     0.62

6   The content is free of grammatical/spelling errors.
        Mean Values C = 3.95   NC = 3.57
        0.38

7+*   The content of the program [reading] is easier to digest in this
        format than in a textbook.
        Mean Values C = 4.27   NC = 3.11
        1.16

Instructional Quality

8+   Directions on the screen [accompanying paper] are easy to follow.
        Mean Values C = 4.57   NC = 3.60
        0.97

9+   Enough information about the program organization [reading] was
        provided.
        Mean Values C = 4.32   NC = 3.20
        1.12

10+   Help is made available throughout the program [reading by using
        the sheets].
        Mean Values C = 4.32   NC = 3.62
        0.70

11+   The program can be operated easily and independently. [I can do
        this reading easily and independently with the materials provided.]
        Mean Values C = 4.22   NC = 3.09
        1.13

12   The tools provided aided in the comprehension of the content.
        Mean Values C = 4.24   NC = 4.00
        0.24

13*   I found the English translation critical to my understanding of the
        text.
        Mean Values C = 4.49   NC = 4.06
        0.43

14*   I found the French translation critical to my understanding the text. [I think definitions in French would have helped my understanding of the text.]

Mean Values C = 3.16   NC = 2.74

0.42

15*   I found the cultural information critical to my understanding the text. [I think more cultural information would have helped my understanding of the text.]

Mean Values C = 3.59   NC = 3.37

0.22

16*   I found the relations information critical to my understanding the text. [I think more information about relations would have helped my understanding of the text.]

Mean Values C = 3.27   NC = 3.54

0.27

17*   I found the audio recording critical to my understanding the text. [I think listening to an audio recording of the text would help my understanding of it.]

Mean Values C = 2.60   NC = 2.83

0.23

Presentation

18   The presentation [reading] is free of programming errors.

Mean Values C = 4.00   NC = 3.51

0.49

19   The program [reading] is free of technical problems.

Mean Values C = 3.97   NC = 3.54

0.43

20+   Screen displays [the handouts] are clear and easy to read.

Mean Values C = 4.46   NC = 3.66

0.80

21   The print size and spacing of text is appropriate.
Mean Values C = 4.40   NC = 3.91
0.49

22+   Important concepts are emphasized or highlighted.
Mean Values C = 3.40   NC = 2.48
0.92

23+   Color is [font size and print are] effectively used.
Mean Values C = 3.59   NC = 3.80
0.20

24   Graphics are crisp, clear, and enhance content. [Pictures enhance the content.]
Mean Values C = 3.89   NC = 3.51
0.38

25   The program [reading] contains appropriate linking from section to section.
Mean Values C = 3.81   NC = 3.40
0.41

Learner Interaction

26+   I could exit and reenter the program at various points. [I could stop and start the reading at various points.]
Mean Values C = 3.62   NC = 4.86
1.24

27+   I could control the rate and sequence of presentation [of my reading this text].
Mean Values C = 4.35   NC = 3.57
0.78

28+   Cues and prompts were available to help answer questions. [Notes were available to help answer questions.]
Mean Values C = 4.24   NC = 2.91
1.33

29+*   I was motivated to continue the program [reading].
Mean Values C = 3.62   NC = 2.68
0.94

30   Program documentation [documentation to the reading] was satisfactory.
Mean Values C = 3.76   NC = 3.26
0.50

Attitude

31+   The program [reading] challenged me.
Mean Values C = 4.11   NC = 4.20
0.09

32   The computer [materials] created a one-on-one environment.
Mean Values C = 3.97   NC = 3.63
0.34

33*   This method of instruction made me want to learn more about what happened next in the story.
Mean Values C = 3.24   NC = 2.71
0.53

34+   It was easy to operate the computer [to use the materials].
Mean Values C = 4.30   NC = 3.40
0.90

35+*   This program [material] used my time efficiently.
Mean Values C = 3.59   NC = 2.80
0.79

36+*   I was satisfied with what I learned.
Mean Values C = 3.54   NC = 2.83
0.71

37+*   Using this method for the content seems superior to traditional
        methods of learning.
        Mean Values C = 3.81   NC = 2.80
        1.01

38+   Efforts were made to suit the program [reading] specifically to me.
        Mean Values C = 3.32   NC = 2.48
        0.84

39   I could work at my own pace.
        Mean Values C = 4.49   NC = 4.03
        0.46

40   I had enough time to learn the concepts critical to my
        understanding of the text.
        Mean Values C = 3.92   NC = 3.46
        0.46

* Questions decided to be important to our study prior to analyzing the data.

+ Questions whose corresponding difference in means (computer versus noncomputer) is > = 0.70 or < 0 (negative difference, i.e., noncomputer mean > computer mean)

Appendix D

Le Journal de Toundi

Maintenant que le révérend père Gilbert m'a dit que je sais lire et écrire couramment, je vais pouvoir tenir comme lui un journal.

— Je ne sais quel plaisir cache cette manière de Blanc, mais essayons toujours.

J'ai jeté un coup d'œil dans le journal de mon bienfaiteur et maître pendant qu'il confessait ses fidèles. C'est un véritable grenier aux souvenirs. Ces Blancs savent tout conserver...J'ai retrouvé ce coup de pied que me donna le père Gilbert parce qu'il m'avait aperçu en train de le singer dans la sacristie. J'en ai senti à nouveau une brûlure aux fesses. C'est curieux, moi qui croyais l'avoir oublié...

*   *   *

Je m'appelle Toundi Ondoua. Je suis le fils de Toundi et de Zama. Depuis que le Père m'a baptisé, il m'a donné le nom de Joseph. Je suis Maka par ma mère et Ndjem par mon père. Ma race fut celle des mangeurs d'hommes. Depuis l'arrivée des Blancs nous avons compris que tous les autres hommes ne sont pas des animaux.

Au village, on dit de moi que j'ai été la cause de la mort de mon père parce que je m'étais réfugié chez un prêtre blanc à la veille de mon initiation où je devais faire connaissance avec le fameux serpent qui veille sur tous ceux de notre race. Le père Gilbert, lui, croit que c'est le Saint-Esprit qui m'a conduit jusqu'à lui. A vrai dire, je ne m'y étais rendu que pour approcher l'homme blanc aux cheveux semblables à la barbe de maïs, habillé d'une robe de femme, qui donnait de bons petits cubes sucrés aux petits Noirs. Nous étions une bande de jeunes païens à suivre le missionnaire qui allait de case en case pour solliciter des adhésions à la religion nouvelle. Il connaissait quelques mots Ndjem, mais il les prononçait si mal qu'il leur donnait un sens obscène. Cela amusait tout le monde, ce qui lui assurait un certain succès. Il nous lançait ses petits cubes sucrés comme on jette du grain aux poules. C'était une véritable table bataille pour s'approprier l'un de ces délicieux morceaux blancs que nous gagnions au prix de genoux écorchés, d'yeux tuméfiés, de plaies douloureuses. Les scènes de distribution dégénéraient parfois en bagarres où s'opposaient nos parents. C'est ainsi que ma mère vint un jour à se battre contre la mère de Tinati, mon compagnon de jeu, parce qu'il m'avait tordu le bras pour me faire lâcher les deux morceaux de sucre que j'avais pu avoir au prix d'une hémorragie nasale. Cette bataille avait failli tourner en massacre car des voisins luttaient contre mon père pour l'empêcher d'aller fendre la tête au père de Tinati qui, lui même, parlait de transpercer l'abdomen de Papa d'un seul coup de sagaie. Quand on eut calmé nos parents, mon père, l'œil mauvais, armé d'un rotin, m'invita à le suivre derrière la case.

— C'est toi, Toundi, la cause de toute cette histoire! Ta gourmandise nous perdra. On dirait que tu ne manges pas assez ici! Tu éprouves encore le besoin, à la veille de ton initiation, de traverser un ruisseau pour aller quémander des morceaux de sucre à cet homme-femme blanc que tu ne connais même pas!

Je le connaissais, lui, mon père! Il avait la magie du fouet. Quand il s'en prenait à ma mère ou à moi, nous en avions au moins pour une semaine à nous remettre. J'étais à une bonne distance de sa chicotte. Il la fit siffler dans l'air et s'avança sur moi. Je marchais à reculons.

— Tu veux t'arrêter, oui? Je n'ai pas de bonnes jambes pour te poursuivre... Tu sais bien que je t'attendrai cent ans pour te donner ta correction. Viens ici pour qu'on en finisse vite!

* * *

— Je n'ai rien fait, Père, pour être battu...protestai-je.

— Aaaaaaaaaakiééééééé!... s'exclama-t-il. Tu oses dire que tu n'as rien fait? Si tu n'avais pas été le gourmand que tu es, si tu n'avais pas le sang des gourmands qui circule dans les veines de ta mère, tu n'aurais pas été à Fia pour disputer, comme un rat que tu es, ces choses sucrées que vous donne ce maudit Blanc! On ne t'aurait pas tordu les bras, ta mère ne se serait pas battue et moi je n'aurais pas éprouvé l'envie d'aller fendre le crâne du vieux Tinati... Je te conseille de t'arrêter!... Si tu fais encore un pas, je considérerai cela comme une injure et que tu peux coucher avec ta mère...

Je m'arrêtai. Il se précipita sur moi et fit siffler le rotin sur mes épaules nues. Je me tortillais comme un ver au soleil.

— Tourne-toi et lève les bras! Je n'ai pas envie de te crever un œil.

— Pardonne-moi, Père! suppliai-je, je ne le ferai plus...

— Tu dis toujours cela quand je commence à te battre. Mais aujourd'hui, je dois te battre jusqu'à ce que je ne sois plus en colère...

Je ne pouvais pas crier car cela aurait pu ameuter les voisins et mes camarades m'auraient traité de fille, ce qui signifiait l'exclusion de notre groupe "Jeunes-qui-seront–bientôt-des-hommes". Mon père me donna un autre coup que j'esquivai de justesse.

— Si tu esquives encore, c'est que tu peux coucher avec ta grand-mère, ma mère!

Pour m'empêcher de me sauver, mon père usait toujours de ce chantage qui m'obligeait à me livrer gentiment à ses coups.

— Je ne t'ai pas insulté et je ne peux pas coucher avec ma mère, ni avec la tienne! Et je ne veux plus être battu et c'est tout!

* * *

— Tu oses me parler sur ce ton! Une goutte de mon liquide qui me parle ainsi! Arrête-toi ou je te maudis!

Mon père suffoquait. Jamais je ne l'avais vu aussi exaspéré... Je continuai ma marche à reculons. Il me poursuivit ainsi derrière les cases pendant une bonne centaine de mètres.

— Bien! lança-t-il, je verrai où tu passeras le nuit! Je dirai à ta mère que tu nous as insultés. Pour entrer dans la case, ton chemin passe par le trou de mon anus.

Sur ce, il me tourna le dos. Je ne savais où me réfugier. J'avais un oncle que je n'aimais pas à cause de ses croûtes de gale. Sa femme sentait, comme lui, le poisson avarié. Il me répugnait d'entrer dans leur masure. Il faisait nuit. La lumière intermittente des lucioles devenait visible. Le bruit des pilons annonçait le repas du soir. Je revins doucement derrière notre case et regardai à travers les lézardes du mur de terre battue. Mon père me tournait le dos. L'oncle dégoûtant était en face de lui. Ils mangeaient... L'arôme du porc-épic que nous avons trouvé à moitié dévoré par les fourmis, pris depuis deux jours à l'un des pièges de mon père, me donnait de l'appétit. Ma mère était réputée au village pour son assaisonnement du porc-épic...

— C'est bien le premier de la saison! dit mon oncle, la bouche pleine.

Sans mot dire, mon père pointa son index au-dessus de sa tête. C'était à cet endroit qu'il alignait tous les crânes des bêtes qu'il prenait au piège.

—Mangez tout, dit ma mère, j'ai gardé la part de Toundi dans la marmite.

Mon père se leva d'un bond et, à son bégaiement, je compris que ça allait barder.

— Apporte la part de Toundi ici! cria mon père. Il ne mangera pas de ce porc-épic. Cela lui apprendra à me désobéir.

— Tu sais, il n'a encore rien mangé depuis ce matin. Que mangera-t-il quand il rentrera?

* * *

—Rien du tout, coupe mon père.

—Si vous voulez qu'il vous obéisse, ajouta mon oncle, privez-le de nourriture... Ce porc- épic est fameux...

Ma mère se leva et leur apporta la marmite. Je vis la main de mon père et celle de mon oncle y plonger. Puis j'entendis ma mère pleurer. Pour la première fois de ma vie, je pensai à tuer mon père.

Je retournai à Fia et... après avoir longtemps hésité, je frappai à la case du prêtre blanc. Je le trouvai en train de manger. Il s'étonna de ma visite. Je lui expliquai par gestes que je voulais partir avec lui. Il riait de toutes ses dents, ce qui donnait à sa bouche une apparence de croissant de lune. Je me tenais coi près de la porte. Il me fit signe d'approcher. Il me donna les restes de son repas qui me parut étrange et délicieux. Par gestes nous poursuivîmes notre conversation. Je compris que j'étais agréé.

C'est ainsi que je devins le boy du révérend père Gilbert.

Le lendemain, la nouvelle parvint à mon père. Je redoutais sa colère... Je l'expliquai au prêtre toujours en gesticulant. Cela l'amusait beaucoup. Il me tapota amicalement l'épaule. Je me sentis protégé.

Mon père vint l'après-midi. Il se borna à me dire que j'étais et resterais son fils, c'est-à-dire sa goutte de liquide... qu'il ne m'en voulait pas et que si je rentrais au bercail, tout serait oublié. Je savais ce que signifiait ce beau discours devant le Blanc. Je lui tirai la langue. Son œil devint mauvais comme d'habitude lorsqu'il se préparait à "m'apprendre à vivre". Mais, avec le père Gilbert, je ne craignais rien. Son regard semblait fasciner mon père qui baissa la tête et s'éloigna tout penaud.

Ma mère vint me voir pendant la nuit. Elle pleurait. Nous pleurâmes ensemble. Elle me dit que j'avais bien fait de quitter la case paternelle, que mon père ne m'aimait pas comme un père devait aimer son fils, qu'elle me bénissait et que si un jour je tombais malade je n'aurais qu'à me baigner dans une rivière pour être guéri...

Le père Gilbert me donna une culotte kaki et un tricot rouge qui firent l'admiration de tous les gamins de Fia qui vinrent demander au prêtre de les emmena avec lui.

Deux jours plus tard, le père Gilbert me prit sur sa motocyclette dont le bruit semait la panique dans tous les villages que nous traversions. Sa tournée avait duré deux semaines. Nous rentrions à la Mission catholique Saint-Pierre de Dangan. J'étais heureux, la vitesse me grisait. J'allais connaître la ville et les Blancs, et vivre comme eux. Je me surpris à me comparer à ces perroquets sauvages que nous attirions au village avec des grains de maïs et qui restaient prisonniers de leur gourmandise. Ma mère disait souvent en riant: "Toundi, ta gourmandise te conduira loin...

Mes parents sont morts. Je ne suis jamais retourné au village.

Ferdinand Oyono. *Une vie de boy.* Paris: Julliard. 1956. Permission granted to use text for educational purposes.

Index to Authors Cited

Index to Topics Cited

Acknowledgments

Standards, page vii. National Standards in Foreign Language Education Project. *Standards for Foreign Language Learning: Preparing for the 21st Century.* Yonkers, NY: National Standards in Foreign Language Education Project.

Figure on page 20, "Communicative Competence" by Celce-Murcia, M., Zoltan, D., and Thurrell, S. In Issues in Applied Linguistics 6(2). Copyright 1995. Reprinted by permission of Issues in Applied Linguistics.

Figure on page 72, "Egan's Stages of Educational Development." From Egan, Kieran. 1979. *Educational Development.* New York: Oxford University Press. Reprinted by permission of Kieran Egan.

Figure on page 73, "Egan's Educational Development Model *." Based on Egan, Kieran. 1979. *Educational Development.* New York: Oxford University Press. Reprinted by permission of Kieran Egan.

Figure on page 75, "The Bennett Model" (originally titled "Content and Process: Balancing Challenge"), Janet M. Bennet. "Cultural Marginality: Identity Issues in Intercultural Training." In *Education for the Intercultural Experience.* Edited by Michael Paige. Reprinted by permission of Intercultural Press, Inc., Yarmouth, ME. Copyright 1993.

Figure on page 76, "The Bennett Model *" (originally titled "A Developmental Model of Intercultural Sensitivity"), Milton J. Bennett. "Towards Ethnorelativism: A Developmental Model of Intercultural Sensitivity." In *Education for the Intercultural Experience.* Edited by Michael Paige. Reprinted by permission of Intercultural Press, Inc. Yarmouth, ME. Copyright 1993.

Figure on page 80, "Byram's Language/Culture Learning Model" by Michael Byram. In *Cultural Studies in Foreign Language Education.* 1989. Multilingual Matters Ltd. Clevedon N. Somerset, England. Reprinted by permission of Multilingual Matters, Clevedon N. Somerset, England. Copyright 1989.

Synopses, pages 95-97, "Assessment Postulates" and "Implications for Culture Learners and Cultural Assessment." Also synopsis, page 105, "An Ethic of Instruction." Drawn from Wiggins, Grant P. 1993. *Assessing Student Performance: Exploring the Purpose and Limits of Testing.* San Francisco: Jossey-Bass. Drawn from Wiggins, Grant P. 1998. *Educative Assessment: Designing Assessments to Inform and Improve Student Performance.* San Francisco: Jossey-Bass. Drawn from Wiggins, Grant P. and Everett Kline. 1998. "Understanding by Design." Presentation at the Collaborative Seminar, January 22-23 at the Headquarters of the American Council on the Teaching of Foreign Languages, Yonkers, NY. Reprinted by permission of Grant P. Wiggins.

Exerpt, page 89. From *Curriculum Planning: A Handbook for Professionals* by David Pratt, copyright © 1994 *by* Harcourt Brace & Company, reprinted by permission of the publisher.

Model page 106 based on Howard Gardner's multiple intelligences model. Drawn from Gardner, Howard. 1993. *Frames of Mind: The Theory of Multiple Intelligences.* Basic Books; and *Multiple Intelligences: The Theory of Practice.* Basic Books.

Standards, page 121. Singerman, Alan J., ed. *Acquiring Cross-Cultural Competence: Four Stages for Students of French.* American Association of Teachers of French National Commission on Cultural Competence. Lincolnwood, IL: National Textbook Company, 1996.